Teacher Education in India

Contemporary Problems and Prospects

Editors
Sesadeba Pany
Sankar Prasad Mohanty

SHIPRA

(2022 PoD, First Published in India in 2013)

Rs. 1250; US$ 42

ISBN: 978-81-7541-682-6

2025 Impression (PoD)

Teacher Education in India:
Contemporary Problems and Prospects

Published by:
SHIPRA PUBLICATIONS
LG 18-19, Pankaj Central Market
I.P. Ext., Patparganj, Delhi 110092, India
91 11 47322068; 9650028065, 9810522367
info@shiprapublication.com
www.shiprapublication.com

Preface

The destiny of India is being shaped in her classrooms-as appears in the introductory lines of the Kothari Education, unequivocally assumes the strategic role played by the teachers in national development. In view of this, the availability of well trained, efficient and dedicated teachers for our education system irrespective of the levels of education has been the most important concern since independence. The teacher education programme in our country is, better to say, still at its adolescence stage and searching for a definite course in terms of its structural and functional aspects. Emphasizing the concern for teachers the National Policy on Education, 1986 states that 'the status of the teacher reflects the socio-cultural ethos of the society; it is said that no people can rise above the level of its teachers'. This statement truly expresses the vital role played by the teachers in the society. The teacher besides his professional skills and competence needs to be humane in nature which has been the major concern for different reports on teacher education since independence.

The teacher education programme today needs a complete change with respect to the National Curriculum Framework, 2005, National curriculum Framework for Teacher Education (NCFTE, 2009) and the Right of Children to Free and Compulsory Education Act, 2009 (RTE-SSA). It is the right time to address on various problems of teacher education like inclusive education, inclusion of ICT, striking a balance between theory and practice, duration of teacher education course, public-private partnership, quality sustenance, role of different quality maintenance supervising agencies and evaluation criteria etc. We are to revitalize our teacher education programme in the context of these concerns for the creation of an egalitarian society. In view of these, an attempt has been made through this book to reflect the vision of the teacher educators of India on various problems of teacher education, since they are concerned with the system, having valuable experiences.

The book contains three parts: Part-I, is devoted to historical perspectives, problems and pedagogical concerns of teacher education; Part-II is devoted to ICT rejuvenations and tech-savvy teachers; and Part-III is devoted to professional developments, curricular issues and frameworks for implementation. Attempt has also been made to focus on problems of teacher education of varied nature, and the editors of the book will be highly obliged to have a highly constructive feedback of the readers. While Part-I deals with pedagogical perspectives in relation to constructivist approach, historical perspectives and development of teacher education (both in-service and preservice), parameters in maintaining the quality teacher education; roles of different stakeholders for the same and the effects of privation of teacher education have been discussed; and the latest report on teacher education (J.S.Verma Report, 2012) have been presented in the papers of*Mohanty, 2012; Katoch,2012;* Part-II is concerned with ICT initiatives in teacher education with role of different technology based learning strategies for teacher education programme. Teacher education curriculum reforms as teacher development is considered as the continuous process of developing and maintaining professional competence in teachers through pre-service, induction training, in-service training and on-going professional development programmes; strategies for professional development of teachers and improvement in quality of education, as Kothari Commission (1964-66) has rightly acknowledged that of all the different factors which influence the quality of education and its contribution to national development; the quality, the competence and character of teachers are undoubtedly the most significant. Because, professional development is the driving force which helps to bring much change in the area of teaching and learning. (Mishra, 2012). The topics related to these concepts have been discussed in Part-III. We hope that the book will be able to acquaint the readers and the researchers about the fundamental problems and concerns of teacher education; and will also sensitize the teacher educators about their prospective roles in the context of the changing pedagogy.

Lastly, we express our indebtedness to all the contributors for their illuminative articles, to the reviewers for their meticulous review and Shipra Publications for publishing this book.

S. Pany
S.P. Mohanty

Contents

PART-I

HISTORICAL PERSPECTIVES, PROBLEMS AND PEDAGOGICAL CONCERNS OF TEACHER EDUCATION

1
Constructivism in Teacher Education: Content and Pedagogical Perspective

Nityananda Pradhan

The Context: Proposed Pedagogical Transformation in NCF 2005

In recent years, constructivism has received considerable attention in educational scholarship, teacher preparation, and policy formation. It has been regarded as a more natural, relevant, productive, and empowering framework for instructing both students and student teachers (Cannella & Reiff, 1994). The National Curriculum Framework, 2005 lamenting on critical lapses in Indian school education has advocated for pedagogical transformation in schools. The major pitfalls, as pointed out by the document, are primacy of teaching over learning, little scope for pupils' deliberation on contemporary life issues, asymmetry between teaching learning and evaluation. The document propounded constructivists' critical pedagogy to promote knowledge construction by learners which involves exploration of the multiple facets of textual concepts and their dynamic natural manifestations through self initiated inquiry and context situated cognitions. Only listening to teachers in classrooms and cramming textual information can not promote life skills among children. Therefore, the school and the conventional class room based instructions should have space and scope for dialogue and discourse to materialize the said goals. School activities and schedules require purposeful contextual planning to provide plenty and diverse activities for experience, deliberations, reflections and contemplation on various life perspectives presented through the text books. A plan of comprehensive education must provide adequate time, space and scope for participation in life in simulations so that socio emotional and moral development take place to the best possible extents. School transformation theoretically is predicated upon on many conditions. This can be easily perceived when we see a school as a complex system operating in a dynamic setup. However, the first and the foremost condition which would make the proposed pedagogical transformation as envisioned in NCF 2005 is the teacher education programme, both pre-service as well as in-service.

What is Constructivism?

Constructivism is an epistemology, a learning or meaning-making theory that offers an explanation of the nature of knowledge and how humans learn. It maintains that individuals create or construct their own understandings or knowledge through the interactions and activities with which they have contact (Cannella & Reiff, 1994; Richardson, 1997). Knowledge is acquired through involvement with content instead of imitation or repetition (Kroll & LaBoskey, 1996). Learning activities in constructivist settings are characterized by active engagement, inquiry, problem solving, and collaboration with others. Rather than a dispenser of knowledge, the teacher is a guide, facilitator and co-explorer, who encourages learners to question, challenge, and formulate their own ideas, opinions, and conclusions. Correct answers and single interpretations are de-emphasized. While there are commonly accepted attributes of constructivism, there are also different interpretations of it. In general, two broad interpretations can be found among contemporary educators: psychological constructivism articulated by Piaget; and social constructivism associated with Vygotsky. Two major issues shape these interpretations: (i) education for individual development versus education for social transformation; and (ii) the degree of influence that social context has on individual cognitive development (Richardson, 1997; Vadeboncoeur, 1997).

Psychological Constructivism

Psychological or Piagetian constructivists generally regard the purpose of education as educating the individual child in a fashion that supports the child's interests and needs; consequently, the child is the subject of study, and individual cognitive development is the emphasis. Learning is primarily an individualistic enterprise. This is a child-centered approach that seeks to identify, through scientific study, the natural path of cognitive development (Vadeboncoeur, 1997). This approach assumes that students come to classrooms with ideas, beliefs, and opinions that need to be altered or modified by a teacher who facilitates this alteration by devising tasks and questions that create dilemmas for students. Knowledge construction occurs as a result of working through these dilemmas. Characteristic instructional practices include: discovery learning and hands-on activities, such as using manipulative student tasks that challenge existing concepts and thinking processes; and questioning techniques that probe students' beliefs and encourage examination and testing of those beliefs (Richardson, 1997).

To a large extent, this approach assumes that development is an ingrained, natural and biological process that is mostly the same for all individuals regardless of gender, class, race, or the social or cultural context in which learning and living take place (Vadeboncoeur, 1997). It is essentially a de-contextualized approach to learning. Critics of the psychological constructivist approach deprecate its lack of attention to the influence of the classroom culture and the broader social context (Vadeboncoeur, 1997).

Social Constructivism

Social or Vygotskian constructivism emphasizes education for social transformation and reflects a theory of human development that situates the individual within a socio-cultural context. Individuals construct knowledge in transaction with the environment, and in the process both the individual and the environment are changed. Schools are the socio-cultural settings where teaching and learning take place and where cultural tools, such as reading, writing, mathematics and certain modes of discourse are utilized (Richardson, 1997). This approach assumes that theory and practice do not develop in a vacuum; they are shaped by dominant cultural assumptions (Martin, 1994; O'Loughlin, 1995). Formal knowledge and the manner of its presentation are influenced by the historical and cultural environment that generated them. To accomplish the goals of social transformation and reconstruction, the context of education must be deconstructed, and the cultural assumptions, power relationships, and historical influences that undergird it must be exposed and, when necessary, altered (Meyers, 1996). Variants of social constructivism include: situated constructivism, social re-constructivism, socio-cultural constructivism, socio-historical constructivism and emancipator constructivism.

Constructivist Frameworks in Teacher Education

Constructivism is primarily a theory of learning, not a theory of teaching (Wolffe & McMullen, 1996). Translating theory to practice is both difficult and imprecise (MacKinnon & Scarf-Seatter, 1997). However, it may inform and influence practice. Constructivist teacher education generally reflects two major traditions: the developmental and social re-constructionist traditions (Canella & Reiff, 1994). programmes influenced by the developmental tradition attempt to teach students how to teach in a constructivist, generally Piagetian, manner. They are characterized by direct instruction in theory and practice, often without opportunities for inquiry, discovery or self-examination. This approach is mostly prescriptive. This approach to teaching is antithetical to the approach student teachers are intended to employ in their future classrooms (Oldfather, Bonds and Bray, 1994).

Programs influenced by social re-constructionist tradition attempt to help teacher education students deconstruct their own prior knowledge and attitudes, comprehend how these understandings evolved, explore the effects they have on actions and behaviour, and consider alternate conceptions and premises that may be more serviceable in teaching. Critical analysis and structured reflection on formal course knowledge and everyday practical experience are incorporated.

Richardson (1997) identifies two factors that appear to affect the approach teachers and teacher educators take in forming constructivist settings: the extent to which the social is acknowledged as a critical factor in learning and individual cognitive development; and the specific content, subject matter or discipline. Some subjects, such as mathematics, are more bounded than others by rules, formulae and procedures. They are more likely to be regarded by teachers as producing problems. Individual interpretations and construction of ideas and concepts are less likely to be encouraged by teachers other than in subjects such as literature and writing.

Implications for Content and Pedagogy

Teaching involves the process of leading learners to understand and use content. While content remains the goal of constructivist teachers, the process of learning becomes both method and goal as well. In the process of learning lie the roots of our understanding of content as well as our goal to create independent learners. The dichotomy between content and process disappears as we take a constructivist approach to knowledge and teaching. Content does not exist outside the process of acquiring that content (Tobin & Tippins, 1993). Controversies exist in taking this position. These controversies go to the very heart of our understanding of content and the ability to teach content to students. As teacher educators, we take a stand on these controversies in how we approach both the process and content of teacher education programs. Teacher educators face a dilemma in differentiating content and process and understanding how they are intertwined.

Perspectives of Content Knowledge

Constructivism challenges the core of our understanding of the nature of content (von Glasersfeld, 1993). The nature of content is the philosophical basis of constructivism. Constructivism as an epistemology or way of knowing is based on a theory of the possibility of knowing objective reality (Staver, 1998). Constructivism questions the separation between the observer and the observations, the knower and the known. We know the world through our experiences through the interface of our sensation and our constructed meanings of those sensations. While we would prefer to believe the world corresponds to our experience of it, constructivism posits that humans interpret the world in ways that see reality (von Glasersfeld, 1989). Where a correspondence view implies that reality exists exactly as we perceive it, a coherence view implies that we actively build a collective, internally coherent understanding of the world that works to explain phenomena (Staver, 1998). These views raise the most controversial aspects of constructivist perspectives. If content is a human construction, it can change over time. Certain content areas are more clearly linked to human experience and interpretation, e.g. the humanities, arts, and social sciences. But the hard sciences, including mathematics, have the greatest difficulty with constructivist epistemology. The humanities and social sciences derive from human creativity and action and seek to interpret and record human progress, whereas the natural/pure sciences purport to exactly map objective reality. A constructivist approach to the nature of content knowledge should affect how teacher educators look at content across many disciplines. English, history, and the social sciences can be seen as the result of personal viewpoints. Mathematics is seen as a social construction, and thus open to discourse as a method for understanding. If we take a constructivist view of the nature of knowledge, then we need to raise questions about the approach teacher educators should take in developing teachers' approaches to knowledge. At the same time, the natural and mathematical sciences provide some of the greatest support for educational practices related to constructivism. In this dichotomy lies a source for continued exploration and discussion between teacher educators and content-area faculty.

Constructivist Approaches to Learning Content

Constructivism brings pedagogical approaches to learning content. Research in cognitive science has supported constructivist theory and progressed to the point that clear implications are apparent in educational practice. Leinhardt (1992) has synthesized the cognitive research on learning that supports constructivism and summarized the implications around three fundamental aspects: multiple forms of knowledge, the role of prior knowledge, and the social nature of knowledge and its acquisition. While each of these aspects has clear implications for school practice, less has been written about how teacher education responds to these understandings about learning.

Institutional Responses

Research on learning has led to the understanding that there are different types and amounts of knowledge. Knowledge varies across content areas as we examine the different arrangements of facts, notations and reasoning in different subjects. Knowledge varies within content areas as one looks at how documentation, arguments or explanations are structured in different disciplines. In addition, metaknowledge (i.e. knowing what and how well you know) is seen as a powerful factor in developing understanding in students (Schoenfeld, 1987). These multiple forms of knowledge highlight the complexity of learning. Knowledge is seen as not just information, but an active process, retained when embedded in some organizing structure (Bereiter, 1985). When students interact with information, using it in solving problems, answering questions, or discussing their interpretations, the information becomes their knowledge. Since knowledge does not exist in isolation, it must be connected to students' prior knowledge and larger contexts in order to be incorporated into their deep understanding. Interdisciplinary approaches can connect the richness of separate disciplines while acknowledging their interrelationships (Martinello & Cook, 2000).

While teacher education has sought to provide more integration of content with process within teacher education courses, the content prospective teachers learn is left separate and inactivated through the teacher education sequence. Traditionally, educators as well as course contents seldom challenge students' prior knowledge and often reinforce a transmission view of knowledge. A compilation of broad knowledge is emphasized over in-depth study that would challenge student misconceptions. Teacher education faculty should work closely with the teachers to plan and implement courses of study that provide strong link between the methods and content of pedagogical studies.

Pedagogical Perspective

Learning involves combining what you know with what was taught, continually connecting prior knowledge with new information (Leinhardt, 1992). This prior knowledge can facilitate, inhibit, or transform learning. Research on the nature of children's science, (the ideas and experiences students bring into class with them), shows that students hold their prior ideas tenaciously (Driver, Guesne, & Tiberghien, 1985; West & Pines, 1985). These alternative conceptions or misconceptions grow out of students' prior experiences with the world around them and often interfere considerably with teachers' attempts to foster learning. Research in mathematics education shows students come to class with effective but alternative routes to mathematics processes that are often confounded by teaching (Carpenter *et al.*, 1989). Research on the construction of history reveal students' tendency to see historical events in terms of individuals' personal intentions and interactions and to ignore the role of societal institutions (Barton, 1997).

The acknowledgment of alternative conceptions held by students helps deeper understandings of the process necessary to deal with student constructions. Teachers need to surface students' prior knowledge, connect to it or challenge it, and allow students to build from and onto their prior knowledge. In order for students to make use of ideas taught by teachers in the ways teachers intend, knowledge must present itself as intelligible, fruitful, and plausible. This is a move away from a discovery approach, where students construct knowledge solely based on their own experience to knowledge construction where students have the opportunity to test their knowledge within a social context (Watson & Konicek, 1990). Cognitively Guided Instruction (Carpenter *et al.*, 1989) emphasizes allowing students to surface their explanations of mathematical processes as the teacher leads students to see alternative routes to solving problems. Scardamalia and Bereiter (1985) have developed models for teaching writing that use a combination of modelling, coaching, scaffolding and fading. The use of narrative has shown to promote students' historical understanding and challenge students' prior conceptions (Levstik & Pappas, 1992).

Teacher education programmes should inform student teachers about the importance of prior experiences and misconceptions in teaching and learning of content. The "apprenticeship of observation" (Lortie, 1975) through lengthy personal experience with schooling prevents pre-service teachers from searching beyond what they already know and from questioning the practices they see (Feiman-Nemser & Buchmann, 1987). Some teacher education programmes promote conceptual change in their students toward viewing schools as they could be, not merely as they are. Experiences that challenge student conceptions of schooling include simulations and experiences in experimental schools.

The social aspect of knowledge provides clear implications for practice. As outlined above, learning is seen to be an active process of knowledge construction and sense making. Beyond that, knowledge is understood as a cultural artefact of people. It is created and transformed by each individual and by groups of people (Vygotsky, 1978). Participating in communities of discourse allows students to clarify, defend, elaborate, evaluate, and argue over the knowledge constructed (Brown, 1994). Many teachers use cooperative learning as a route to building communities of discourse in their classrooms. Cooperative learning has been shown to be a powerful vehicle to improve learning outcomes for students (Slavin, 1996).

Teacher education has a clear role in clarifying a vision of a social environment supportive to learning. Pre-service teacher education courses can model collaboration between and among the teacher and students. Instructional conversations within the framework of classic Socratic seminar can help instructor and students to explore problems together. Pairing students for field experience placements in schools is one way to promote peer collaboration that fosters deeper understandings of classroom situations (Hausfather, Outlaw, & Strehle, 1996). Pairing allows more opportunities for students to get feedback on their classroom behaviours.

These findings from cognitive science research help to understand the difficulty of separating content from process in learning. Research in teaching has identified the linking of content with the process of teaching. Such links occur as the teacher continually restructures subject matter knowledge for the purpose of teaching (Cochran, DeRuiter, & King, 1993).

Pedagogical Content Knowledge

Shulman (1986) introduced the term pedagogical content knowledge (PCK) as "the ways of representing and formulating the subject that makes it comprehensible to others" (p. 9). This goes beyond knowledge of the content per se to include issues of teaching the content, including typical curricular choices, common learning difficulties and student conceptions in the specific subject. Shulman included PCK in the broader knowledge base for teaching, which included content knowledge, PCK, curriculum knowledge, general pedagogy, learners and their characteristics, educational contexts, and educational purposes (Shulman, 1987). PCK involves the transformation of content knowledge by teachers in ways that allow learners to construct knowledge during classroom practice. Teachers derive PCK from their understandings of content, their own teaching practice, and their own schooling experience. As such, PCK is closely intertwined with both content knowledge and pedagogical process knowledge (Van Driel, Verloop, & De Vos, 1998). Research in pedagogical content knowledge reinforces the research in cognitive science (Cochran, DeRuiter, and King, 1993). Teacher education programmes can enhance the development of PCK in student teachers by modelling and sharing teaching decisions and strategies with students. Faculty should have opportunities to demonstrate and reflect on how they use PCK in their own teaching (Cochran, DeRuiter, and King, 1993).

Although it is difficult to separate PCK from content knowledge, a thorough and coherent understanding of content is necessary for effective PCK (Van Driel, Verloop, & De Vos, 1998). Teacher education programmes can assist pre-service teachers in constructing a deep understanding of disciplinary content from a teaching perspective. A teacher education programme which balances attention to the process of learning with the content being learned can ultimately result in helping teachers be able to understand better both their content and the learning of their students. Too often content is taught without any attention to process, or process is taught without a deep understanding of the content involved. Teacher education programmes seek to find the balance.

Lessons from the Field: What Research Says?

Review of research (1990 to 2009) on constructivist teacher education (Dangel, 2009: http://www.ineducation.ca/category/article-type/articles) reveals a growing but fragmented body of research and links it to practice in teacher education. It provides a guide for future research, programme development, and policy and practice development which is consistent with empirical evidence. An analysis of the research suggests a variety of effects. Some of the findings include:

Student teachers as well as teacher educators found increased understanding of the theoretical underpinnings of constructivism and changes in epistemological beliefs (Al-Weher, 2004; Andersen & Piazza, 1996; Black & Ammon, 1992; Cheng, Chan, Tang, & Cheng, 2009; Graham *et al.*, 1997, Lesar, Benner, & Habel, 1996).

Social interaction and collaboration were key experiences for pre-service teachers and teacher educators (Al-Weher, 2004; Fosnot, 1996; Graham *et al.*, 1997; Gunstone *et al.*, 1993; Jadallah, 1996; Magliaro *et al.*, 1996; Sherman & MacDonald, 2007).

Constructivist teacher education programme enhanced pedagogical understanding of student teachers. Pre-service teachers reported increasing their: (a) skills to develop classroom community (Beck & Kosnik, 2001); (b) views of learner-centeredness as essential to teaching (Condon, Clyde, Kyle, & Hovda, 1993; Graham *et al.*, 1997); (c) their use of inquiry-based teaching approaches (Marek, Laubach, & Pederson, 2003); and (d) their ability to set up learning environments for children to take responsibility for learning (Levin, 2003).

Short-term interventions had an impact on student teachers' pedagogical understanding. In the Mayer-Smith and Mitchell (1997) study, most (13 of the 16) pre-service teachers were able to distinguish didactic from learner-centered teaching approaches and demonstrated a familiarity with teaching for understanding. They also viewed teachers' and pupils' questions as essential to promote and challenge thinking, increase motivation, relate content to pupils' interests and experiences and examine pupils' understandings. In Jadallah's (1996) study, pre-service teachers were able to relate pupil motivation to the extent a lesson promoted active participation, subject matter which caused students to experience cognitive dissonance, and subject matter which related to students' past experiences.

Pre-service teachers reported the importance of active involvement in reconstructing knowledge and recognized the need to tailor communication to meet the needs of learners (Dhindsa and Anderson, 2004; Steele, 1994; Chen, 2001; Stofflet and Stoddart, 1994). Both Steele (1994) and Chen (2001) found that prospective teachers increased their understanding of constructivist pedagogical strategies and the importance of establishing a supportive and risk-free climate for learning. Stofflet and Stoddart (1994) found that pre-service teachers in an elementary science methods course gave stronger pedagogical responses and provided rationales for their pedagogy. They wrote lesson plans that demonstrated coherent understandings of constructivist pedagogy.

Constructivist teacher education programmes found to have positive impact on student teachers' classroom practice (Jadallah, 1996; Stofflet and Stoddart, 1994; Chen, 2001; Mayer-Smith and Mitchell, 1997). Jadallah (1996) used videotapes to investigate pre-service teachers' practice in the field and found that they taught lessons based on pupil's interests and involved children in experiential learning and guided discovery lessons. They also encouraged active involvement of pupils in lessons. Likewise, Stofflet and Stoddart (1994) and Chen (2001) found that pre-service teachers used constructivist pedagogy more consistently in practice, e.g., guided discovery activities and experimentation, a reduced amount of lecturing and increased questioning, and opportunities for children to discuss their ideas. In observing pre-service teachers during their field placements, Mayer-Smith and Mitchell (1997) noticed that pre-service teachers experimented with a range of constructivist strategies in their teaching, including probing the prior views of pupils, incorporating in-depth discussions, having pupils' examine their beliefs, and using role-play.

Pre-service teacher education programme was reported to have changed the student teachers' beliefs and understanding of content (Hand and Peterson, 1995; Luera and Otto, 2005; Fosnot, 1996; Graham, Hudson-Ross and McWhorter, 1997; Gunstone, Slattery, Baird, & Northfield, 1993). In terms of subject-matter, Hand and Peterson (1995) and Luera and Otto (2005) found that pre-service teachers changed their views on teaching and learning science and increased their understanding of science topics. Fosnot (1996) found that pre-service teachers broadened their definitions of mathematics. Authors of two studies (Graham, Hudson-Ross and McWhorter, 1997; Gunstone, Slattery, Baird, & Northfield, 1993) discussed pre-service teachers' growth in terms of their overall intellectual development.

Challenges

The major challenge constructivism presents to teachers and teacher educators is the task of translating a learning theory into a theory of teaching (MacKinnon & Scarff-Seatter, 1997), which in turn raises questions about what teachers need to know and be able to do. For teacher educators, among other tasks, this involves balancing the need to acknowledge the different discipline-specific requirements of teaching with the need to model constructivist methods in teacher education courses and practicum. Richardson (1997) also notes the limits of a perspective on teaching that values students' understandings at the expense of right answers. Student knowledge becomes idiosyncratic; 30 different students may arrive at 30 different understandings or interpretations of a concept, all of which are not appropriate.

Several authors cite the importance of teacher educators' modelling constructivist approaches that engage students in interdisciplinary exploration, collaborative activity, and field-based opportunities for experiential learning, reflection, and self-examination (Kaufman, 1996; Kroll and LaBosky, 1996) if future teachers are to be able to employ these strategies in schools.

To derive culturally relevant and socially just pedagogy and practice from constructivist epistemologies, Martin (1994) and Vadeboncoeur (1997) urge teacher educators to deconstruct and scrutinize cultural assumptions that underlie various interpretations of constructivism to expose how social beliefs have influenced the development of theory and practices. Without such scrutiny, societal inequities and historical forms of oppression may perpetuate in constructivist classrooms.

A final challenge faced by educators is the pitfall of regarding constructivism as the only viable theoretical framework for teaching and learning. It is one way of thinking about how knowledge and understanding are formed, but it is not the only way. Nor are various interpretations of constructivism necessarily incompatible with one another (MacKinnon and Scarff-Seatter, 1997; Oldfather, Bonds, and Bray, 1994). Prospective teachers should be exposed to varying perspectives and given opportunities to develop the discretion needed to implement their choices.

Conclusion

Constructivist approaches to teacher education must deal with the issues of content and process, acknowledging the vital link between content and its acquisition. Constructivism challenges some basic understandings of content knowledge. At the same time, research supporting constructivist approaches brings insights to teacher education practice that makes for more powerful teaching and student understanding of content. An understanding of the nature of pedagogical content knowledge leads teacher educators to help students integrate their experiences in content courses with their experiences in teacher education courses. Examples in teacher education programmes reinforce these understandings. These examples should share an understanding that content and process are inseparable. Teacher education programmes consciously link method courses with content with purpose to help student teachers to think in different ways about content. Modelling by teacher education faculty engages student teachers with content while they learn strategies to teach that content. Content is negotiated with students with an emphasis on concepts over facts. Courses are blocked across content areas to model interdisciplinary teaching and learning. Finally, efforts are made to increase collaboration with arts and sciences faculty toward creating a seamless teacher education program.

Teacher education provides a multiplier effect. As the model that lead our students to understand content deeply and to view content and process as inseparable aspects of knowledge construction approaches , our students gain the perspectives and abilities to move their students to deeper understandings of content. Powerful teacher education should help students at all levels of schooling for better appreciations of the world around them. A constructivist approach shows that content and process are not dichotomous. As more teachers come to that understanding, many more students will benefit.

REFERENCES

Al-Weher, M. (2004). The Effect of a Training Course Based on Constructivism on Student Teachers' Perceptions of the Teaching/Learning Process. *Asia-Pacific Journal of Teacher Education,* 32(2), 169-184.

Anderson, D. and Piazza, J. (1996). Changing Beliefs: Teaching and Learning Mathematics in Constructivist Pre-service Classrooms. *Action in Teacher Education,* 18(2), 51-62.

Barton, K.C. (1997). "Bossed Around by the Queen:" Elementary Students' Understanding of Individuals and Institutions in History. *Journal of Curriculum and Supervision,* 12 (4), 290-314.

Beck, C., and Kosnik, C. (2001). From Cohort to Community in a Preservice Teacher Education Program. *Teaching and Teacher Education, 17*, 925-948.

Bereiter, C. (1985). Toward a Solution of the Learning Paradox. *Review of Educational Research,* 55, 201-226.

Black, A., and Ammon, P. (1992). A Developmental-Constructivist Approach to Teacher Education. *Journal of Teacher Education,* 43(5), 323-335.

Brown, A.L. (1994). The Advancement of Learning. *Educational Researcher*, 23(8), 4-12.

Cannella, G.S., and Reiff, J.C. (1994). Individual Constructivist Teacher Education: Teachers as Empowered Learners. *Teacher Education Quarterly* 21(3), 27-38. EJ 498 429

Carpenter, T.P., Fennema, E., Peterson, P.L., Chiang, C.P., and Loef, M. (1989). Using Knowledge of Children's Mathematics Thinking in Classroom Teaching: An Experimental Study. *American Educational Research Journal*, 26(4), 499-531.

Chen, S. (2001). Constructing a Constructivist Teacher Education: A Taiwan Experience. In Y. Cheng, K. Chow, and K. Tsui (Eds.), *New Teacher Education for the Future: International Perspectives* (p. 261-290). Norwell, MA: Kluwer Academic Publishers.

Cheng, M., Chan, K, Tang, S., and Cheng, A. (2009). Pre-service Teacher Education Students' Epistemological Beliefs and their Conceptions of Teaching. *Teaching and Teacher Education, 25*, 319-327.

Cochran, K.F., DeRuiter, J.A., and King, R.A. (1993). Pedagogical Content Knowing: An Integrative Model for Teacher Preparation. *Journal of Teacher Education,* 44(4), 263-272.

Condon, M.W.F., Clyde, J.A., Kyle, D.W., and Hovda, R.A. (1993). A Constructivist Basis for Teaching and Teacher Education: A Framework for programme Development and Research on Graduates. *Journal of Teacher Education,* 44(5), 273-278.

Dhindsa, H., and Anderson, O. (2004). Using a Conceptual Change Approach to help Pre-service Science Teachers Reorganize their Knowledge Structures for Constructivist Teaching. *Journal of Science Teacher Education,* 15(1), 63-85.

Driver, R., Guesne, E. and Tiberghien, A. (Eds.) (1985). *Children's Ideas in Science.* Philadelphia, PA: Open University Press.

Feiman-Nemser, S. and Buchmann, M. (1987). When is Student Teaching Teacher Education? *Teaching and Teacher Education*, 3(4), 255-273.

Fosnot, C.T. (1996). Teachers Construct Constructivism: The Center for Constructivist Teaching/Teacher Preparation Project. In C.T. Fosnot (Ed.), *Constructivism:*

Theory, Perspectives and Practices (p. 175-192). New York, NY: Teachers College Press.

Graham, P., Hudson-Ross, S., and McWhorter, P. (1997). Building Nets: Evolution of a Collaborative Inquiry Community within a High School English Teacher Education Program. *English Education,* 29(2), 91-129.

Gunstone, R., Slattery, M., Baird, J., and Northfield, J. (1993). A Case Study Exploration of Development in Pre-service Teachers. *Science Education,* 77(1), 47-73.

Hand, B., and Peterson, R. (1995). The Development, Trial and Evaluation of a Constructivist Teaching and Learning Approach in a Pre-service Science Teacher Education Program. *Research in Science Education,* 25(1), 75-88.

Hausfather, S.J. (1996). Vygotsky and Schooling: Creating a Social Context for Learning. *Action in Teacher Education,* 18(2), 1-10.

Hausfather, S.J., Outlaw, M.E., and Strehle, E.L. (1996). Relationships as a Foundation: Emerging field Experiences within Multiple College-school Partnerships. In T. Warren (Ed.), *Partnerships in Teacher Education: Schools and Colleges Working Together* (pp. 27-41). Lanham, MD: University Press of America.

Jadallah, E. (1996). Reflective Theory and practice: A Constructivist Process for Curriculum and Instructional Decisions. *Action in Teacher Education,* 18(2), 73-85.

Kaufman, D. (1996). Constructivist-based Experiential Learning in Teacher Education. *Action in Teacher Education* 18(2), 40-49. EJ 536 845.

Kroll, L.R., and LaBosky, V.K. (1996). Practicing what we Preach: Constructivism in a Teacher Education Program. *Action in Teacher Education* 18(2), 63-72. EJ 536 947.

MacKinnon, A., and Scarff-Seatter, C. (1997). Constructivism: Contradictions and Confusion in Teacher Education. In V. Richardson (Ed.), *Constructivist Teacher Education: Building New Understandings* (pp. 38-55). Washington, DC: Falmer Press.

Martin, R.J. (1994). Multicultural Social Reconstructionist Education: Design for Diversity in Teacher Education. *Teacher Education Quarterly* 21(3), 77-89. EJ 492 141

Myers, C.B. (1996, April). Beyond pdss: Schools as Professional Learning Communities. A Proposal Based on an Analysis of pds Efforts of the 1990's. Paper presented at the Annual Meeting of the American Educational Research Association, New York. ED 400 227

Leinhardt, G. (1992). What research on Learning Tells Us about Teaching. *Educational Leadership* 49 (7) 20-25.

Lesar, S., Benner, S., and Habel, J. (1996, April). Preparing Elementary Education Teachers for Inclusive Settings: A Constructivist Teacher Education Program. Paper Presented at the Meeting of the American Educational Research Association, New York.

Levin, B. (2003). *Case Studies of Teacher Development.* Mahwah, NJ: Lawrence Erlbaum and Associates.

Levstik, L.S. and Pappas, C.C. (1992). New Directions for Studying Historical Understanding. *Theory and Research in Social Education,* 20(4), 369-385.

Lortie, D. (1975). Schoolteacher: A sociological Study. Chicago: University of Chicago Press.

Luera, G., and Otto, C. (2005). Developing and Evaluation of an Inquiry Based Elementary Science Teacher Education programme Reflecting Current Reform Movements. *Journal of Science Teacher Education,* 241-258.

Magliaro, S., Murphy, S., Sawyers, J., Altieri, L., and Nienkark, L. (1996, April). Reinventing Teacher Education: An Examination of the Social Construction of Learning in an Elementary Education Program. Paper presented at the Meeting of the American Educational Research Association, New York.

Marek, K., Laubach, T., and Pederson, J. (2003). Pre-service Elementary School Teachers' Understandings of Theory Based Science Education. *Journal of Science Teacher Education,* 14(3), 147-159.

Martinello, M.L. and Cook, G.E. (2000). *Interdisciplinary Inquiry in Teaching and Learning* (2nd Edition). Upper Saddle River, NJ: Prentice-Hall, Inc.

Mayer-Smith, J., and Mitchell, I. (1997). Teaching about Constructivism: Using Approaches Informed by Constructivism. In V. Richardson (Ed.), *Constructivist teacher education* (p. 135-152). Washington, DC: Falmer Press.

NCERT (2005): National Curriculum Framework-2005, New Delhi.

Oldfather, P., Bonds, S., and Bray, T. (1994). Drawing the Circle: Collaborative Mind Mapping as a Process for Developing a Constructivist Teacher Education Program. *Teacher Education Quarterly* 21(3), 5-13. EJ 492 137

O'Loughlin, M. (1995). Daring the Imagination: Unlocking Voices of Dissent and Possibility in Teaching. *Theory into Practice* 24(2), 107-116. EJ 512 860

Richardson, V. (1997). Constructivist Teaching and Teacher Education: Theory and Practice. In V. Richardson (Ed.), *Constructivist Teacher Education: Building New Understandings* (pp. 3-14). Washington, DC: Falmer Press.

Scardamalia, M., and Bereiter, C. (1985). Fostering the Development of Self-Regulation in Children's Knowledge Processing. In S. Chipman, J. Segal, and R. Glaser, (Eds.), *Thinking and Learning Skills: Research and Open Questions.* Hillsdale NJ: Erlbaum.

Schoenfeld, A.H. (1987). What's all the Fuss about Metacognition? In A.H. Schoenfeld (Ed.), *Cognitive Science and Mathematics Education* (pp. 189-253). New York: W.H. Freeman.

Sherman, A., and MacDonald, L. (2007). Pre-service Teachers' Experiences with a Science Education Module. *Journal of Science Teacher Education, 18*, 525-541.

Shulman, L.S. (1986). Those who Understand: Knowledge Growth in Teaching. *Educational Researcher*, 15, 4-14.

Slavin, R.E. (1996). Research on Cooperative Learning and Achievement: What we Know, what we Need to Know. *Contemporary Educational Psychology*, 21(1), 43-69.

Staver, J.R. (1998). Constructivism: Sound Theory for Explicating the Practice of Science and Science Teaching. *Journal of Research in Science Teaching*, 35(5), 501-520.

Steele, D. (1994, April). Helping Preservice Teachers Confront their Conceptions about Mathematics Teaching and Learning. Paper presented at the American Education Research Association, New Orleans, LA.

Stofflett, R., and Stoddart, T. (1994). The Ability to Understand and Use Conceptual Change Pedagogy as a Function of Prior Content Learning Experience. *Journal of Research in Science Teaching,* 31(1), 31-51.

Tobin, K., and Tippins, D. (1993). Constructivism as a Referent for Teaching and Learning. In K. Tobin (Ed.) *The Practice of Constructivism in Science Education.* Hillsdale, NJ: Erlbaum.

Vadeboncoeur, J. (1997). Child Development and the Purpose of Education: A Historical Context for Constructivism in Teacher Education. In V. Richardson (Ed.), *Constructivist Teacher Education: Building New Understandings* (pp. 15-37). Washington, DC: Falmer Press.

Van Driel, J.H., Verloop, N., and De Vos, W. (1998). Developing Science Teachers' Pedagogical Content Knowledge. *Journal of Research in Science Teaching*, 35(6), 673-695.

von Glaserfeld, E. (1993). Questions and Answers about Radical Constructivism. In K. Tobin (Ed.) *The Practice of Constructivism in Science Education* (pp. 23-38). Hillsdale, NJ: Erlbaum.

von Glaserfeld, E. (1989). Cognition, Construction of Knowledge, and Teaching. *Synthese*, 80, 121-140.

Vygotsky, L.S. (1978). Mind in Society: The Development of Higher Psychological Processes. Cambridge, MA: Harvard University Press.

Vygotsky, L.S. (1978). *Mind in Society: The Development of Higher Psychological Processes*. Cambridge, MA: Harvard University Press.

Watson, B. and Konicek, R. (1990). *Teaching for Conceptual Change: Confronting Children's Experience*. Phi Delta Kappan, 71(9), 680-685.

West, L.H., and Pines, A.L. (Eds.) (1985). *Cognitive Structure and Conceptual Change*. Orlando, FL: Academic Press.

2
Quality Secondary Teacher Education Programme: Some Considerations

Sesadeba Pany

The socio-economic and political development of any society is dependent upon a well coordinated teacher education programme. The teacher training programme receives such paramount importance in the context of the magic role played by teachers in the classroom. The teacher is the real social-architect who can really shape the destiny of India by imparting need based education to the future generation of the society. As such, the quality of living of people is directly proportional to the quality of education programme. In the era of knowledge explosion all the countries virtually try to impart quality education which is highly essential for the emergence of a learning society. In this context, the National Council of Teacher Education (NCTE) in its document in 1998 has emphasized that teachers are the torchbearers in creating social cohesion and national integration by revealing and elaborating the secrets of attaining higher values in life. The teachers having a futuristic vision can only lead the society towards an egalitarian one.

Teacher Education: The Backdrop

The concept of teacher education is not of recent origin in India. Though the origin of the modern teacher education programme can be traced back to early 19th century, such programme was having a strong background on Indian soil since long. In ancient India the educational system was mainly spiritual in nature and the Brahmins were solely in the charge of acquiring knowledge and transmitting it to the upcoming generation. In this context, we can quote Prof. R.P. Singh (1970) points out: 'One thing is however evident that there were certain Brahmin families where teaching was a hereditary profession. There is no evidence to hold the view that teacher training existed in the formal sense, known to us. But surely the Brahmins knew about their future calling and learnt their subjects keeping the future in mind'. During the Vedic periods the 'Rishis' or 'Munis' were called as Gurus, Acharyas or teacher. Such teachers were really the storehouse of wisdom and enriched vision; and on a hereditary basis their future generation were practicing the same profession. Each Brahmin family was working just like a school and their prime mission was the propagation of knowledge to the coming generation. They were imparting complete education and only the successful brilliant students later on were establishing their independent Ashram as schools for the transmission of knowledge. The system of education was quite rigorous and only the meritorious students were given the status of the Guru later on. But with the passage of time due to some unavoidable circumstances like foreign aggression our indigenous system collapsed and the modern teacher education programme emerged with the assistance of the East India Company. However, credit goes to wood's despatch 1854 for taking initiation in establishing teacher training institutions in India in the form of Normal school to train the primary teachers in the Madras presidency in the year 1856. Further in 1882 the Indian Education Commission recommended training for secondary school teachers and consequently by the end of 19th century six training colleges were established in Madras, Lahore, Kurseong, Allahabad, Jabalpur, and Rajmundry. Later on the independent India on the basis of the recommendation of various commissions established different levels of teacher training institutions throughout India (649 training schools and 42 Secondary training colleges) and presently the numbers of secondary teacher training institutions are approximately more than 10,000. But some fundamental questions arise here such as—Why there are so many teacher training colleges? And, are they really capable of providing quality teacher education? Such mushroom growth of teacher training institutions is only due to the privatization and liberalization of teacher training programme. Such rapid expansion of teacher training institutions results in the deterioration of the quality of training causing irreparable loss to human resource development. Therefore, unless immediate attempt is taken to ensure quality teacher education programme, the country is bound to face intellectual crisis.

Quality Teacher Education: The Concept

The term quality is a very commonly used term in the field of teacher education. Though it is a relative term but it can be defined with the help of its basic indicators. Any system which is beneficial to the society, has the potential to eradicate the earlier wrong practices and unanimously accepted by different categories of citizens leaving aside their selfish interest may be conceived as the qualitative one. As such, quality refers to excellence. The quality teacher education programme can very well be understood through a conceptual analysis of its three basic components like input, process and output. These three components are related to each other and quality in aspect leads to quality in another one. Quality input in teacher education include quality teachers having sound theoretical knowledge and pedagogical skills, attractive and well equipped building, availability of standard teaching learning materials and aids, well equipped library, need based and relevant curriculum; and meritorious teacher trainees having the proper aptitude for teaching. Quality process in teacher education programme is concerned with the proper method of transacting the curriculum, practical based training with constructive feed-back system and democratic teacher-student interaction system. The quality output aspect is judged in terms of pedagogical skills, personal characteristic and enriched teaching aptitude of the pupil teachers. It is almost impossible to impart quality teacher education in the absence of a sweet co-ordination among all these elements.

Fig. 2.1: Parameters of Quality Teacher Education

Besides these three fundamental aspects of quality teacher education, there are some other allied aspects and agencies which play a very decisive role in ensuring quality. The pre-service teacher training institutions need a complete change with regard to its structural as well as the functional aspects.

Structural Redesigning of the Teacher Education Programme

The preservice teacher education programme in different states of India varies considerably with regard to its duration as well as admission procedure. Keeping in mind the thrust areas highlighted by the NCF-2005 and the NCFTE-2009 in terms of the development of content knowledge as well as the pedagogical competencies a basic structural change is required which can provide necessary scaffoldings for quality teacher education programmes. Some of the suggestions are follows:

1. Without sound theoretical knowledge competency in practice is a distant dream. In addition to this we all experience a radical change in the school curriculum in terms of its contents as well as difficulty level. Hence the existing duration of teacher education programme need be modified as suggested by the report of Hon'ble Justice J.S. Verma (2012) i.e. introduction of four years integrated programme after 10+2 or two years training programme after graduation.
2. Admission of teacher trainees at different levels of teacher training programme need be through the conduct of teaching aptitude tests in order to ensure quality entrants to the profession. But most of the state governments with the pressure of the private college management when their seats lie vacant simply cancel the policy of teaching aptitude tests compromising with the quality of teacher training programme. This situation arises due to the unplanned opening of teacher training institutions.
3. The number of teacher training colleges need be restricted keeping in mind the supply and demand figure of teachers at different levels for the maintenance of quality of teacher training institutions as well as the schools.
4. Keeping in mind the increased innovative content load at the primary and secondary level, consideration may be made with regard to enhancing the entry level qualifications of the teacher trainees at different levels of training programme.
5. We find uneven distribution of teacher training colleges throughout India, which need be as per the distribution of population. The number of teacher training colleges in different states have been presented in the following table:

Redesigning of Teacher Education Curriculum

The present teacher education at all the stages need be changed keeping in mind the recommendations of the National Curriculum Framework for Teacher Education (NCFTE, 2009). According to the report issues related to inclusive education, perspectives for equitable and sustainable development, gender perspectives, role of community knowledge in education and ICT in schooling as well as e-learning need be central to teacher education curriculum development. Hon'ble justice J.S. Verma in his report (August, 2012) has clearly

State Wise List of B.Ed. Colleges

S. No.	*State*	*No. of B.Ed. Colleges*	*Population*
1.	Uttar Pradesh	1108	199,581,477
2.	Maharashtra	347	112,372,972
3.	Bihar	60	103,804,637
4.	West Bengal	132	91,347,736
5.	Andhra Pradesh	623	84,665,533
6.	Madhya Pradesh	375	72,597,565
7.	Tamil Nadu	667	72,138,958
8.	Rajasthan	697	68,621,012
9.	Karnataka	393	61,130,704
10.	Gujarat	285	60,383,628
11.	Odisha	16	41,947,358
12.	Kerala	188	33,387,677
13.	Jharkhand	55	32,966,238
14.	Assam	48	31,169,272
15.	Punjab	195	27,704,236
16.	Haryana	1056	25,353,081
17.	Chhattisgarh	09	25,540,196
18.	Uttarakhand	69	10,116,752
19.	Himachal Pradesh	74	6,856,509
20.	Tripura	03	3,671,032
21.	Meghalaya	04	2,964,007
22.	Manipur	06	2,721,756
23.	Nagaland	03	1,980,602
24.	Goa	04	1,457,723
25.	Arunachal Pradesh	04	1,382,611
26.	Mizoram	01	1,091,014
27.	Sikkim	03	607,688
28.	Delhi	37	16,753,235
29.	Puducherry	30	1,244,464
30.	Chandigarh	02	1,054,686
31.	Andaman & Nicobar Islands	02	379,944
32.	Dadar& Nagar haveli	01	342853
33.	Daman and Diu	02	242,911
34.	Lakshadweep	01	64,429

advocated the implementation of the recommendations of NCFTE-2009 on teacher education curriculum like

1. The inclusion of disciplinary (subject) content engagement in courses on pedagogy.
2. The inclusion of the nature, philosophy and history of discipline in specific pedagogy courses to engage student teachers with epistemological basis of different school subjects.
3. The inclusion of learner assessment as part of pedagogical approaches to develop perspective and a repertoire of skills in teachers.
4. Shift in the focus from 'concepts of educational psychology', such as learning theories to concepts related to children's development,

children's learning and thinking patterns, thus contextualizing teachers' knowledge.

5. Introduction of courses that engage student-teachers with contemporary Indian issues within inter-disciplinary frameworks so as to locate education and the learner in a socio-cultural, economic and political context with a thrust on diversity.
6. Integration of field based study in theory courses so as to enable teachers to think praxis.
7. Design of practicum courses that enable observing and studying children in 'real' contexts; provide hands on experience of curriculum/ text analysis and design; field tours for getting first-hand experience of diverse socio-cultural and socio-economic contexts.
8. Introduction of courses of language proficiency for the developing teacher.
9. Instituting Teacher Learning Centers for grounding the education of pre-service students within immediate classroom contexts, the wider societal context and learner diversity.
10. Setting up of laboratory schools as part of the education of teachers.

The teacher education programme need a structural reform along with change in its functional aspects to ensure quality of the programme. So far as the functional aspect is concerned the various regulating authorities like NCTE, NAAC, UGC, Universities and State governments have to play a very decisive role in this regard and as such the roles of such agencies for quality maintenance have been discussed in the succeeding sections.

National Council for Teacher Education

The National Council for the Teacher Education (NCTE) is responsible for maintaining quality of teacher education programme in India. It came into force in 1995 as a statutory body by the parliamentary act in 1993. The basic responsibility of NCTE is to lay down norms—the standards for teacher training institutions with regard to appointment of teaching and non – teaching staffs, infrastructure which include size of the classroom, building, library, laboratories, playground, number of teaching days, entry level qualifications of teacher trainees and curriculum etc. The training institutions fulfilling these conditions are given recognition by NCTE. Further, the teacher training institutions are also bound to submit the performance appraisal report each year to NCTE which helps NCTE to ensure quality in those institutions in terms of suggestion for improvement or withdrawing recognition if there is any violation of norms. But in spite of all the attempts made by NCTE to maintain quality of teacher education programme, all the attempts go in vain due to the private managements as well as the step motherly attitude of some of the state governments.

What NCTE can do?

However considering the mushroom growth of the teacher training institutions and gross violation of the norms and standards, the NCTE should focus attention on the following considerations:

(a) No compromise with the norms and standards as fixed by NCTE (if we compromise with the norms by giving relaxation for one, two or three years, are we not doing injustice to teacher trainees produced during those period by compromising with the quality?)

(b) Surprise visit of NCTE regional and central team to confirm the truthfulness of information provided by the institution during the time of recognition.

(c) There should not be frequent change in the qualification of lecturers appointed in the teacher training institutions.

(d) The NCTE visiting team should constitute experts from different discipline like Revenue Inspectors from revenue department for land measurement purpose, a lawyer and journalists. (Preferably experts from other states)

(e) There should be video recording of the entire visit and the report of the visit need be finalized on the spot and should be made public.

(f) The NCERT pattern of two years B.Ed degree having sufficient scope for practical work should be followed in all the teacher training institutions and M.Ed degree should be of two years duration just like any other post graduate degree (As suggested by the Hon'ble J.S. Verma Commission Report, August-2012).

(g) The M.Ed pass outs should be appointed as teacher educators in the DIETs whereas the M.A. Education candidates should be appointed in higher education institutions.

(h) In many cases the name of a single lecturer is also reflected in more than one colleges. Therefore, the NCTE need be vigilant in this regard and a nationwide network need be introduced in its website.

(i) NCTE should open a separate portal for the teacher trainees, teachers and parents so that they can lodge their complaints to NCTE well in time and the matter need be viewed seriously by the NCTE with immediate effect.

Universities

Universities are considered as the affiliating bodies for different colleges. Initially the university gives provisional affiliation to the teacher training colleges and later on by considering their nature of work and other conditions laid down by the university, they are given permanent affiliation. Generally the universities by means of the entrance test and counseling fulfils the seats of B.Ed colleges, conduct examination and give certificates. As such, the university has full control over the training colleges. But in reality what happens? If the universities have so many powers regarding the maintenance of quality, then why are most of the teacher training colleges playing with the future of the teacher-trainees with under qualified staffs, ill maintained library and improper infrastructure etc? The responsibility of maintenance of quality in such institutions will be fixed on whom? On the NCTE or on the concerned universities? In view of the mushroom growth of teacher training institutions and degradation of quality, the concerned universities should focus their attention on the following aspects:

(a) Entrance examination should be conducted to admit students to the teacher training institutions.
(b) Entrance examination should consist of two major aspects like (i) teaching aptitude of the students and (ii) content related knowledge of the students in the concerned teaching subjects they will opt for.
(c) Conditions of provisional affiliation should be very strict especially subject to the fulfillment of the conditions relating to appointment of qualified staff, building, library and financial matters and NCTE norm should not be violated in this regard.
(d) The number of specified teaching days need be strictly observed in all the teacher training institutions.
(e) The university should make the provision of surprise visit to each teacher training institution at least twice a year (during the teaching days).
(f) The university should approve the lecturers of all the training colleges and their yearly progress in terms of research and development should be properly recorded.
(g) Only some selected institutions should be allowed to run the M.Ed course—those are having necessary infrastructure, enriched library and qualified teaching facilities.
(h) There should be the provision of inter college transfer among the approved staffs in order to stop the monopoly of the college managements.
(i) The colleges should be asked to deposit the salary of each staff in the university account and salary need be released by the university. Annual financial audit should be done by the concerned state government and it should match the audit made by the college management itself, otherwise appropriate disciplinary action should be taken against the corrupt officials.

(j) All the financial power should be rested with the principal of the college to reduce the monopoly of the colleges.
(k) No college should be allowed to run its college without approved principal and teaching staff. If approved principal and teaching staff is not appointed then the college should be fined per month basis i.e. Rs. 60,000 for principal and Rs. 35,000 per teaching staff.
(l) The attendance system of the teachers and the students should be taken through biometric device and it should be made online.

State Government

The state governments play a vital role in the quantitative and qualitative development of any educational system in general and that of the teacher-training institutions in particular. Nobody can open teacher-training institution without the consent of the concerned state government in terms of No Objection Certificate (NOC). The NOC is the basic criterion to obtain affiliation from the university. Hence, the state governments need be very cautious and have a realistic vision while giving NOC to open such colleges. But in reality the case is quite different. Due to the presence of some corrupt officials the process of obtaining NOC has been very easy. Therefore, if at all we want to save our nation and provide quality education then the concerned authorities should not come under the influence of any illegal pressure while giving NOC to any organization. In this context, the state government should take into consideration the following aspects before giving NOC for the opening of any new teacher training institution:

(a) Consider the number of existing teacher training institutions and give NOC to another one if the situation demands for so.
(b) The department of higher education should inspect these institutions at regular interval and undertake proper follow-up action.
(c) The government should fix up uniform fees for admission in these institutions.
(d) The government should ensure that the teaching faculties of such institutions are not ill paid and under qualified.
(e) The government should carry out surprise inspection to different teacher training institutions in order to ensure the implementation of rules and regulations of the statutory bodies.
(f) Colleges found guilty need be given exemplary punishment in terms of heavy fine (five times of annual turnover) or by closing the colleges forever.
(g) As the teacher training institutions play a vital role in the human resource development of the country, the state government should be very strict towards such institutions with regard to the fulfillment of norms and standards.

National Assessment and Accreditation Council (NAAC)

With a view to maintain quality in the higher educational institutions, the central government established NAAC in 1994 on the basis of the recommendations of NPE-1986. The major function of NAAC is to label the higher educational institutions on the basis of quality concern. Such accreditation is given on the basis of rigorous process of assessment which generally proceeds through three stages like, self appraisal report by the institution concerned, assessment of the self appraisal report by means of field investigation by the team of experts of NAAC and the final accreditation by NAAC. Such accreditation is generally given for a period of five years. As such, the NAAC if properly acts can definitely ensure the quality of teacher training institutions to a great extent.

Further, keeping in view the increasing number of the institutions— teacher training or any other higher education institutions—the NAAC should establish its regional centers for its smooth functioning. However all the teacher training institutions should come under the purview of NAAC and the NCTE, and the concerned universities and state governments should give due weight to the NAAC report. Transparency need be maintained in the process of NAAC accreditation and it should also collect information from different sources to confirm the information as furnished by the concerned colleges.

University Grants Commission

The University Grants Commission is considered as the highest regulating authority of the higher education system in India. It has to lay definite norms for teacher education institutions all over India, and other bodies like NCTE and NCERT should also frame their norms in the light of that of the UGC. UGC should also ensure the implementation of its scale of pay and other provisions through its regular inspection of the colleges. The UGC can also sponsor eligible lecturers and principals to various teacher training colleges for the maintenance of quality staff and teaching-learning process. Besides this for the development of research skills and promotion of research and innovation in the field of teacher education the UGC is expected to change its rules and opportunity should be given to one and all irrespective of the private or government owned college for carrying out research work with the financial assistance of the commission. Further the UGC should take initiatives in linking the teacher training institutions with the universities and if possible by establishing separate teacher training universities in each state.

Conclusion

Teacher training institutions are a must in India but it is high time to control the mushroom growth of such institutions otherwise we may cause irreparable loss to our human resources. It is presently seen that in some states there are more than 1200 private teacher training colleges whereas in others not a single one (Orissa) and in the government sector the seats are so few that students go to other states for B.Ed degree. Hence each state government should come forward with a proper policy with the regard to the quantitative and qualitative development of the teacher training institutions. All the national and state level agencies like NCTE, UGC, NAAC, University and state governments should be true to the implementation of the norms and the standards as set by themselves if they really want to save this nation and create a learning society, but unfortunately in India in most of the cases the norms and standards fixed for teacher training institutions are simply maintained in pen and papers and in reality the scenario is quite the reverse. Therefore, it is the right time on the part of related quality maintaining agencies to be alert towards the honest implementation of proper policies, otherwise quality teacher education in India may be a distant dream than reality.

REFERENCES

Bhushan, S. (2007). A New Liberal Agenda of Knowledge Commission, *University News*, Vol. 45. No. 25 p. 1

Gupta, A.K. and Gupta, R. (2007). Students' Feedback for Quality Assessment: Challenges and Tasks Ahead, *University News*, Vol. 45. No. 30 p. 5.

Mohanty, A.K. and Pani, A. (2005). Landmark in the Development of Teacher Education in India, *University News*, Vol. 43. No. 18 p. 14

Nigavekar, Arun (2001). Transformation for Quality in Higher Education, *University News*, Vol. 39. No. 28 p. 13

Singh, L.C. and Mishra, S. (2005). Quality Concern in Teacher Education, *University News*, Vol. 43. No. 18 p. 29.

Upadhyaya, S.K. and Upadhyaya. V. (2005). Quality Concern Indicators of Teacher Education, *University News*, Vol. 43. No. 18 p. 43.

3
Historical Perspective of Teacher Education and Capacity Building of Teachers through In-Service Training

Sankar Prasad Mohanty

Teacher education as a programme of education, research and training of persons to teach from pre-primary to higher education level as defined by National Council for Teacher Education. It is related to the development of teacher proficiency and competence which enables the teacher to meet the requirements of the profession and face the challenges in the profession. Teacher Education includes three aspects i.e., teaching skills, pedagogy and professional skills. Teaching skills comprise of different techniques, approaches and strategies that helps the teachers for planning and imparting instruction, providing appropriate motivations; reinforcing and conducting effective student's assessment. Besides, it includes classroom management skills, core teaching skills; preparation and use of TLMs and methods of transaction in the classroom, providing scope for pupil-teacher interaction; interaction with peers; school community relations etc. Teacher education has three phases: Pre-service, Induction and In-service (International Encyclopedia of Teaching and Teacher education, 1987). The age-old talk 'Teachers are born, not made' has been changed as teacher education believes in 'Teachers are made, not born, because the teacher is taught both knowledge and skills of teaching'.

Teacher Education does not end in training institutions, but it is a continuous process from the entry into the profession till the retirement. The development of a teacher does not cease when he leaves the training college; he now begins to learn from a different kind of experience. In ancient India scholars and teachers used to meet and discuss topics of mutual interest. These discussions were made by the members of the same school of thought as well as by exponents of different schools of thoughts. We have innumerable examples of pundits of different religions travelling long distance to meet and discuss the problems with pundits of other places.

The in-service education of secondary school teachers at the beginning of this century consisted mainly of refresher courses, lectures, and conferences.

These were generally arranged during the vacation period at a centrally located place or the teacher training institution and were seldom a regular feature of the school program. Most of these activities were spasmodic responses to the recommendations of the various commissions that were appointed from time to time to study the problems of the existing educational system.

Historical Perspective of Teacher Education in India

The history of teacher education in India is as old as the history of education itself. The history of Indian teacher education may be divided into five parts:

- Vedic Period : 1200 B.C to 600 B.C
- Buddhist Period : 600 B.C to 1200 A.D
- Muslim Period : 1200 A.D to 1700 A.D
- British Period : 1700 A.D to 1947 A.D
- Independent period : 1947 A.D to Current period

Vedic Period

In Vedic period, Brahmins served as teachers of the community devoting themselves to the work of acquisition, conversation and promoting of knowledge and its transmission from one generation to another. It was their duty to learn, to teach. The system of education was Gurukul-centered concerned with teaching of *Vedas*. Brahmins used to earn their livelihood by teaching. It was a hereditary process. In this connection Professor R.P. Singh (1970) writes: "One thing is however evident that there were certain Brahmin families where teaching was a hereditary profession.... There is no evidence to hold the view that teacher training existed in the formal sense, known to us. But surely the Brahmins knew about their future calling and learnt their subjects keeping the future in mind".

In later Vedic age when the three Vedas—Samveda, Yajurveda and Atharvaveda—and other Vedic literature also came into existence, teaching was still continued in the time-honoured system of oral tradition, but in the course of time teachers had the access to other means also to enhance their education. Gradually several types of institutions known as *'Sakhas'*, *'Charaòas'*, *'Parishads'*, *'Kulas'*, *'Gotras'* and the like developed. All of these were of the nature of assemblies, academies, literary or religious guilds, serving as schools of Vedic learning in which knowledge was conserved, commented upon and communicated by and to the successive generations of teachers and pupils. Thus in later Vedic period, teachers were better equipped to enhance and develop their education.

Buddhist Period

Training of the teachers became more elaborate and thorough during Buddhist Period. A monk or a *'Bhikkhu'* was placed under the in-charge-ship of two superiors, qualified by learning, character and standing, which were called the '*Upadhyaya*' and '*Acharya*'. Upadhyaya was entrusted with the duty of instructing the young Bhikkhu in the sacred texts and doctrines, while the '*Acharya*' assumed the responsibility for his conduct and discipline. He was therefore also known as '*Karmacharya*'. This period of training or dependence under the two teachers was for at least ten years after which this monk was considered ready to give 'Nissaya' to others. Teaching was considered as the noblest profession during Buddhist period.

Muslim Period

The chief aim of the Muslim rulers in India was to propagate their religion. It was very difficult for them to have any idea of teacher education. There was no formal system of teacher training. Education was a public affair. Educational institutions were called Madrasha where students were taught by *Molvies*. Education was mainly teaching of *Quran*. Educated people available in the country or abroad from Arabia were appointed as Molvies in the educational institutions.

British Period

- **Teachers' Training Institutions for training teachers were first started by Danish Missionaries:** A normal training school was established by William Carey at Serampur (West Bengal) in 1802. Thereafter, Calcutta School Society established in 1819 got a grant of Rs. 500 per month from the Board of Directors in early 1825 for the training to teachers of native schools. The Native Educational Society of Bombay, for instance, trained 24 teachers for primary schools in 1826 and a training class was started at Elphinston Institution in 1829 as primary schools increased. In these training efforts however, there was emphasis on the improvement of knowledge of the subject matter and not on the methods of teaching as the traditions and views in favour of academic excellence reflected strongly.
- **Monitorial system (1830):** The idea of formal teachers' training originated out of an indigenous technique called '*Monitorial System*' which was based on the principle of '*Mutual Instruction*' or '*Bell-Lancaster method*' the British educators Dr Andrew Bell and Joseph Lancaster who both independently developed it. The class was being split up into small groups and one brilliant pupil (Monitor) was being placed as the in charge of the class. The monitors gained some proficiency in teaching and class control, which enabled them to teach independently in their later life.
- **The Woods Despatch (1854):** It is popularly known as '*Magna Charta of English Education in India*' which advocated the need

of establishing teacher's training institutions and of giving stipends to pupil-teachers for first time. In addition to proposing certain new schemes, the Despatch considered the question of securing properly qualified teachers for schools in each presidency. During the 30 years following the Despatch, there were only two training institutions for secondary (English) school teachers for the whole of India. These teachers were trained for schools with English as the medium of instruction. The training school at Madras was established as early as 1856, and the one at Lahore was started in 1880. Even at these two schools, students with different levels of attainment were all grouped together as one class and were put through the same course. Moreover, there were no practicing schools for these teacher trainees.

- **The Hunter Commission (1882):** By the recommendation of the commission, the importance of training to teachers was accepted by all concerned, still there was a controversy in England as to what type of training should be introduced in India. Should it be the pattern of the French Normal Schools or that of the German Schools…? For this reason there was slow progress in teachers' training even after twenty years following the report of the Hunter Commission. Hence, by 1901-1902, there were six training colleges located at Saidapet, Rejamahendry, Kurslong, Allahabad, Lahore, and Jubbulpore. A certificate examination for secondary teachers was organized in every province in India. Madras, one of the educationally progressive states of India, had by then the L.T. (Licentiate of Teaching) Degree.
- **Resolution on Educational Policy (1904):** Lord Curzon's resolution initiated a new era in the training of secondary teachers. His orders were for improving the training colleges as well as for increasing the output of trained secondary teachers. On the basis of his recommendation, four training colleges were established: Bombay (1906); Calcutta (1908); Patna (1909); and Dacca (1910). The Jabbalpore training class was developed into a college in 1911. By 1912, there were 15 training institutions for secondary school teachers, giving instruction to nearly 1,400 students.
- **The Government Resolution on Educational Policy (1913):** Subsequently, Government of India clearly stated in the resolution on Educational policy the following: "Eventually, under Modern system of education, no teacher should be allowed to teach without a certificate that has qualified to do so".
- **The Calcutta University (Sadler) Commission of (1917):** The popularly known Sadler Commission was appointed under the

chairmanship of Michael Sadler. The report emphasized the role of universities to set up Department of Education for the professional training of secondary teachers and need to establish a demonstration school attached to each training college.

- **The Hartog Committee (1929):** The Committee made some important recommendations regarding the training of primary teachers. As a result of these declarations, the teacher training institutions in India developed steadily, with improved libraries, and better equipped laboratories. Practicing schools for trainees were also made accessible. On the recommendation of the committee the system of teacher training was re-oriented on more progressive lines. In 1932, a new degree B.Ed was instituted for the first time by Andhra University and in 1936, Bombay University started for the first time Post graduate degree M.Ed in Education.

Independent Period

The independence of India on the 15th August 1947 marks a defining moment in the history of our nation. India's independence, division of the country and related disturbances took place almost simultaneously and drew the attention of national leaders. Transformation of the *'economy of scarcity'* into the *'economy of plenty'*, and reducing unemployment of the youth and food shortage became their main priorities. The first step in this direction was setting up of the University Education Commission (1948), which made valuable suggestions regarding pre-service and in-service education of teachers and linking the programme of teacher preparation with the university system.

- **University Education Commission (1948-49):** The Government of India appointed the commission under the chairmanship of Dr. S. Radhakrishnan. The commission submitted its report in 1949. The commission was mainly concerned with the university education, but it has made recommendations for teachers training also.

    i. Teacher training colleges should be remodeled—more time should be given to practice teaching and weightage to practical examination than theory.
    ii. In the training colleges teachers should be recruited from those who possess sufficient teaching experience.
    iii. The theory courses should be flexible and adaptable to local needs and circumstances.

- **Secondary Education Commission (1952-53):** The Government of India appointed the Commission under the chairmanship of Dr. A.L. Mudaliar. The commission strongly recommended the improvement of working conditions in the training colleges. Valuable suggestions made by the commission were:

i. There should be two years course for non-graduates and one year training course for graduates.
ii. The pupil teachers should be trained in one or two extracurricular activities also.
iii. The commission also stressed the importance of refresher courses, short term intensive courses and specialized courses, workshops and conferences for in service teachers.

- **The Review Committee on Education (1960)** made major recommendations about post-graduate studies in education and research, education of administrators and qualifications of teacher educators. Most of these recommendations were accepted and implemented. Many other committees were appointed to look into teacher education from different perspectives. Only some of the suggestions were carried out because teacher education was no one's exclusive responsibility. The Center, the States, the universities, and public and private enterprise looked after teacher education. Besides, its problems were not examined in totality. The availability of resources for teacher education was also a problem. Further, teacher education was not accorded adequate importance in the agenda of education.
- **NCERT:** There was a need for a planned programme for teacher education towards implementation of the multipurpose schools with trained, qualified, competent teachers. With this aim in view, under the National Council for Educational Research and Training (1961) four regional colleges of education, in four regions—Ajmer, Bhopal, Bhubaneswar and Mysore were established in 1963. The characteristics of these teachers' education institutions and programme have been:

  i. Design and development of integrated courses of four year duration in a different areas.
  ii. Establishment of demonstration multi-purpose schools to work in synergy with the Regional Institute of Educations to function as educational laboratories in teachers preparations.
  iii. A fully professionalized academic schedule involving interaction with community during three summer vacations available in the duration of four years of the teacher education programme to focus on the role of teachers as agent of social change.
- **The Education Commission (1964-66)** was appointed under the chairmanship of Dr. D.S. Kothari who had pointed out clearly the

major weaknesses in the existing system of professional education visualizing weaknesses in teacher training programme. The commission made many recommendations which may be clarified into the following groups:

i. Removing isolation of teacher training from the main academic life.
ii. Improving the quality of teacher's training programme.
iii. Expansion of teacher training facilities.
iv. Making adequate provision for continuing professional education of all teachers.
v. Creating appropriate agencies for the maintenance of standards both at the Centre and States.

- **The National Commission on Teachers (1983)** studied in depth the problems of teacher education and the status of teachers in society. Its main recommendations were directed at enhancing the period of training, change in selection procedure of teachers, making the pedagogy of teacher education meaningful leading to enrichment of the theory courses and practical work. It suggested changes in the structure of M.Ed. programme also. On the basis of these suggestions, another curriculum framework was issued in 1988 but it could not catch national attention because the work on NPE (1986) had already started, and which opened new vistas in teacher education.

"Education has continued to evolve, diversify and extend its coverage since the dawn of history. Every country develops its system of education to express and promote its unique socio-cultural identity and also to meet the challenges of time" NPE, 1986. In the revised National Policy on Education in 1992, the following was emphasized "the Government of India will also review, every five years; the progresses made and recommend guidelines for further development".

- **The Acharya Ramamurthy Review Committee (1990)** explicitly stated that "in-service and refresher courses should be related to the specific needs of the teachers. In-service education should take due care of the future needs of teacher growth; evaluation and follow up should be part of the scheme".
- **The Yashpal Committee Report (1993)** on Learning without Burden noted "...inadequate programmes of teacher preparation lead to unsatisfactory quality of learning in schools. ...The content of the programme should be restructured to ensure its relevance to the changing needs of school education. The emphasis in these

programmes should be on enabling the trainees to acquire the ability for self-learning and independent thinking."

- **The National Policy on Education (NPE), 1986** and the Programme of Action there under envisaged a National Council for Teacher Education with statutory status and necessary resources as a first step for overhauling the system of teacher education. The National Council for Teacher Education as a statutory body came into existence in pursuance of the National Council for Teacher Education Act, 1993 on the 17th August, 1995, established by the Government of India for the maintenance of standards and improvement of the quality of teacher education in the country. The objective of the council are:
    i. To achieve planned and coordinated development of teacher education system throughout the country.
    ii. To regulate and maintain norms and standards in the teacher education system.

The first step for achieving quality standards was the publication in 1998 of the document *"Curriculum Framework for Quality Teacher Education"* which highlighted the importance of Information and Communication Technology (ICT) and Value Education in teacher education programme.

The National Council for Teacher Education has to initiate suitable measures to make teacher education at various levels responsive to such developments as well as to quality concerns in future. Education of teachers not only facilitates improvement of school education by preparing competent, committed and professionally well qualified teachers who can meet the demand of the system, but also functions as a bridge between schooling and higher education. It has to meet twin demands: (a) challenges of the education system including higher education, and (b) the ever-changing demands of the social system. The role of teacher education as a process of nation building is universally recognized. Its objective is man making and producing enlightened citizens. But teacher education in India, because of its history and also due to various factors beyond its control, has by and large been confined to school education only.

However, India possesses one of the largest systems of teacher education. Besides, the university departments of education and their affiliated colleges, government and aided institutions, private and self-financing colleges and open universities are also engaged in this venture. The programmes are almost identical but the standard varies. Certain institutions are being run with motives other than educational. In certain areas, the supply of teachers far exceeds the demand while in others there is acute shortage and unqualified teachers are working under different names. The manpower planning is practically absent in teacher education. The situation at the elementary level in certain states is comparable to international standards, where DIETs, CTEs and IASEs are making tangible impact on pre-and in-service teacher education.

Historical Background of In-Service Teacher Education in India

The origin of in-service education for teachers in India can be traced back to the Vedic period and to the 6th and 7th centuries A.D., when the Nalanda, Takhyashila, Ujjain universities were at their glorious peak. Teachers from different parts of the country used to assemble in the '*Gosthies*' and the '*Vad Vivads*' (which are the Sanskrit terms for seminars and discussions respectively) in order to exchange their experience. '*Swadhyaya*' (Self-Study) was also recognized as one of the means of in-service education. Not only men but also women and foreign scholars participated in these discussions. We have the classical examples of discussions held by '*Yagnivalkya*' and his wife or by Chinese or Muslims pilgrims with Indian scholars. Discussions were held by participants on their own initiative, but example were not wanting of kings, queens and nobles taking the initiatives in organizing such discussions at their courts and Durbars (Koul, 1964).

Resolution on Educational Policy, 1904: The first reference was made to the need of the programme of in-service education of teachers in the Government of India policy Resolution in 1904 (Lord Curzon's Resolution on Educational Policy). At the time of the resolution there was only one Teacher College at Madras in the whole country.

> "Every possible care should be taken to maintain a connection between the training college and the school, so that the student on leaving the college and entering upon his career as a teacher may not neglect to practice the methods which he has been taught, and may not (as sometimes happens) be prevented from doing so and forced to fall into line with the more mechanical methods of his untrained colleagues. The trained students whom the college has sent out should be occasionally brought together again and the inspecting staff should co-operate with the training college authorities in seeing that the influence of the college makes itself felt in the schools" (36, para 39).

Resolution on Educational Policy, 1913: The Resolution on Educational Policy of 1913 laid down the major principles for the expansion and improvement of primary education and also recommended in-service education for village teachers. The trend at that time was toward an increase in the quality rather than the quantity of the teachers at the primary level. The resolution stated:

> "As teachers left to themselves in villages are liable to deteriorate, there are great advantages in periodical repetition and improvement courses for primary school teachers during the school vacations (37, para 11)."

The Hartog Committee Report, 1929: The Hartog Committee of 1929, made further recommendations about the training as well as in-service education of primary teachers. The report of the committee helped little towards the progress of primary education for the next twenty years or so and some of the valuable suggestions of the committee such as improved salaries for teachers, improvement of curricula, progress in in-service education, and tutorial work in colleges were neglected.

University Education Commission Report, 1949: Stressed on the need for in-service education, remarked about the utilization of the vacation period for in-service program, the committee stated "at present neither students nor the teachers utilize vacation; for most of them vacation is a period of want of occupation".

Secondary Education Commission Report, 1953: Regarding the in-service education, the committee was of the following opinion:

> However excellent the programme of teacher-training may be, it does not by itself produce an excellent teacher. It can only engender the knowledge, skills and attitudes which will enable the teacher to begin his task with a reasonable degree of confidence and with the minimum amount of experience. Increased efficiency will come through experience critically analyzed and through individual and group efforts at improvement. The teacher-training institution should accept its responsibility for assisting in this in-service stage of teacher-training (38, p. 169).

The SEC recommended for arrangement of (1) refresher courses, (2) short intensive courses in special subjects, (3) practical training in workshop, (4) seminars and professional conferences as a normal part of work of teachers' training colleges. The commission also recommended for a base of institutional responsibility towards in-service training for teachers. More specifically, the commission recommended for programme for extension services for the secondary teachers. As a result All India Council for Secondary Education was established to provide in-service education to secondary teachers. International Secondary Education Project Team of the Government of India gave further stimulus to the need of in-service education for secondary school teachers.

Historically, the first structural arrangement of in-service education was made during the period 1952-58 by establishing extension services department in about one hundred teachers' training colleges.

International Secondary Education Project Team Report, 1954: Government of India appointed this Project Team in 1954, to study the various steps and procedures needed for implementing the major recommendations of the Secondary Education Commission. The report stated:

> We recommend that education departments consider ways and means of helping teachers to obtain in-service training and recognizing the improvement in their professional and academic qualifications by suitable salary increment (p. 5).

The International Team suggested special in-service training courses immediately

> "......for teachers of technical, vocational and other special subjects, who are already in service but for those who have not been trained we recommend short intensive courses in the theory and practice of Education" (40, p. 47).

The first in-service programme on record in Madras State was a refresher course, arranged by the Teachers' College, Saidapet, Madras, in 1859.

National Seminar on the education of primary teachers in India in 1960: The first National Seminar on the education of primary teachers in India in 1960 recommended the opening of extension service centres for primary school, and accordingly 30 centres were opened in 1962 and 15 more were added in 1965. The responsibility of guiding these programmes at the central level was entrusted to the National Institute of Basic Education, one of the constituent departments of NCERT. Another important step in this direction has been the establishment in 1964, of State Institute of Education in the 16 states changed with the main responsibility of improving of elementary education, by providing in-service education programmes for supervisors of primary schools and teacher educator in primary teacher training institutions. The objectives of extension service centres were to improve elementary schools through the in-service growth of teachers training programme by providing teacher educators an opportunity to be in touch with the actual conditions in the schools.

NCERT, extension service centres, 1962: Under the auspices of NCERT, three extension service centres were established in the state of Odisha in the year 1962, one extension service centre was set up at Salipur in the campus of Salipur Training School in the district of Cuttack and another at Chhendipada, in the campus of Chhendipada training school in the district of Dhenkanal (presently in Angul District). The third one was attached to the State Institute of Education, Bhubaneswar, which was opened later. Each extension service centre used to take fifty primary schools as cooperative schools and impart in-servive education to the primary school teachers through various seminars, workshops, meetings and discussions etc. There was an extension educator known as the coordinator who used to coordinate the planning, implementation and follow up of the in-service training programme.

Indian Education Commission, 1964-66: The commission also recommended that the large scale programme of in-service education of teachers should be organized by universities, training institutes and teachers' organizations at all levels so that every teacher would receive at least two or three months on-service education in every five years of service. In-service teacher education programme should be the responsibility of the Sates and the State Institute of Education.

The National Policy on Education (NPE), 1986 brought about a remarkable contribution in the field of teacher education in India in general and in Odisha in particular. "Teacher Education is a condensed process and its pre-service and in-service components are inseparable. As the first step, the system of Teacher Education will be overhauled. The new programmes of Teacher Education will emphasize continuing Education and the need for teachers to meet the thrusts envisaged in this policy" (NPE, 1986). Accordingly, the District Institutes of Education and Training (DIET) were established with the capability to organize pre-service and in-service course for Elementary School Teachers and for the personnel working in non-formal and Adult Education.

Sarva Shiksha Abhiyan (SSA), 2000-2001: Sarva Shiksha Abhiyan (SSA) was introduced in 2000-2001 as the flagship programme of Government of India's flagship programme for achievement of Universalization of Elementary Education (UEE) in a time bound manner, as mandated by the 86th amendment to the Constitution of India making free and compulsory Education to the Children of 6-14 years age group. A Fundamental Right. SSA is implemented as India's main programme for universalizing elementary education. Its overall goals include universal access and retention, bridging of gender and social category gaps in education, enhancement of learning levels of children and capacity building of teachers through in-service training.

Capacity Building of Teachers through In-Service Training under SSA

SSA laid its emphasis on capacity building of teachers through regular training programmes which includes regular annual in-service training for teachers. The amended SSA framework gives more emphasis to practical classroom activities related training programme based on a split-up model in which every teacher has to undergo minimum 20 days in-service training through the calendar year. The split-up model was designed for providing:

(a) 10 days institutional training at BRCs level, and another 10 days specifically at cluster/school level in order to ensure follow-up, peer learning and experience practical classroom transactions.
(b) 30 days induction training for newly recruited trained teachers to orient them to their roles and responsibilities, the expectation of the SSA programme and specific state/district priorities in quality education.
(c) 60 days training for teachers that have not received pre service training in order to provide customized distance mode programmes for such teachers to acquire progressive qualifications in-service mode.
(d) 10 days Training for BRC and CRC coordinators and resource persons each year.

Guidelines for In-Service Training Programme

The guidelines for such annual in-service training programme under SSA were developed by National Council for Educational Research and Training in 2006 in its book '*The Reflective Teacher*'. These guidelines are as following:

(a) The training should be based on 'the constructivist approach' as advocated in NCF 2005. It emphasizes on the teacher as a 'facilitator' instead of 'transmitter' 'who elicits a variety of learning experiences in and out of the classroom to enable the children for construction of knowledge out of such activities and experiences.
(b) A *'split up'* model of in-service training in which 6-8 days training at the BRC/DIET level and 2 days training through actual observation of classroom situations. Thereafter, teachers are expected to return to their school settings for 2-3 months, to try out the methodologies and ideas acquired during the training. At the end of the training programme, they once again return to the BRC/DIET for 2 days to share their experience and reflect on the new ideas before they complete the training.
(c) Training of teachers in areas such as art and heritage crafts, health and physical education, work education and education for peace, besides training in basic subjects like language, EVS and Mathematics as recommended in NCF 2005.
(d) Identification of training needs and development of appropriate training modules through BRGs/DRGs/SRGs. The training design should

emphasize local, contextual and specificities in the teaching learning situation.

On the basis of the guidelines all the states have developed their training modules with reference to the local training needs and core aspects such as: Subject-specific content, Classroom processes and pedagogical improvement, Learning Enhancement Programme, Development and use of TLMs, Continuous and comprehensive assessment, Inclusive education, including education of children with special needs, SC/ST, gender issues, tribal children, Data management (use of DISE, QMT), Teacher attitudes and motivation, Training of HMs, Computer training and Other topics like curriculum/textbooks, NCF 2005, classroom management, life skills, value education or extracurricular activities, etc.

J.S. Verma Commission-2011-12

The high powered Commission was constituted in 2011 by the Hon'ble Supreme Court under the Chairmanship of Hon'ble Justice J.S. Verma, the former Chief Justice of India. The Commission included eight members including one member secretary and submitted its report on August, 2012. While analyzing the quality of pre-service teacher education programme, it is reported that most of teacher education programme (B.Ed and D.Ed) do not adequately engage with subject knowledge. The aspects are most crucial in pre-service teacher education such as the entrants to the teaching profession, quality of curriculum content, mode of teacher preparation, quality of teacher educators, curricular transaction and pedagogical aspects; and quality of teacher assessment.

Regarding the entrants to the teaching profession, the TET has been implemented due to the poor quality teacher education programme and poor content knowledge by the pass outs. Thus the Commission recommends the government should make initiations for implementing a pre-entry test during the admission into teacher education programme. Even the content knowledge in both B.Ed and D.Ed programme is of very poor quality. New methods and current innovations in teaching are neglected. The traditional practice teaching has occupied a prime place. The trainees are more engaged in decorating the lesson plans instead of reading and reflecting the ideas in it. They do not adhere to the purpose of practice teaching, which should be taken care of on the basis of reflective mode with connection to life and development of the children for which the teacher training programme is designed. Practice teachings are not properly organized as required by the course.

Besides, the Commission has noticed that nearly 90 per cent teacher education institutions are in private sector and 80 per cent of the students enrolled are in state responsibilities. Obviously, the market demand is very large and to fulfill the demand the private teacher education institutions prepare teachers with less emphasis of curricular transactions for fulfilling the objectives of NCF, 2005 and RTE Act-2009.

While this is so on the one hand, on the other hand, Commission highlights that the success of in-service teacher education depends on four aspects such as content of training, overall ethos of training venue, resourcefulness of the trainers and receptivity with involvement of trainees. Thus, selection of the trainers or faculties occupies the prime place. The state government should take necessary steps for selection of the faculties. The selected core faculties must be provided extensive training to conduct interactive training session, organization of debates, discussions, projects, experiments and evaluation trainee's performance and giving feedback to training designers and course writers.

Conclusion

It is true that teachers are the backbone of education system in any country. The need of teachers' professional development is always accepted for the improvement of education all over the world in 21st century. Thus both pre-service and in-service is important for the professional development of teachers. Sometimes it has been seen that the trained graduates are employed in service sectors other than the teaching profession which seems to be wastage of resources. Hence, in comparison to pre-service training, in-service training is vital for teachers and it should be only way of providing training. The selection of teachers should not be based on their pre-service training, rather training should be provided after joining in the profession. However, teachers' training is vital for professional development.

REFERENCE

Acharya Ramamurthy Review Committee Report (1990). *Towards an Enlightened and Humane Society.* MHRD, GoI.

Chattopadhyaya Committee Report (1983-95). *The Teacher and Society*. MHRD, GoI.

Dunking, Michael, J. (1987). *The International Encyclopedia of Teaching and Teacher Education.* Oxford, Pergaman Press.

Koul, G.N. (1964). *Better Schools of India.* New Delhi: Orient Longmans.

Ministry of Education (1948-49). *Report of the University Education Commission.* New Delhi, Government of India.

Ministry of Education (1953): *Report of the Secondary (1952-53),* New Delhi, Government of India.

Ministry of Education (1966): *Education and National Development: Report of the Commission (1964-66).* New Delhi, Government of India.

Mohanty, J. (2003) *Teacher Education.* Deep and Deep Publications Pvt. Ltd., New Delhi.

MHRD (1992). National Policy of Education New Delhi: GoI.

MHRD (1986). National Policy on Education, New Delhi: GoI.

MHRD (2012). *Vision of Teacher Education in India Quality and Regulatory Perspective,* Report of High Powered Commission on Teacher Education, Volume, 1-3 MHRD, GoI.

National Commission on Teachers-1 (1983-85): *Teacher and Society*. Delhi, Government of India Press.

NCERT (2006-07). *The Reflective Teacher*, New Delhi.

Report of the Education Commission (1964-66). *Education and National Development. Ministry of Education*. GoI.

Singh, R.P. (2010). *Dialogue with Teacher Educators: Teaching Content, Modes and Its Nature,* Delhi, Shipra Publications.

Saxena, N.R., Mishra, B.K. and Mohanty, R.K. (2005). *Teacher Education*. Meerut, Surya Publications.

Singh. R.P. (1970), *Education in Ancient and Medieval India*. Delhi, Arya Book Depot.

Yashpal Committee Report (1993). *Learning Without Burden*. MHRD, GoI.

4

Quality Measures in the Context of Present Indian Teacher Education System

J D Singh

Teacher education is the process of providing teachers and potential teachers with the skills and knowledge necessary to teach effectively in a classroom environment. Quality of education plays pivotal role in the process of development of nations. Hence, quality concerns in education are national priorities for all nations. Quality is multiple perspectives and is not a unitary concept (Newton 2007, p. 14). The dimensions of quality in education include achieving pre-determined targets and objectives. Enlightened, emancipated and empowered teachers lead communities and nations in their march towards better and higher quality of life.

Keeping in view the quality of education, ASER (2011) Report says that more than 50 per cent students of V standard are unable to read, write and do mathematical calculations of II standard in India. According to London Times Higher Education (2009)-Quacquarelli Symonds (QS) World University rankings, no Indian university features among the first hundred. But universities in East Asia have been included in the first hundred. Hong Kong has three, ranked at 24, 35 and 46; Singapore two ranked at 30 and 73; South Korea two ranked at 47 and 69 and Taiwan one in the 95th position. Notably, China's Tsinghua University and Peking University are ranked at 49 and 52 respectively. There is no Indian university in the rankings from 100 to 200. It is only when one moves on to the next 100 that we find the Indian Institute of Technology, Kanpur at 237; IIT Madras at 284 and the University of Delhi at 291. Therefore, the present situation of Indian education is not very good and for this situation, teachers, teacher education institution and various agencies from elementary to professional education are responsible.

Education is the essential foundation of a thriving and innovative society. The quality of education in a society is no less important for economic development. As competition among economies becomes more intense, the importance of education as the key to future success intensifies. One of the best ways to achieve quality is to enhance Teacher Education programmes so as to train high quality teachers for schools. The quality of teachers and training programmes is, to a large extent, determined by who are attracted to enter the profession and how they are trained. The task of bringing qualitative change of the teacher education system in itself is a huge and challenging one. The community expects teachers to be sufficiently knowledgeable in the subjects they teach and proficient in pedagogy.

Development of Teacher Education

Teachers are the torch bearers in creating social cohesion, national integration and a learning society. They not only disseminate knowledge but also create and generate new knowledge. Teacher education refers to the policies and procedures designed to equip prospective teachers with the knowledge, attitudes, behaviours, and skills they require to perform their tasks effectively in the classrooms, school and wider community. It aims at imparting professional skills and techniques to the teachers under training. Various Commissions and Committees appointed by the Central and the State Governments in recent decades have invariably emphasized the need for quality teacher education suited to the needs of the educational system. The Secondary Education Commission (1953) observed that a major factor responsible for the educational reconstruction at the secondary stage is teachers' professional training. The Education Commission (1964-66) stressed that 'in a world based on science and technology it is education that determines the level of prosperity, welfare and security of the people' and that 'a sound programme of professional education of teachers is essential for the qualitative improvement of education'.

The National Commission on Teachers (1983) studied in depth the problems of teacher education and the status of teachers in society. Its main recommendations were directed at enhancing the period of training, change in selection procedure of teachers, making the pedagogy of teacher education meaningful leading to enrichment of the theory courses and practical work. It suggested changes in the structure of M.Ed. programme also. On the basis of these suggestions, another curriculum framework was issued in 1988 but it could not catch national attention because the work on NPE (1986) had already started, and opened new vistas in teacher education. In pursuance of the NPE 1986, a major step was taken by the Central Government to enhance the professional capacity of a large number of teacher education institutions. The DIETs are charged with the responsibility of organising pre-service and in-service programmes in addition to being the nodal resource centres for elementary education at district level. Likewise, Colleges of Teacher Education (CTEs) and Institutions of Advanced Study in Education (IASEs) have been given the responsibility of introducing innovations in teacher education programmes at the secondary and higher education. NPE (1986) was followed by a Programme of Action (1986), which provided details about the needed transformation of policy into action. Its emphasis was on the enrichment of both in-service and the pre-service teacher education programmes and new as well as alternative models of teacher preparation.

As a statutory body responsible for the coordination and maintenance of standards in teacher education, NCTE issued a Curriculum Framework for Quality Teacher Education in 1998. Before issuing it, the Council sought and ensured a national consensus in its favour. This is a comprehensive document that deals with almost all aspects of teacher education including its context, concerns and also the social philosophy of teacher education in Indian society which contemplates a synthesis between unity and diversity, freedom and compulsion, social planning and individual initiative. Its salient features were:

- Increased duration and multiple models of teacher education.
- Updating of theoretical and practical components of teacher education by giving new orientation and adding new inputs to the existing programmes.
- Emphasis on developing professionalism, commitment, competencies and performance skills.
- Optimal utilization of the potentialities of community, university and information and communication technology for preparation of teachers.
- Making provisions for preparation of teachers for the neglected sections of society.
- Suggesting alternative educational programmes for teachers of gifted children, teachers of senior secondary schools and specialized programme of education for teacher educators.

Besides, there were other suggestions too which were well received by the nation. Some of its recommendations were implemented. But all of them could not be put into practice due to various reasons.

Some Major Problems in Teacher Education

The teacher-student relationship is far more complex and demanding than ever before. The implication of this more diversified role for the teacher is what impelled a new view of the process of teacher education and training. Thus, teacher education is seen as a continuous process, beginning with a phase of initial training and continuing throughout the teacher's professional life throughout regular and sustained periods of in-service training. India possesses one of the largest systems of teacher education. Besides, the university departments of education and their affiliated colleges, government and aided institutions, private and self-financing colleges and open universities are also engaged in this venture. The programmes are almost identical but the standard varies. Certain institutions are being run with motives other than educational. In certain areas, the supply of teachers far exceeds the demand while in others there is acute shortage and unqualified teachers are working under different names. The manpower planning is practically absent in teacher education. The situation at the elementary level in certain states is comparable to international standards, where DIETs, CTEs and IASEs are making tangible impact on pre and in-service teacher education. But the same cannot be said about the preparation of secondary, vocational and pre-school teachers.

Advanced Study in Education could offer doctoral research and other types of programmes. A few other training colleges have been designated as Colleges of Teacher Education. One elementary teacher training institution in every district has been designated as District Institute of Education and Training. The Government of India takes burden for a few years, after which the concerned State government takes over. In most of the cases, the scheme reflects a huge wastage of material as well as human resources. While some of these institutions do not function with heads and faculty members having at least B.Ed. qualification, a few function without adequate work load, as the concerned State Governments do not give funds for conducting in-service programmes for school teachers. The scheme also gives support to State Councils of Educational Research and Training that even has Directors without a B.Ed. qualification or school teaching experience. The Regional Colleges of Education of the National Council of Educational Research and Training have been running their courses with the help of contract teachers who are paid on hourly basis. This is not a case of paucity of fund, but a case of ineffective management.

During the last two decades, the teacher education curricula have received severe criticism and their weaknesses have been well exposed. The students are not exposed to the realities of school and community. Internship, practice of teaching, practical activities and supplementary educational activities are not paid proper attention. The curriculum, pedagogy and evaluation of teacher education need improvement and radical transformation. Some educationists and social activists call it vapid and irrelevant because they do not address the needs of contemporary Indian schools and society. They do not prepare teachers who can impart quality education in our schools. One often hears that there is little difference between the performance of trained and that of untrained teachers because of the outdated and defective curriculum. To some extent, these charges may be somewhat exaggerated; but often they seem to be correct.

During the last decade, new thrusts have been posed due to rapid changes in the educational, political, social and economic contexts at the national and international levels. Curriculum reconstruction has also become imperative in the light of some perceptible gaps in teacher education. Teacher education by and large, is conventional in its nature and purpose. The integration of theory and practice and consequent curricular response to the requirements of the school system still remains inadequate. Teachers are prepared in competencies and skills which do not necessarily equip them for becoming professionally effective. Their familiarity with latest educational developments remains insufficient. Organised and stimulatory learning experiences whenever available, rarely contribute to enhancing teachers' capacities for self-directed lifelong learning. The system still prepares teachers who do not necessarily become professionally competent and committed at the completion of initial teacher preparation programmes. A large number of teacher training institutions do not practice what they preach. Several of the skills acquired and methodologies learnt are seldom practiced in actual school system. The National Knowledge Commission's final report states: "The training of teachers is a major area of concern at present, since both pre-service and in-service training of school teachers is extremely inadequate and also poorly managed in most states" (NKC 2009, pp. 44-45).

Frequently criticized as being theoretical in its nature, the curriculum of teacher education is only partially theoretical. It is information loaded which are disconnected from each other. The curriculum framework of 1998 pointed out this weakness to an extent but the situation could not improve for reasons known to all. There is the pressing need to integrate scattered information for giving them the shape of a discipline capable of promoting educational theory and practice. During the last five decades certain efforts have been made to indigenize the system. The gaps, however, are still wide and visible. The imperatives for building the bridges may be as follows:

- build a national system of teacher education based on India's cultural ethos, its unity and diversity synchronizing with change and continuity;
- facilitate the realization of the constitutional goals and emergence of the new social order;
- prepare professionally competent teachers to perform their roles effectively as per needs of the society; and
- upgrade the standard of teacher education, enhance the professional and social status of teachers and develop amongst them a sense of commitment.

These are but a few of the major concerns which call for an immediate action. A comprehensive, dynamic and responsive system of teacher education needs to be continually evolved keeping the overall scenario in view.

Measures for Improving Quality of Teacher Education

Quality of an institution or a programme is generally considered on the basis of placement of its products. It is ascertained from quality of material and human resources. Various factors that affect quality are: finance, sincerity of faculty and students and management, skills of management, skills of teaching of faculty members, and quality of brain of students. In order to accelerate qualitative improvement in higher education, National Knowledge Commission (2009, p. 166) recommended establishment of 30 new Central universities, 16 in States where they do not exist and 14 as World class universities (all India admissions, course credits, regular syllabi revision, incentives for faculty, strong linkage with industry and research institutions, no affiliated colleges, outsource nonteaching functions (p. 166). The main indicator of the quality of teacher education can be visualized in terms of its products the learners achievement both in scholastic and co-scholastic areas i.e. the performance in various subjects of study and habits, attitudes, values and life skills necessary for becoming a good citizen. The factors associated with success in these areas, which relate to conditions of learning and learning environment, are also sometimes considered as indicators of quality of teacher education. Quality is the most important concern of the teacher education programmes. Quality of teaching also depends on certain physical resources such as provision for power point presentation, internet browsing, Xeroxing therein. Availability of such facilities motivates the teachers to become more effective that upgrades the level of curriculum transaction. The need of teacher man power planning has resulted in mushrooming growth of teacher education throughout the country. It's the right time that every educationist should take care, that quantitative expansion should not slip the quality.

- To enhance the quality in teacher education;
- To provide professional development for practicing in-service teachers by updating their knowledge and skills;
- Effectiveness of the new initiatives curricular reforms;
- Intensive use of ICT for school education and also involvement of the community;
- To adopt innovative Teaching strategies in teacher education and Improving educational administration practices;
- To evolve strategies to enhance professional competency in teacher education;
- To provide expert advice to local schools upon request;
- To analyse the future of teacher education institutions;
- To provide infrastructure facility in teacher education;
- Teacher education and professional competence of teacher educators;

- Spreading sense of ethical values in teacher education; and
- Modern and latest communication and knowledge management for quality teacher education.

Conclusion

The task of bringing qualitative change in the teacher education system in itself is a huge and challenging one. Quality issues in teacher education revolve around the quality of infrastructure and support services, opportunity time, teacher characteristics and teacher motivation, pre-service and in-service education of teachers, curriculum and teaching-learning materials, classroom processes, pupil evaluation, monitoring and supervision etc. Indeed, improvement of quality in these parameters and its sustenance is a matter of grave concern for the whole system of education. Academic and professional skills are not independent of each other. Teacher Education curricula have to integrate and blend them into a composite whole likes the curricula of other sciences. The reconstruction of teacher education curricula has become a pressing need of the hour. It has to be transformed from information based to experience based. The National Council for Teacher Education, NAAC and other relating agencies have not done remarkable job in context of quality teacher education. They have to initiate suitable measures for making teacher education at various levels responsive to such developments as well as to quality concerns in future keeping in view goal of national development.

REFERENCE

Academic Ranking of World Universities (AWRU) http://www.arwu.org/

International Network of Quality Assurance Agencies in Higher Education http://www.inqaahe.org/index.php

National Knowledge Commission (2009) Final Report (2006-09). Govt. of India, New Delhi.

Chapman, D. and Adams, D. (2002) *The Quality of Education: Dimensions and Strategies*. IIEP, Paris.

Delors Jacques (1996) *Learning: The Treasure Within: Report of the International Commission on Education for Twenty-first Century*, Paris: UNESCO:

National Council for Teacher Education (1998) *Curriculum Framework forQuality Teacher Education*, New Delhi: NCTE.

NCERT (1978) *Teacher Education Curriculum a Framework*, New Delhi: NCERT.

NCTE (1988) *National Curriculum Framework for Teacher Education*, NewDelhi, NCERT.

5
Pedagogical Rejuvenation of Teacher Education in India: Some Challenges

Gyanendra Kumar Rout

Enlightened, emancipated and empowered teachers lead communities and nations in their march towards better and higher quality of life. They reveal and elaborate the secrets of attaining higher values in life and nurture empathy for the fellow beings. Teachers are the torch bearers in creating social cohesion, national integration and a learning society. They not only disseminate knowledge but also create and generate new knowledge. They are responsible for acculturating role of education. No nation can even marginally slacken its efforts in giving necessary professional inputs to its teachers and along with that due status to their stature and profession.

The educational expansion, universalisation of elementary education, vocationalisation of secondary education, higher and professional education and overall quality of education are major challenges before the country. Evidently the quality of education is a direct consequence and outcome of the quality of teachers and teacher education system. The task of bringing qualitative change in institutional efficacy of the teacher education system in itself is a huge and challenging one. The last five decades have witnessed several attempts to change, modify and indigenise the inherited system of teacher education. The system however continues to function more or less on the same principles, similar content and approaches characterised by continuity and unwillingness to change. Over the years the magnitude of the task has increased manifold.

Teacher education is an integral component of the educational system. It is intimately connected with society and is conditioned by the ethos, culture and character of a nation. The constitutional goals, the directive principles of the state policy, the socio-economic problems and the growth of knowledge, the emerging expectations and the changes operating in education, etc. call for an appropriate response from a futuristic education system and provide the perspective within which teacher education programmes need to be viewed.

Scenario of Teacher Education

When India attained freedom, the then existing educational system was accepted as such because it was thought that an abrupt departure from the same would be disturbing and destabilising. Thus a predisposition to retain the system acquired preponderance and all that was envisaged by way of changes was its rearrangement. Consequently, education including teacher education largely remained isolated from the needs and aspirations of the people. During the last five decades certain efforts have been made to indigenize the system. The gaps, however, are still wide and visible. The imperatives for building the bridges may be as follows:

- build a national system of teacher education based on India's cultural ethos, its unity and diversity synchronizing with change and continuity.
- facilitate the realization of the constitutional goals and emergence of the new social order.
- prepare professionally competent teachers to perform their roles effectively as per needs of the society.
- upgrade the standard of teacher education, enhance the professional and social status of teachers and develop amongst them a sense of commitment.

These are but a few of the major concerns which call for an immediate action. A comprehensive, dynamic and responsive system of teacher education needs to be continually evolved keeping the overall scenario in view.

The need for improved levels of educational participation for overall progress is well recognised. The key role of educational institutions in realising it is reflected in a variety of initiatives taken to transform the nature and function of education — both formal as well as non-formal. Universal accessibility to quality education is considered essential for development. This has necessitated improvement in the system of teacher education so as to prepare quality teachers.

Various Commissions and Committees appointed by the Central and the State Governments in recent decades have invariably emphasised the need for quality teacher education suited to the needs of the educational system. The Secondary Education Commission (1953) observed that a major factor responsible for the educational reconstruction at the secondary stage is teachers' professional training. The Education Commission (1964-66) stressed that 'in a world based on science and technology it is education that determines the level of prosperity, welfare and security of the people' and that 'a sound programme of professional education of teachers is essential for the qualitative improvement of education.'

India has a large system of education. There are nearly 5.98 lakh Primary Schools, 1.76 lakh Elementary Schools and 98 thousand High/Higher Secondary Schools in the country, about 1300 teacher education institutions for elementary teachers and nearly 700 colleges of education/university departments preparing teachers for secondary and higher secondary schools. Out of about 4.52 million teachers in the country nearly 3 million are teaching at the primary/elementary level. A sizeable number of them are untrained or under-trained. In certain regions, like the North-East, there are even under- qualified teachers. As far as in-service education is concerned the situation is not very encouraging. It is estimated that on an average 40 per cent of the teachers are provided in-service teacher education once over a period of five years. Regarding non-formal education, though a number of models are in vogue in various states in the country, much more needs to be done to prepare teachers and other functionaries for the system.

The Programme of Action (POA 1992) has emphasised teacher education as a continuous process, its pre-service and in-service components being inseparable. The POA, among others, has pointed out the following in respect of teacher education:

- The quality of pre-service education has not only not improved with recent developments in pedagogical science, but has actually shown signs of deterioration;
- Teacher education programmes consist mainly of pre-service teacher training, with practically no systematic programmes of in-service training, facilities for which are lacking.
- There has been an increase in sub-standard institutions of teacher education and there are numerous reports of gross malpractices; and
- The support system provided by the State Councils of Educational Research and Training (SCERTs) and the University Departments of Education has been insufficient and there is no support system below the state level.

In pursuance of the NPE 1986, a major step was taken by the Central Government to enhance the professional capacity of a large number of teacher education institutions. Nearly 430 District Institutes of Education and Training (DIETs) have already been established by 1997-98. The DIETs are charged with the responsibility of organising pre-service and in-service programmes in addition to being the nodal resource centres for elementary education at district level. Likewise, Colleges of Teacher Education (CTEs) and Institutions of Advanced Study in Education (IASEs) have been given the responsibility of introducing innovations in teacher education programmes at the secondary and higher secondary stages and in vocational education.

The National Council for Teacher Education (NCTE) as a non-statutory body took several steps as regards quality improvement in teacher education. Its major contribution was to prepare Teacher Education Curriculum Framework in 2009. Consequently, teacher education curricula witnessed changes in teacher preparation programmes in various universities and boards in the country.

During the last decade, new thrusts have been posed due to rapid changes in the educational, political, social and economic contexts at the national and international levels. Curriculum reconstruction has also become imperative in the light of some perceptible gaps in teacher education. Teacher education by and large, is conventional in its nature and purpose. The integration of theory and practice and consequent curricular response to the requirements of the school system still remains inadequate. Teachers are prepared in competencies and skills which do not necessarily equip them for becoming professionally effective. Their familiarity with latest educational developments remains insufficient. Organised and stipulatory learning experiences whenever available, rarely contribute to enhancing teachers' capacities for self-directed lifelong learning. The system still prepares teachers who do not necessarily become professionally competent and committed at the completion of initial teacher preparation programmes. A large number of teacher training institutions do not practice what they preach. Several of the skills acquired and methodologies learnt are seldom practiced in actual school system. This highlights the need to bring realism and dynamism in the curriculum.

Pedagogical Rejuvenation of Teacher Education: The National Curriculum Framework for Teacher Education 2009

A major effort to rejuvenate school education as well as teacher education towards modernisation, contextualisation and professionalisation has been made in 2005 and 2009 through the National Curriculum Framework for School Education (2005), and National Curriculum Framework for Teacher Education (2009) respectively. During recent years, the epistemology of learning has undergone a major change i.e. learning does not involve discovering the reality, but constructing the reality. Knowledge and cognitions are to be constructed and affects are to be felt. Learning is no more passive absorption of knowledge and ideas, but the construction of ideas developed on one's personal experiences. Emphasis has now shifted towards constructivist approach of learning. Learning is also perceived as an integral part of learner's physical, social, and cultural contexts. This concept has come to be known as situated cognition and is the guiding principle of the National curriculum Framework for School Education (2005) developed by the NCERT. The NCF 2005 expects a teacher to be the facilitator of students' learning in a manner that helps them to construct knowledge and meaning utilising their individual experiences. The whole pedagogical approach of teacher education programme, therefore, needs to be reoriented from traditional behaviourist to constructivist discourses. The National Curriculum Framework for Teacher Education (2009) developed by NCTE tries to ensure that teacher education courses are reoriented to align with the epistemological shift envisaged in the NCF 2005 and develop teachers as facilitators of learning. It includes the contexts, concerns and visions of teacher education which calls for preparing teachers for learning society, empowering teachers in learning to learn, and making teacher education liberal, humanistic and responsive to the demands of inclusive education. It has tried to incorporate the changing school contexts and demands in the light of recently implemented Right to Education Act (RTE 2009), issue of academic burden of students, and universalisation of secondary education that have implication for teacher education. The major concerns addressed by this framework include inclusive education, ensuring equitable and sustainable development, utilising community knowledge in education, and integration of ICT and e-learning in the curriculum of teacher education which is in tune with the thrust of NCF 2005 and the needs of contemporary Indian society.

Therefore, the traditional approach to teacher preparation based on philosophical, sociological and psychological orientation of courses has given way to 'carefully crafted curriculum design that draws upon theoretical and empirical knowledge as well as student teachers' 'experiential knowledge' (NCFTE 2009, p. 24). Three broad curricular areas identified by this framework are: (A) Foundations of Education which includes courses under three rubrics, namely, Learner Studies, Contemporary Studies and Educational Studies; (B) Curriculum and Pedagogy including Curriculum Studies and Pedagogic Studies; and (C) School Internship, leading to the development of a broad repertoire of perspective, professional capacities, teacher sensibilities and skills (NCFTE 2009, p. 24). An attempt has been made through this curriculum framework to not only address the issues, concerns and pedagogical shifts visualised by NCF 2005, but also organise the entire teacher education curriculum as an organic and integrated whole.

This framework envisages a two year teacher preparation programme along with the four year integrated teacher education courses. It is felt that longer duration of teacher preparation will provide enough time and opportunity for self-study, reflection and engagement with teachers, students, classrooms and pedagogic activities that is essential for developing professionalism in teachers. It also tries to address the criticism regarding the unrelatedness of theoretical discourses of teacher education institutions to the classroom realities by incorporating the socio-cultural contexts of education, giving more weightage to the field experience of student teachers in all courses through practicum, visits to innovative centres of pedagogy and learning, classroom based research, longer duration of internship i.e. minimum duration of six to ten weeks for a two year programme (four days per week), and 15-20 weeks for a four year programme, including an initial phase of one week for observing a regular classroom with a regular teacher. It also emphasises developing unit plan and maintaining Reflective Journals which is currently missing from our teacher education programmes, especially, at the secondary level dynamism in the curriculum.

Constitutional Goals

The Constitution of India solemnly resolves "to constitute India into a sovereign, socialist, secular and democratic republic and secure to all its citizens: justice—social, economic and political; liberty of thought, expression, faith, belief and worship; equality of status and of opportunity; and to promote among them all fraternity assuring the dignity of the individual and the integrity of the nation." These are the main goals which the nation expects to be realized through education. Teacher preparation must not lose sight of this basic thrust so as to empower teachers to inculcate the same among the students.

In order to reinforce faith in democratic socialism, secularism, justice, liberty, freedom etc. the role of education needs to be understood in its true perspective. Democracy is a process of building consensus among the citizens on matters of common concern. It expects high mortality from them, protects the interest and preserves their uniqueness, dignity and individuality. Quality of democracy depends on its citizens willing to discharge their responsibilities towards the self, the family, the community, the nation and humanity at large. Democracy is a way of life and its values need to be imbibed through education and practised in the day-to-day life. Democratic socialism attempts to achieve a synthesis between individual freedom and social compulsion and combines liberty with responsibility and authority with accountability. The Indian situation demands citizens capable of making conscious and purposive efforts directed towards social cohesion and living together harmoniously.

Indian Society is plural and heterogeneous with an underlying current of unity. The imposition of a homogeneous and uniform curriculum of teacher education may prove counterproductive under this situation. Except for identifying certain basics and essentials, regional autonomy must be exercised for developing region/culture specific curriculum of teacher education. Indian reality demands that plurality should be used for strengthening national solidarity and social cohesion.

The Indian state is secular. The Indian society, however, is religious. To resolve this dichotomy between the state and polity, the principle of equal respect for all the religions has been accepted. This is the essence of Indian secularism. The teachers themselves have to internalise the imperatives of secularism in national context and interpret the same effectively to the learners. That alone would develop the right attitudes among all citizens irrespective of their own backgrounds. In India religion is also the source of value and morality. The teachers have to develop values and morality in a different context. Teacher education has to respond to this reality. Justice, liberty, equality of status and of opportunity and promoting fraternity constitute another set of inter-related goals. Justice protects the rights of the weak and ensures impartiality. To ensure justice and fulfil the constitutional commitments in this regard, certain positive and legal provisions have been made by the state. Special measures such as reservation in educational institutions, financial support, scholarships, hostel facilities, etc. have been extended to the under-privileged groups like Scheduled Castes, Scheduled Tribes, Other Backward Classes etc. It implies change in attitudes and values through education, in which the role of teachers needs to be stressed. Liberty of thought, expression, faith, belief and worship is another constitutional goal which education is expected to help realise. Indian Constitution ensures equality of status and opportunity to all its citizens. The objective is to minimise social and economic disparities, inequality of power and life chances by positive discrimination in favour of the weak. The education of teachers should equip them with the competencies needed to deal with discrimination, disparities and inequalities. Fraternity stands for acceptance of universal brotherhood, respect for human personality and feeling of oneness irrespective of linguistic, racial, cultural and religious diversities.

Teacher Education and Problems of the Nation

It is universally acknowledged that education is an effective means for social reconstruction and to a great extent it offers solutions to the problems a society is faced with. These problems may be economic, social, cultural, political, moral, ecological and educational. Since the teachers play a major role in education of children, their own education becomes a matter of vital concern. Teacher education must, therefore, create necessary awareness among teachers about their new roles and responsibilities.

Education of teachers needs to strengthen and stress upon the main attributes of a profession, such as, the systematic theory, rigourous training over a specified duration, authority, community sanction, ethical code and culture, generating knowledge through research and specialisation. It is acknowledged that formal professional training on continuous basis is necessary for becoming a good teacher as it caters to the development of one's personality and sharpening of communication skills and commitment to a code of conduct.

Economic Problems

Poverty, unemployment, and low rate of growth and productivity are some of the major economic problems of the country which have led to the compulsions of the backward economy. These problems seek immediate solution and demand a realistic co-ordination between economic planning and manpower planning. Education can help find solutions if it is properly coordinated with manpower needs. Introduction of work education and vocationalisation of education in secondary schools will have to be given a modern and meaningful direction. The attitude towards work culture needs a transformation. The Indian society needs education with special emphasis on science and technology, vocational inputs and realistic work experiences. Teacher education curriculum, therefore, has to promote such attitudes as are necessary for the emergence of a new economic order. Alongwith the vocational competencies and skills, a new work culture will have to be created which necessarily involves the inculcation of dignity of work, the spirit of self-reliance and scientific temper among students. The courses of teacher education need to be enriched to enable teachers to understand the attributes of modernity and development.

Social Problems

Casteism, communalism and regionalism are some of the problems in the body politic of the society which misguide the youth. Increasing delinquency, violence, terrorism and fissiparous tendencies and use of inappropriate means to get one's ends served are threats to the national integration and social cohesion. Democracy, violence and terrorism cannot coexist. Education has to develop a peace loving personality and the programme of teacher education has to contribute in this regard.

The explosion of population with all its allied disturbing trends is not only neutralising the economic gains but also creating many problems for the country. Indian society still suffers from evils like child labour, child marriage, untouchability, discriminatory treatment to women, violation of human rights, etc. and most of the people are unaware of their legal rights. Modern model of development which puts man against nature by making it an object of exploitation has disturbed the harmony and equilibrium between the two. Its consequences are visible in serious environmental degradation, pollution and ecological imbalances. Strengthening national and social cohesion in a diverse and plural society, accelerating the process of economic growth, improving the life of the downtrodden and the people living below the poverty line, removing the widely prevalent ignorance, superstition and prejudices from the masses, inculcating scientific temper and developing a critical awareness about the social realities of Indian life are some of the issues which call for immediate attention. Teachers and the teacher educators have a special role to play in such efforts.

Problems of Cultural Reconstruction

Education is the process of transmission of dynamic and responsive components of cultural heritage and its continuous enrichment. There is a need to reinterpret the Indian culture in its distinct identity and composite strength. Its capacity to absorb the sublime from the other cultures needs to be highlighted. The teachers will have to play their role in cultural transmission and reconstruction.

Crises of Values and Morality

There has been a persistent erosion of values in the society. In the present day context certain values need to be redefined and reinstalled. There are situations when the values imparted and inculcated in schools are not generally practised in society. Value education demands a planned and purposive approach. It is through education and as of necessity through teacher education programmes that the task of inculcating values can be substantially accomplished. Whereas values are emotive, the other related significant dimension is that of moral education which is essentially conative in character. Morals are situation-specific and demand immediate decision and action and yet there are morals which are considered to be eternal and universal. Through committed teachers, the art of ensuring moral development in a secular, multi-religious and multi-ethnic society needs to be cultivated.

Problems within Educational System

The nation has yet to fulfill the constitutional commitment to provide free and compulsory education to all children till they attain 14 years of age. India is also a party to the global commitment for achieving the goal of Education for All by the year 2000. The education system however, has to respond to several major issues and problems which have hindered the progress in this regard. Maintenance of educational standards against the pressure of increasing enrolment, relevance and quality of school education, efficacy of school functioning under the decentralized role of political power through the enactment of Panchayati Raj Act are some of the pertinent issues. In addition, specific requirements and need of social and economical groups of the society and of the minority communities, vocationalization of education, scientific and technological literacy, alienation of youth, rush for urbanization, perceived urban orientation of educational system and its inflexibility to respond to rural, tribal and regional requirements are some of the dominant issues. These would determine the nature and shape of teacher education programmes and the efficacy and functioning of teachers in their new and emerging multifaceted roles.

Isolation of Teacher Education

Teacher education institutions which were considered 'islands of isolation' have gradually developed linkages with schools, peer institutions, universities and other institutions of higher learning as also the community. However, much remains to be done in this direction. The curriculum of the school, its actual transactional modalities, examination system, management processes and its ethos need to be the main thrust areas of teacher education programmes. To achieve these ends, teacher educators need to be made conversant with various aspects of school experiences. It is observed in day-to-day functioning that teacher educators often tend to lose contact with content areas relevant to their own disciplines resulting into gaps in communication and latest information. It is, therefore, a felt need in the present-day context that teacher education institutions keep in continuous touch with institutions of higher learning and peer institutions for effective transmission of knowledge and its upgradation.

The breaking of isolation from the community is essential for enabling teachers and teacher educators to reconstruct pedagogical and educational principles and practices in the light of experiences gained from mutually beneficial community interactions. Teacher as a professional and intellectual cannot remain indifferent to the events that are taking place in society. The academic and social issues are inter-related and inter-dependent. In contemporary context, the role of the teacher is no longer confined to teaching alone. The teachers are expected to play an active role in the developmental activities responding to the progress of the community.

Expanding Scope of Teacher Education

Education of teachers is not an end in itself. Its target is the school. Any change in the nature, purpose, quality and character of the school demands a concomitant change in teacher education, specially in its curriculum. The implementation of the 10 + 2 scheme at the school level has transformed the complexion of education to a considerable extent from the pre-primary to the + 2 stage. There has been an increase not only in the quantum of knowledge, but also in its nature and purpose. In addition, new transactional techniques and strategies have also been evolved. Certain new subjects have replaced the old ones whereas some others have changed their context, content, orientation, theme and philosophy. These changes at the school level, out of necessity, demand a new pedagogy and evaluation techniques. But the changes at the level of teacher education have not adequately responded to the emerging realities at the school level. All that the teachers are expected to do in their work places need to be reflected in the teacher education activities and programmes.

The teaching community has to face the challenges thrown by science and technology. There has been an explosion not only of scientific and technological knowledge but also in the means and techniques of acquiring knowledge. The scientific researches and developments related to theories of heredity, learning, mental health, neurology, attention, motivation etc. can no longer be treated alien to teacher education programmes.

Evolving a Culture-Specific Pedagogy

Every region and state has its typical cultural identity, and there is a need to utilise the same as a basis for developing meaningful, relevant pedagogies. Since there is no one universal way in which the children learn, there is a strong need for looking into the cultural context in which a child is placed. A child in a tribal society may process information in an altogether different manner as compared to the one from the urban area and high socio-economic stratum. Pedagogy, therefore, should be culture-specific. Cultural practices such as story-telling, dramatics, puppetry, folk-play, community living, etc. should become a strong basis of pedagogy instead of using one uniform, mechanistic way of student learning. Cultural specificity should get embedded in the pedagogical practices which should be evolved for tribal, rural, urban communities and other ethnic groups.

Inseparability of Pre-service and In-service Education

Learning society visualizes education as a continuing activity. This is equally applicable to teacher education. The policy stipulation on inseparability of the pre-service and in-service education of teachers and emphasis on continuing education need to be given pragmatic shape at the implementation stage. The curriculum of pre-service and in-service teacher education has to be redesigned to maintain continuity between the two. Teachers who are being educated today will have to devote major part of their life to education during the twentyfirst century. If the present rate of explosion of knowledge continues, in a few years the teachers will find themselves in a world where their present knowledge and teaching skills to an extent would become obsolete. They will have to face the challenge of electronic media and information technology.

Research and Innovation

One of the major inputs towards enhancing the quality of teaching and learning in schools as well as the teacher education institutions would be the extent to which research outputs and the outcomes of innovations are utilized by the system. Researches on teacher education have been and are being conducted in universities, national level institutions and other establishments but their utility for the teacher educator or the classroom teacher remains rather low. Majority of the researches are undertaken to obtain a degree and hence the focus on its possible utility and relevance gets misplaced. The situation is compounded by non-availability of appropriate dissemination mechanisms, like journals, publication of findings in different forms and opportunities to the target group to get an access to these. Institutional capabilities and resources need to be augmented, enabling them to undertake relevant researches.

There is a definite requirement of bringing in research methods and methodologies in appropriate form in teacher education at preservice and in-service programmes. To an extent, it finds a place in master level courses in education though in some universities the same is not insisted upon. The structure and design of future courses and programmes need to take this aspect into account. Preparation of teacher educators can no longer be completed without adequate grounding in various aspects of research. Researches must respond to policy issues, curriculum issues, evaluative procedures and practices, training strategies, classroom practices etc. The areas of teacher preparation for children with special needs, gifted children and children from groups with specific cultural, social and economic needs can no longer be ignored. Surveys and studies also need to be encouraged. These may be exploratory or diagnostic in nature. The new initiatives and innovations need to be encouraged and studied. Wherever considered appropriate, these could be brought into the system of teacher education for wider and gainful use.

The concept of field interaction and laboratory area approach in the context of establishment of DIETs is indeed timely. Researches, innovations and surveys must become an integral part of the training programmes of teacher education institutions irrespective of the stages. The trainees need to be familiarised with innovations in general and innovative practices in teacher education in particular.

Other Critical Concerns

The factors and forces influencing teacher education are many, some of which have been discussed in the preceding sections, certain others are being mentioned hereunder:

- Gradual change-over from conventional programmes of teacher education to integrated courses to ensure greater professionalism.
- increased duration of teacher education programmes to accommodate proper assimilation of emerging professional inputs.
- stage-specific theoretical and practical components, transactional strategies and evaluation.
- Plans and programmes of teacher education to respond to the expected role performance of teacher.
- Flexible and pragmatic approach to plans and programmes of teacher education.
- Proper planning and orientation of education of teacher educators.

Spectrum of Institutional Function

In the light of context and concerns teacher education institutions will acquire a wider spectrum of functions and greater responsibilities. Resolution of specific functions from the spectrum will have to be made depending upon the institutional capabilities. It is visualised that the following institutional functions will have to be undertaken by different institutions according to availability of resources:

- Develop capability to provide for both pre-service and in-service education.
- Provide training and orientation programmes to the functionaries of alternative educational strategies aimed at achieving universal elementary education and eradication of illiteracy.
- Organise programmes for heads of schools and school complexes and supervisory staff.
- Offer courses for community leaders, voluntary agencies and parents.
- Provide academic support to schools and other agencies engaged in education of children and adults.
- Undertake research and experiments with innovative educational ideas.
- Act as a resource centre for education for a specific area.
- Offer counselling and guidance services.
- Organise need-based programmes for educational administrators, planners, curriculum designers, evaluators etc.
- Impart training for other areas of education, like physical education and special education.
- Act as a link between the school and the university system.

Commitment and Performance in Teacher Education

A major concern in school education is the quality and relevance of education being imparted to young learners. Every learner is supposed to acquire mastery level learning in identified competency areas. NCTE has analysed the existing curriculum of teacher education from the point of view of competency areas. It has emerged that to enhance the quality of school education, equal emphasis needs to be given to competencies, commitment and willingness to perform. A curriculum framework based upon competencies, commitments and performance has been developed. Competency areas namely, contextual competencies, conceptual, content, transactional, related to other educational activities, developing teaching learning material, evaluation, management, working with parents and working with community and other agencies, have been identified as critical to teacher preparation at elementary stage.

Acquisition of competencies alone will not be sufficient until and unless the teacher is fully committed. Teacher commitment areas identified include commitment to the learner, commitment to the society, commitment to the profession, commitment to attaining excellence for professional actions and commitment to basic values.

Along with competency and commitment areas, performance areas have also been identified. These include classroom performance, school level performance, performance in the out-of school educational activities, parents related performance and community related performance. Teacher education institutions could identify details in each of the three major categories. For each competency, commitment and performance area, the existing curriculum needs to be analyzed. Whenever certain unit of curriculum is taken up for transaction, its relationship to commitment and performance has to be examined. Such an approach would provide an opportunity to the training institutions to prepare teachers who are not only competent but also committed and both these aspects are reflected in their performance leading to higher learning attainments by all children.

Conclusion

Teacher education has to be conceived as an integral part of educational and social system and must primarily respond to the requirements of the school system. It can no longer remain conventional and static but should transform itself to a progressive dynamic and responsive system. National values and goals need to be meaningfully reflected and their inculcation attempted with care and caution. The theoretical and practical components need to be balanced appropriately. The theory and practice of education has to be enriched with the latest research findings not only in the field of education but also in the allied disciplines and areas. While it is essential to develop identified competencies to prepare effective teachers it is equally necessary to develop commitment and build capacity to perform as integral part of teacher preparation. The teachers have to keep abreast of the latest developments not only in their field of specialisation but also in areas of educational developments and social and cultural issues through continuous in-service orientation. Emphasis on continuing life-long learning has to become an essential concern of teacher education. A nation concerned with erosion of values needs teachers who are professionally committed and prepared to present a value-based model of interaction with their learners. The basic tenets identified in the national basic education scheme—Head, Heart and Hand need now to be linked to another 'H' - highways. Information highways, websites and internet are going to become terms of common usage in teacher education. For sound mind we need strong hand and a vibrant heart. Areas like physical education and vocational education will continue to gain greater emphasis in years to come and will serve as the basis for developing competencies and skills in addition to commitments and values. A comprehensive theoretical base is essential for a teacher to assume professional role and develop capacity to conceptualise inputs from other disciplines as well and evolve strategies to utilise them. A true professional is capable of perceiving complexities and uncertainties in the society, has a thorough grasp of the subject, possesses skills to make critical diagnosis, takes decisions and has courage and conviction to implement such decisions.

REFERENCES

MHRD (1985) *Challenges of Education*. New Delhi. Govt. of India.

MHRD (1986) National Policy on Education, New Delhi. Govt. of India.

Ministry of Education (1948-49): *Report of the University Education Commission*. New Delhi, Government of India.

Ministry of Education (1953) *Report of the Secondary Education Commission (1952-53)*, New Delhi, Government of India.

Ministry of Education (1966) *Education and National Development: Report of the Commission (1964-66)*. New Delhi, Government of India.

National Commission on Teachers-1 (1983-85) *Teacher and Society*. Delhi, Government of India Press.

National Council for Teacher Education (1998): *Curriculum Framework for Quality Teacher Education*, New Delhi, NCTE.

NCERT (1978) *Teacher Education Curriculum a Framework*. New Delhi, NCERT.

NCTE (1988) *National Curriculum Framework for Teacher Education*, New Delhi, NCERT.

NCTE (2005) *National Curriculum Framework for School Education*, New Delhi, NCERT

NCTE (2009) *National Curriculum Framework for Teacher Education*, New Delhi, NCERT.

Raina, V.K. (1995) Teacher Educators in India: In Search of an Identify. *Journal of Teacher Education*, no. 46, p. 45-52.

Raina, V.K. (1999) Indegenizing Teacher Education in Developing Countries: The Indian Context. *Prospects*, Vol. Xxiv (1) p. 5-25.

Shotton, J.R.1 (1997) No Master High or Low: Challenging the Pedagogy of the Oppressed in Ved Prakash (ed.) *Teacher Empowerment and School Effectiveness at Primary Stage*, NCERT, New Delhi.

Shulman, I.S. (1987): Knowledge and Teaching: Foundations of New Reforms. *Harvard Educational Review*, 57(1), pp. 4-14.

Saxena N.R., Mishra B.K., Mohanthy R.K. (1998) *Teacher Education*, Surya Publications, Meerut.

World Bank, (1997). *Primary Education in India*. Washington DC, The World Bank.

6
Understanding Teacher Education and Teaching in Constructivist Perspectives: Principles and Practices

Mayadhar Sahu

> "Scientific observation has established that education is not what the teacher gives; education is a natural process spontaneously carried out by the human individual, and is acquired not by listening to words but by experiences upon the environment. The task of the teacher becomes that of preparing a series of motives of cultural activity, spread over a specially prepared environment, and then refraining from obtrusive interference. Human teachers can only help the great work that is being done, as servants help the master. Doing so, they will be witnesses to the unfolding of the human soul and to the rising of a New Man who will not be a victim of events, but will have the clarity of vision to direct and shape the future of human society."
>
> —*Maria Montessori*

There is a paradigm shift in the teaching learning process in the 21st century. Child education and schooling has become a challenge before the teachers, parents, and policy makers. This is not due to the growing demands of the society but due to the change of perspectives in child pedagogy and innovative ideas which germinate in the field of educational research. The new movement of constructivism has brought new perspectives, strategies in child learning and education. The guiding principle of education in 21st century is based on the following points;

- Connecting knowledge to life outside the school.
- Ensuring that learning is shifted away from rote methods.
- Enriching the curriculum to provide for overall development of children rather than remain textbook centric.
- Making examinations more flexible and integrated into classroom life.
- Learner's engagement and learners voices are given utmost priorities.

- Teacher works as a facilitator in teaching learning process.
- Knowledge cannot be 'given' by the teacher, rather can be "constructed" by the child himself.

Behaviourism has been dominating the teaching learning process since long, making the learner a passive listener of knowledge. It has neither helped the learner to identify his potentialities nor to flourish his talents. In a teacher centric environment, learners have been a victim. It has never concerned about child's innate potentialities, rather pinned talents at its buds. Individual differences among the learners have never been bridged in behaviourism. Conception of constructivism has given a new direction and insight to modern teaching learning practices. It has put the learner at the centre of learning and focussed on the construction of knowledge by learner. Constructivism has undoubtedly revolutionalised the modern teaching learning practices. Constructivism is basically a theory based on observation and scientific study about how people learn. It says that people construct their own understanding and knowledge of the world, through experiencing things and reflecting on those experiences. Constructivism is a student-centered approach that places responsibility on students to take charge of their learning experiences. In the classroom, the constructivist view of learning can point towards a number of different teaching practices. In the most general sense, it usually means encouraging students to use active techniques (experiments, real-world problem solving) to create more knowledge and then to reflect on and talk about what they are doing and how their understanding is changing. The teacher makes sure she understands the students' pre-existing conceptions, and guides the activity to address them and then build on them. Teachers create activities and assignments that foster the creation of knowledge. Students are challenged to produce reality based products such as portfolios and papers. Formalization of the theory of constructivism is generally attributed to Jean Piaget, who articulated mechanisms by which knowledge is internalized by learners. He suggested that through processes of accommodation and assimilation, individuals construct new knowledge from their experiences. When individuals assimilate, they incorporate the new experience into an already existing framework without changing that framework. This may occur when individuals' experiences are aligned with their internal representations of the world, but may also occur as a failure to change a faulty understanding; for example, they may not notice events, may misunderstand input from others, or may decide that an event is a fluke and is therefore unimportant as information about the world. In contrast, when individuals' experiences contradict their internal representations, they may change their perceptions of the experiences to fit their internal representations. According to the theory, accommodation is the process of reframing one's mental representation of the external world to fit new experiences. Accommodation can be understood as the mechanism by which failure leads to learning: when we act on the expectation that the world operates in one way and it violates our expectations, we often fail, but by accommodating this new experience and reframing our model of the way the world works, we learn from the experience of failure, or others' failure. It is important to note that constructivism is not a particular pedagogy. In fact, constructivism is a theory describing how learning happens, regardless of whether learners are using their experiences to understand a lecture or following the instructions for building a model airplane. In both cases, the theory of constructivism suggests that learners construct knowledge out of their experiences.

The constructivist educational philosophy operates on four major assumptions:

- Knowledge depends on past constructions. Piagets cognitive processes confirm this which explained that one's cognitive structure operates in assimilation and accommodation of knowledge and learning. We know the world through our mental framework and we transform and interpret new information through this framework. Constructions come through systems of assimilation and accommodation into our existing mental framework
- Learning is an organic process of invention, not mechanical.
- Meaningful learning occurs through reflection and scaffolding of new knowledge upon existing framework of knowledge.

Our past experiences about 'learning' is primarily based on behaviouristic models. It conceived learning as response strengthening. According to this view, learning occurs when learner strengthens or weakens an association between a stimulus and a response. This first view developed in the first half of 20th century. The role of learner is to passively receive rewards and punishments. The instructional designer role is to create environments where the learner repeatedly is cued to give a simple response, which is immediately followed by a feedback. The second view of learning is that learning is knowledge acquisition. It is based on behaviouristic model. Learning occurs when a learner places new information in long-term memory. This view was developed in 1950s, 1960s and 1970s and was based largely on the study of human learning in artificial laboratory settings. The role of the learner is to passively acquire information, and the teacher's job is to present information, such as in textbooks and lectures. According to this view, information is a commodity that can be transmitted directly from teacher to learner. The instructional designer's role is to create environments in which the learner is exposed to a large amount of information through textbooks, lectures and computer based multimedia programmes. Learning is knowledge construction.

Learning occurs when a leaner actively constructs a knowledge representation in working memory. This view emerged in 1980s and 1990s and was based on largely on the study of human learning in increasingly realistic settings. According to this view, the learner is a sense maker, whereas the teacher is a cognitive guide who provides guidance and modeling on authentic academic tasks. The instructional designer's role is to create environments in which the learner interacts meaningfully with academic material.

Past vs. Present

Traditional Classroom	*Constructivist Classroom*
• Curriculum begins with the parts of the whole. • Emphasizes basic skills • Strict adherence to fixed curriculum is highly valued. • Materials are primarily textbooks and workbooks. • Learning is based on repetition. • Teacher's role is directive, rooted in authority. • Assessment is through testing correct answers. • Knowledge is seen as inert. • Students work primarily alone	• Rooted in negotiation. • Pursuit of student questions and interests is valued. • Materials include primary sources of material and manipulative materials. • Learning is interactive, building on what the student already knows. • Teacher's role is interactive, product. • Assessment includes student works, observations, and points of view, as well as tests. Process is as important as Curriculum emphasizes big concepts, beginning with the whole and expanding to include the parts. • Knowledge is seen as dynamic, ever changing with our experiences. • Students work primarily in groups.

The Learner in Constructivist Classroom

- ***The importance of the background and culture*:** Social constructivism or socioculturalism encourages the learner to arrive at his or her version of the truth, influenced by his or her background, culture or embedded worldview.
- ***Learner is responsible*:** It is argued that the responsibility of learning should reside increasingly with the learner (Glasersfeld, 1989). Social constructivism thus emphasizes the importance of the learner being actively involved in the learning process, unlike previous educational viewpoints where the responsibility is rested with the instructor to teach and where the learner played a passive, receptive role.
- ***The Harkness Discussion Method*:** It is called the "Harkness" discussion method because it was developed at Phillips Exeter Academy with funds donated in the 1930s by Edward Harkness. This is also named after the Harkness monster and involves students seated in a circle, motivating and controlling their own discussion. The teacher acts as little as possible.

- ***High motivation is must*:** The most crucial thing regarding the nature of learner is that he should have high motivation for learning. According to Von Glasersfeld (1989) sustaining motivation to learn is strongly dependent on the learner's confidence in his or her potential for learning.

Nature and Perspectives of Constructivist of Learning

- ***Learning is active*:** The student is the person who creates new understanding for him/herself. The teacher coach, moderates, suggests, but allows the students room to experiment, ask questions, try things that don't work. Learning activities require the students' full participation (like hands-on experiments). An important part of the learning process is that students reflect on, and talk about, their activities. Students also help set their own goals and means of assessment.
- ***Learning is reflective*:** Students control their own learning process, and they lead the way by reflecting on their experiences. This process makes them experts of their own learning. The teacher helps create situations where the students feel safe questioning and reflecting on their own processes.
- ***Collaborative learning*:** There are many reasons why collaboration contributes to learning. The main reason it is used so much in constructivism is that students learn about learning not only from themselves, but also from their peers. When students review and reflect on their learning processes together, they can pick up strategies and methods from one another. **Enquiry based learning**: The main activity in a constructivist classroom is solving problems. Students use inquiry methods to ask questions, investigate a topic, and use a variety of resources to find solutions and answers.

Constructivist Classroom: The Teacher and Learner

Teacher encourages student's initiatives and gives freedom and encouragement.

- The teacher asks open-ended questions and allows wait time for responses.
- Teacher emphasizes Higher-level thinking and reasoning.
- Students are engaged in dialogue with the teacher and with each other.
- Students are engaged in experiences that challenge hypotheses and encourage discussion.
- The class uses raw data, primary sources, manipulative, physical, and interactive materials.
- There is reciprocal learning environment in the classroom.

- Critical Exploration (Duckworth, 2006) The two components of critical exploration are curriculum development and pedagogy. In this method teachers find ways to encourage their students to explore the subject matter and express their thoughts on the material (Duckworth).
- Focus on Inquiry-based learning.
- There is emphasis on Problem-based learning
- Cognitive apprenticeships, various methods involving collaboration or group work, cooperative learning (reciprocal questioning, Jigsaw Classroom, structured controversies) are emphasized.

Assessing Learners Progress and Performances

Some assessment strategies include:

- Oral discussions. The teacher presents students with a "focus" question and allows an open discussion on the topic.
- Concept Mapping. In this activity, students list and categorize the concepts and ideas relating to a topic.
- Hands-on activities. These encourage students to manipulate their environments or a particular learning tool. Teachers can use a checklist and observation to assess student success with the particular material.
- Pre-testing. This allows a teacher to determine what knowledge students bring to a new topic and thus will be helpful in directing the course of study.

Instructors as Facilitators

According to the social constructivism approach, instructors have to adapt to the role of facilitators and not teachers (Bauersfeld, 1995). Whereas a teacher gives a didactic lecture that covers the subject matter, a facilitator helps the learner to get to his or her own understanding of the content. In the former scenario the learner plays a passive role and in the latter scenario the learner plays an active role in the learning process. The emphasis thus turns away from the instructor and the content, and towards the learner (Gamoran, Secada & Marrett, 1998). This dramatic change of role implies that a facilitator needs to display a totally different set of skills than a teacher (Brownstein, 2001). A teacher tells, a facilitator asks; a teacher lectures from the front, a facilitator supports from the back; a teacher gives answers according to a set curriculum, a facilitator provides guidelines and creates the environment for the learner to arrive at his or her own conclusions; a teacher mostly gives a monologue, a facilitator is in continuous dialogue with the learners (Rhodes and Bellamy, 1999). A facilitator should also be able to adapt the learning experience 'in mid-air' by taking the initiative to steer the learning experience to where the learners want to create value.

The learning environment should also be designed to support and challenge the learner's thinking (Di Vesta, 1987). While it is advocated to give the learner ownership of the problem and solution process, it is not the case that any activity or any solution is adequate. The critical goal is to support the learner in becoming an effective thinker. This can be achieved by assuming multiple roles such as consultant and coach.

Constructivist Classroom: An Example

We can take an example to understand the nature of constructivist classroom.

Students study astronomy and science in general by using observations of telescopic plates and a computer simulation of the sky to construct and test interpretations of astronomical phenomena. Students examine and make measurements on photographic plates from observatory telescopes and computer simulations of the sky (Observation), then relate these analyses to reference materials (Contextualization) containing what is known about astronomical objects (i.e., stars, planets, etc.). The teacher initially talks through how he would analyze and interpret examples of such astronomical data (Cognitive Apprenticeship) then the students form groups to work on some data (Collaboration), while the teacher coaches and advises them as they proceed. The students develop their own hypotheses and test them against the astronomical data (Interpretation Construction). Students defend their hypotheses using their analyses and reference materials both within and between the groups, and such argumentation together with background readings exposes them to various ways to interpret the data (Multiple Interpretations). As they proceed through the course, the students see how basic principles of astronomy, physics and chemistry can be used to make sense of different sets of astronomical data (Multiple Manifestations).

What We will Gain?

Education works best when it concentrates on thinking and understanding, rather than on rote memorization. Constructivism concentrates on learning how to think and understand.

- Constructivist learning is transferable. In constructivist classrooms, students create organizing principles that they can take with them to other learning settings.
- Children learn more, and enjoy learning more when they are actively involved, rather than passive listeners.
- Constructivism promotes social and communication skills by creating a classroom environment that emphasizes collaboration and exchange of ideas.

- Constructivism gives students ownership of what they learn, since learning is based on students' questions and explorations. Engaging the creative instincts develops students' abilities to express knowledge through a variety of ways. The students are also more likely to retain and transfer the new knowledge to real life. Students in constructivist classrooms learn to question things and to apply their natural curiosity to the world.
- Critics say that the collaborative aspects of constructivist classrooms tend to produce a "tyranny of the majority," in which a few students' voices or interpretations dominate the group's conclusions. It's elitist. Critics say that constructivists, by rejecting evaluation through testing and other external criteria, have made themselves unaccountable for their students' progress.

It is obvious that constructivism has brought a new vision and insight in to schooling. It has put the learner at the center of learning and teacher as facilitator of learning. Its strategies and approaches focuses on meaningfulness and participatory, cooperative learning. All the teaching community especially classroom teachers need to understand the essence and goodness of constructivism as a philosophy of teaching and psychology of learning. They need to change their mindset and learn new skills for implementing this innovative strategy in our classroom.

REFERENCES

Jonassen, D.H. (1999). Constructing learning environments on the web: Engaging students in meaningful learning. EdTech 99: Educational Technology Conference and Exhibition 1999: Thinking Schools, Learning Nation.

Walker, M *et al.* (2008). A bright spark: open teaching of science using Faraday's lectures on candles. *Journal of Chemical Education*, 85 (1): 59–63.

Piaget, J., and Inhelder, B. (1969). *The Psychology of the child.* New York: USA. Basic Books, Inc.

Vygotsky, L.S. (1978). *Mind In Society: The Development of Higher Psychological Processes*. Cambridge: MA, Harvard University Press.

Bain, Ken. (2004). *What the Best College Teachers Do. Cambridge*, MA: Harvard University Press.

Mayer, R. (2004). Should There Be a Three-Strikes Rule Against Pure Discovery Learning?. *American Psychologist*, 59(1), 14–19

Kirschner, P.A., Sweller, J., and Clark, R.E. (2006). Why minimal guidance during instruction does not work: an analysis of the failure of constructivist, discovery, problem-based, experiential, and inquiry-based teaching. *Educational Psychologist* 41 (2): 75–86.

NCERT. (2005). *National Curriculum Framework-2005*. New Delhi: India.

7
Teacher Education Programme: Some Challenges and Concerns

Ajay Kumar Attri

As an integral part of educational system, teacher education in India has to be responsive to socio-cultural ethos and national development. It does not consist of institution-based activities only. Its scope has broadened and its objectives have become more focused during the last thirty years. Therefore, it is expected to engage itself in all endeavors of social and national reconstruction and regeneration, address itself to the social and educational problems, fulfill the expectations of the people, accelerate the process of nation building and assist in the realization of constitutional goals. It is true that considerable achievements have been made in all these directions. Teacher education cannot remain indifferent to its context and major concerns. The Indian Constitution provides a long-term perspective on our educational system including that of teacher education. The founding fathers of Indian Constitution solemnly resolved 'to constitute India into a sovereign, socialist, secular and democratic republic and to secure to all its citizens: justice-social, economic and political; liberty of thought, expression, faith, belief and worship, equality of status and opportunity; and to promote among them all fraternity assuring the dignity of the individual and the integrity of the nation'. If teachers are to make positive contribution to the realization of the constitutional goals, pre-service and in-service education of teachers needs to give up its neutral stance and commit itself to attaining these goals. To develop the skills and competencies of students for getting through the examination would not be enough. Teachers must understand the importance of the constitution in its true perspective in the light of Indian cultural ethos and integrate it with the philosophy of education. In the absence of such an attempt, transplantation of ideologies and ideas may prove counter-productive. The concepts used in the Constitution are essential politico-philosophical and socio-psychological visualizations and they permeate and transcend changing needs of the time. Teacher education curricula would accordingly need to be restructured. Teacher education curricula at all stages need to emphasize the cultural, political and economic unity of the country. The contribution of different racial, religious, social, linguistic and regional groups in developing India's composite culture and nationhood need to be clearly discussed in teacher education institutions. Students need to be acquainted with the commonalities of different religions, languages, art, architecture, music, dance and drama. Misconceptions regarding other's faiths and way of life need to be removed. Scientific temper should be developed among students for eliminating superstitions that have struck deep roots in the mind of the people. Exchange of teachers and their educators from one region to another may also to be arranged. The identity of minorities has to be preserved but teacher education should try to bring them into the mainstream of national life. Ignorance of different kinds which develop suspicion among individuals and groups need to be removed. Instead of group loyalty, teachers and teacher educators should inculcate patriotic feelings. In addition to the realization of the constitutional goals, teacher education has to take part in the efforts for solving of socio-economic problems and make its contributions to the arduous task of nation building.

Some Challenges and Concerns in Teacher Education

Teacher education has to be receptive to the problems faced by educational system in general and the school education in particular. Besides, teacher education is essentially a context-sensitive activity. It has to respond to various changes in its social, political, and economic as well as cultural contexts. Developments in science and technology during the last two decades have transformed human life and the world. New technologies related to storage and communication of information have impacted the instructional process, given rise to e-learning and re-defined the concept of library and library service. Education that does not review and rethink its content and processes soon loses its relevance. These concerns give rise to educational challenges i.e. challenges from within the educational system. The well-established tradition of teaching and learning in India has retained its inherent strength even under adverse circumstances. The post-independence period was characterized by major efforts being made to nurture and transform teacher education. The system of teacher preparation has come under considerable pressure as a result of the expansion and growth of school education, through efforts to universalize elementary education. Having inherited a foreign model of teacher preparation at the time of independence from Britain in 1946, major efforts have been made to adapt and update the teacher education curriculum to local needs, to make it more context based, responsive and dynamic with regard to best meeting the particular needs of India. The current system of teacher education is supported by a network of national, provincial and district level resource institutions working together to enhance the quality and effectiveness of teacher preparation programmes at the pre-service level and also through in-service programmes for serving teachers throughout the country.

Teacher education as a whole needs urgent and comprehensive reform. There is a need to bring greater convergence between professional preparation and continuing professional development of teachers at all stages of schooling in terms of level, duration and structure. Considering the complexity and significance of teaching as a professional practice, it is imperative that the entire enterprise of teacher education should be raised to a university level and that the duration and rigour of programmes should be appropriately enhanced. Some challenges and concerns in teacher education are as follows:

Professionalism

The most significant quality perspective is the need to realize the importance of the teacher preparation programme to ensure professionalism in the processes and practices. This professionalism can be achieved only by total commitment, devotion and continuous efforts on enhancing quality in transaction. It is also essential to understand the learner's growth and development in the context of latest theories of medical and neurological sciences. The perception of emotional quotient has to be internalized by teachers. Thus quality in education rests in teacher education programme as teachers are the most critical agent of change, responsible for growth, development and progress of societies and communities. As teachers are acknowledged the crucial role not only in education but also in national development so teacher preparation programme need to built on the four pillars of education i.e. Learning to know, Learning to do, Learning to live together and Learning to be.

Problems of Education of the Country

Teacher education has to support the efforts for the solution of problems of education of the country. These problems can be divided into two categories: problems of education as a whole with special reference to school education and problems of teacher education itself. The latter includes general problems as well as those caused by school education curricula which put the responsibility of its implementation on teachers.

Well Qualified and Properly Trained Teachers

The country has to fulfill its constitutional commitment of providing universal elementary education to all and achieve the obliteration of illiteracy. Education is a fundamental right. To meet this obligation many programmes have been initiated. For achieving the target, the country needs well-qualified and properly trained teachers. The system has to prepare them and also train under qualified teachers professionally. Unprecedented expansion of teacher education institutions and programmes during the past few years characterizes the teacher education scenario of today. With increasing school enrolments and the launch of Indian primary education development programmes like Operation Blackboard, District Primary Education Programme, Sarva Shiksha Abhiyan and Universalization of Elementary Education, there was a natural increase in the demand for teachers. Added to this, the backlog of untrained teachers in the system and the essential requirement of pre-service teacher certification for appointment as a teacher led to mounting pressure on existing institutional capacity. The demand far exceeding supply, market forces have taken over unprecedented rise in the number of teacher education institutions in most parts of the country.

Linkages

Teacher education institutions need to forge stronger links with the system of education and also with the community they serve. In very specific terms these linkages may take the form of (a) linkages between Teacher education institutions and other university departments (b) linkages between sister Teacher education institutions, (c) linkages with school education system and school clusters and (d) linkages with community and its resources. Community linked teacher education, research and extension programmes need to be undertaken. Teacher education institutions and teachers may invite the experts from community, if available, and educators may be encouraged to participate in the activities of the community and vice-versa. In India, need-based selective approach has to be adopted by teacher education. Blind adaptation of alien experiments may prove counter- productive and wastage of precious resources. The guiding principle in this respect has to be the concept of 'working with community' and in this age of international competition, teacher education should not lag behind.

Certain Emerging and Innovative Concerns

In addition to these, there are a few other emerging concerns which teacher education cannot afford to ignore. The national curriculum framework for school education (2000) and that of 2005 have certain expectations from teacher education, which have been well articulated in these documents. Information and communication technology (ICT), open learning systems, value education, development of life skills, healthy, and productive living, integration of subjects and three language formula are the major concerns of these documents. With the commencement and explosion of Information and Communication Technology (ICT), there is a growing demand that it be included in school education. Teacher education has been structured to orient and sensitize the teacher to distinguish between developmentally appropriate and detrimental uses of ICT. It needs to also equip teachers with competence to use ICT for their own professional development. It is also the case that across different national contexts, and indeed within countries, there are differences in expectations for schooling. Key stakeholders, employers and parents have become more vocal about the skills and attitudes they expect schools to develop. This is, of course, not unconnected to the challenges brought about by economic globalization. In countries with mature economies, like the US, UK, Canada and Australia, there are concerns about skills at both ends of the spectrum – a lack of adequate literacy and numeracy skills, especially among disadvantaged groups; and insufficient high-quality science and mathematics graduates to fuel technological change. The rate of technological change, especially in information and communications technologies (ICT), has also increased. This change provides new platforms for enhancing teaching and learning, an opportunity poorly used so far despite the rise of several online universities. The technology is also giving rise to new forms of social networking which in time will challenge the notion of a brick-and-mortar school as a necessary site for teaching and learning to occur. Already, young people today are learning a great deal in non-formal contexts, and it is possible to put the contents of a year's worth of textbooks into a tablet PC.

Teacher and Quality in Teacher Education

The development of the country rests on the shoulders of teachers because they shape the youth in the classrooms of scholars and colleges. Thus the Quality of teachers is directly dependent on the quality of teacher education. The destiny of India lies in its classroom. This has been rightly said by the Education Commission Report, 1964-66. This implies that teacher, who is the organizer and controller of the classroom, is mostly responsible for the future of India. He is building future citizens of the country. As he moulds the children so the country will be moulded. From this point of view, a lot of responsibility lies with the teacher to discharge his duties effectively. So the teachers must be properly equipped with necessary knowledge, skills and abilities to deal with children. It is in this context that education of teachers becomes most important in any country. The quality of education we provide to our children depends on the quality of education of teachers we inject into the education system, which in turn depends on the quality of teacher education programme. Only competent, committed and resourceful teachers can give quality education. Quality is not just the quantum of knowledge imparted to students but also the effectiveness with which they are able to apply that knowledge in meeting the challenges of tomorrow. Quality of teacher education programme also depends on the quality of teaching. For this there is an urgent need for a comprehensive review of the curriculum. There is a need for training teachers in community health, guidance and counseling, research, strategies, competitions, personal development and student support services. Training in the use of computers has become a major priority for teachers both nationally and internationally. A well-developed programme of professional development is, therefore, required, to enable the teacher educators to develop these skills. To produce human resources with high quality, we need education with a high quality. In fact according to the demand of the global challenges, we need to improve the quality of education and develop educational standards that contain global and international issues. The purpose of teacher education is to produce teachers who have professional competencies. The role of teachers is no longer confined to teaching alone. They need to be thorough professionals, fully equipped with high academic standard, pedagogical and practical skills. Recognizing the global perspectives in education, the Jacquas Delores Commission in its report "Learning: The Treasure Within" (UNESCO, 1996) highlights challenges that are to be responded to by teacher and teacher preparation system. The programmes of teacher education for various stages need to be restructured and modernized in their input, process and output to make the system quality-oriented. The development of the country rests on the shoulders of teachers because they shape the youth in the classrooms of scholars and colleges. Thus the Quality of teachers is directly dependent on the quality in teacher education. Quality is not merely a measure of efficiency. It also has value dimension. Quality in education includes a concern for quality of life in all its dimensions Therefore, teacher education should concentrate on the issues such as the right leadership, expertise and effective transformation ofknowledge into wisdom, which places the nation on a higher level of prosperity and peace. This type of orientation is the need of the hour in teacher education.

The Education Market

The new contexts in which education systems have to operate can be quite succinctly stated. An older geo-political framework of internationalism has given way to an ever-deepening globalization process, primarily but not exclusively in the economic sphere. Trade barriers have come down and capital, labour and technology flows have increased dramatically and changed financial and industrial production and consumption patterns. Fuelled by a still dominant neo-liberal agenda, education processes have entered the marketplace as a commodity, to be priced, marketed and sold to willing buyers. The increasing rate of corporatization of universities, the import and export of academic programmes, the increasing presence of the private sector in education, the rise of private and international schools are examples of this trend. For example, more Indian and Chinese students than ever before are travelling abroad to study; at the same time, the number of students from the West studying in China and India is also increasing.

Technological Advancement

All regions of the world are in the middle of a technological, scientific and information revolution. New Information technologies produce important changes in all dimensions of social and cultural life. Their impact on education is two-fold. On the one hand, information technologies constitute an instrument which can be of help in the learning process and in educational management, while on the other, the use of these technologies has become the content of teaching in itself. E-learning also provide future and existing teachers with access to rich information resources, tools, training programmes, online communities of practice, and opportunities to collaborate with other educators around the world. So supervising teachers must also be skilled in the use of e-learning so that they can model its use to enhance the learning of their students.

Status and Training of Teachers

The status of teachers and their working conditions among regions and within them are different. Better packages would improve the status of teachers and of education in society. These packages include the provision of adequate welfare programmes, including pension schemes and employment packages ensuring good living conditions, more clearly defined hours of work etc. Quality of teacher education is a product of the knowledge, skills and competencies working in perfect harmony to produce good students. For this teacher educators in training institutions should reexamine their textual materials and curriculum contents. Every teacher educator should be trained and competent:

- in the use of ICT - Internet, media, appropriate institutional technologies.
- in selecting, organizing and using learning resources.
- in the use of communication skills.
- to understand expectations of the community.
- to undertake action research for qualitative improvement of classroom teaching.

Teaching Moral Character

The importance of character education is gaining momentum among politicians and educators. The relative neglect of moral character education in the formal pre-service teacher curriculum has at least two proximal causes. The first is the daunting surfeit of training objectives that already crowd the academic curriculum of teaching majors. The second cause is the puzzling phenomena whereby stakeholders—parents and school boards—expect schools to address the character of students, but nobody wants to be caught teaching values. The allergic fear of moral education is that one should be asked "whose values?" are being taught. Yet values are embedded inextricably in school and classroom life. Teachers implicitly impart values when they select and exclude topics; when they insist on correct answers; when they encourage students to seek the truth of the matter; when they establish classroom routines, form groups, enforce discipline, encourage excellence. Teachers mould certain forms of social life within classrooms, and influence students' experience of community and school membership. Moral values saturate the daily life of classrooms. Character formation is intrinsic to classrooms and schools and an inescapable part of the teacher's craft. The dilemma that faces teacher educators, then, is whether it is acceptable to allow character education to remain part of a school's hidden curriculum, or whether advocacy for the value commitments immanent to education and teaching should be transparent, intentional, and public.

Research and Innovation

There is a need to increase research that documents practices reflectively and analytically—whether it is of programmes or of individual classrooms – so that it can be included in the body of knowledge available for study to student teachers. University departments and research institutions need to undertake such research. In addition there is a need to innovate with different models of teacher education. Institutional capacity and capability to innovate and create are a pre-requisite for the pursuit of excellence. Hence in the present scenario a lot of impetus has been given to research. Many teacher educators are encouraged to take up either major or minor research projects.

Inclusive Education

There are two kinds of exclusion prevalent in schools; one is the exclusion of the child with disabilities and the second is the social exclusion of children who come from socially and economically deprived backgrounds. There is a dire need to equip teachers to overcome their biases in these regards and positively handle these challenges. The Persons with Disabilities (PWD) Act of 2005 provides for free and compulsory education up to the age of 18 years for all children with disabilities. The education of socially and economically disadvantaged groups, especially the SCs, STs and minorities has remained a primary national concern of education for several years. The enrolment and retention of girls and therefore their participation has also remained behind those of boys. Teachers will have to be specially equipped if the social deprivation has to be overcome through education.

Aggression and Violence among Students

Educators should objectively discuss and identify the causes of aggression, violence and disorder in their expository presentations. Students should be convinced that use of aggression, violence, terrorism, subversive activities have no place in a civil society. Teacher education needs to build a strong bulwark against these practices and ideologies. This is a real challenge for teacher education.

Problem of Selection

Defects of selection procedure lead to deterioration of the quality of teachers. Better selection method would not only improve the quality of training but also save the personal and social wastage. Some suggestions are mentioned: (a) Candidates should be interviewed (b) Test of General Knowledge should be applied (c) Test in school subjects (d) Test of language (e) Test of intelligence should be administered (f) Aptitude; interest and attitude inventory should be administered (g) A well direct guidance service should be provided.

Deficiencies of Small Time Period Provided for Teacher's Training

In India, the teacher training period is of one year after the graduation—the effective session being of eight to nine months. The main purpose of teacher education programme is to develop healthy attitude, broad based interest and values. This is not possible during the short duration of nine months.

Incompetency of Student Teachers

The existing training programme does not provide adequate opportunities to the student teachers to develop competency because the organizers of teacher's training programme are not aware of the existing problems of schools. Therefore there should be a close matching between the work schedule of the teacher in a school and the programme adopted for teacher preparation in a training college.

Problems of Practice Teaching

The ratio of marks between theory and practice generally remains 5:2 although teaching practice plays a significant role in B.Ed. programme. In spite of all kinds of elaborate arrangements regarding practice in teaching, student teachers are non-serious to the task of teaching, and are deficient in sense of duty, irresponsible, aimless, indifferent to children, lacking innovative measure in teaching—which are great obstacles in the development of pedagogical skills.

Problem of Supervision of Teaching

The supervisory organization for practice teaching aims at bringing improvement in the instructional activity of the student teachers by using various techniques and practical skills in teaching and helping them develop confidence in facing the classroom situations. This is done through following types of supervisions:

i. *Supervision before classroom teaching:* It aims at guiding in planning their lessons, learning to organize contents, formulating suitable gestures and developing other related skills. At present the lesson plans are checked superficially and no discussion is made by the subject method specialist.

ii. *Supervision during the classroom teaching:* It is done by teachers who are not method specialist generally. These supervisors offer descriptive type of criticism, while constructive type is desirable. Their remarks are related to the general personality of the student teachers. The percentage of lessons supervised by the subject method specialist varies from 5 per cent to 25 per cent due to faulty staffing pattern, lack of time, too many lessons to be supervised, defective time table etc. Here, the school teacher should be assisted by the college supervisor in his work. Frequent conferences and consultations between them will help to relate them to practice and the student teacher will improve the performance in a realistic school setting.

Faulty Methods of Teaching

In India teacher educators are averse to innovation and experimentation in the use of methods of teaching. Their acquaintance with modern class-room communication devices is negligible.

Learners at Central Place

These expectations suggest that teacher operates in a larger context and its dynamics as well as concerns impinge upon her functioning. That is to say, a teacher has to be responsive and sensitive to the social contexts of education, the various disparities in the background of learners as well as in the macro national and global contexts, national concerns for achieving the goals of equity, parity, social justice and also excellence. To be able to realize such expectations, Teacher Education has to comprise such features as would enable the student teachers to care for children, and who love to be with them; Understand children within social, cultural and political contexts; View learning as a search for meaning out of personal experience; Understand the way learning occurs, possible ways of creating conductive conditions for learning, differences among students in respect of the kind, pace and styles of learning. The NCF 2005 requires a teacher to be a facilitator of children's learning in a manner that the child is helped to construct his/her knowledge. Education is not a mechanical activity of information transmission and teachers are not information dispensers. Teachers have to increasingly play the role of crucial mediating agents through whom curriculum is transacted. The confluence of the two processes of globalization and technological change is having a tremendous impact on the students who go to school today. On the one hand, global economic opportunities and the necessity to learn 21st century skills have raised the academic bar. The new human capital paradigm is no longer just about having extended years of schooling to prepare students for industrial jobs; it is about content mastery, deep disciplinary understanding as well as acquiring the soft skills of communication, initiative, resilience, group dynamics and problem-solving abilities, among others.

Lack of Proper Facilities

In India, the teacher education programme is being given a step-motherly treatment. About 20 per cent of the teacher education institutions are being run in rented buildings without any facility for an experimental school or laboratory, library and other equipments necessary for a good teacher education department. There are no separate hostel facilities for student teachers.

Conclusion

Professional development needs to be understood as activities that lead to changes in knowledge and skills that more effectively respond to the problems of practice. It is predicated on the belief that such enhanced competencies will lead to improved student learning. Related to this is the idea that schools are valuable sites for teacher learning and that learning together with others in the school and in more extended networks of teachers will provide powerful learning opportunities. The courses of studies both in theory and practice should be reorganized. For this a pragmatic research should be conducted to see what should be the course structure which will be helpful for realization of the goals of teacher education. The method of teaching in the teacher education departments should be such that it inspires a sense of appreciation among other departments of the universities and colleges: A teacher education department should therefore, conduct special innovative programmes in the following directions: Seminar, combining of seminar and discussions with lectures, team teaching panel discussion and projects sponsored by the faculty members for improvement of learning in various spheres. For development of professional attitude it will be advisable to recognize the college of education as unit in themselves. Such an institution should be equipped with facilities for organizing various types of activities such as daily assembly programmes, community living, social work, library organization and other curricular activities, which promote democratic spirit of mutual appreciation and fellow feeling. The admission procedures of B.Ed. should be completely systematized and steps should be taken to make it fool proof against tempering and meddling as far as possible. Positive attitude and increased information during teacher training help in effective implementation of important measures. The role and shape of teacher education is easy to visualize but difficult to accomplish. There is a gap between theory and practice; so we have to develop such type of teacher training programmes which can fulfill the requirement of present need of society and country which could fulfill the larger goals of human empowerment in the wake of globalization in knowledge explosion.

REFERENCES

Cho, Y. (2008). *Innovations in Training New Teachers: The Development of Korean Education through a New System for Colleges of Education.* South Korean submission to the Alliance, College of Education, Seoul National University.

Cochran-Smith, M. (2004). The problem of teacher education. *Journal of Teacher Education,* 55(4), 295–299.

Mohanty, Jagannath (2003). *Teacher Education.* Deep & Deep Publications Pvt. Ltd., New Delhi.

Ramnath K.N., (2007). *Global Trends in Teacher Education*, New Delhi A.P.H. Publishing Corporation.

Saxena, N.R., Mishra, B.K., Mohanty, R.K. (2005). *Teacher Education*, Meerut.

Sharma, Shashi Prabha (2003). *Teacher Education: Principles, Theories and Practices.* Kanishka Publishers, New Delhi.

Vashist, S.R. (2003). *Professional Education of Teachers*, Mangal Deep Publications, Jaipur.

8
Teachers in the Global World: New Horizons

Taruna Malhotra

Following the tremendous impact of information technology and globalization, there are drastic contextual changes and paradigm shifts in conceptualizing knowledge and education (Beare & Slaughter 1993), (Cheng 2001s). Some important examples of these changes and shifts in education include 'de monopolization' of teaching—a shift from teacher centered teaching to student centered learning, the emphasis on life long learning and development of multiple intelligence, shift from subject specific to cross-disciplinary curriculum, the breaking down of geographical barriers and enabling of world class education through various forms of e-learning and redefinition of the body of knowledge worth pursuing as well as the way to acquire it. Correspondingly, the expected role of the teacher in global world has also changed fundamentally such that it is very different from the traditional mode (Cheng 2001).

Teacher in Modern and Traditional Paradigms

Traditionally, teachers were perceived mainly as the knowledge providers to students, but now teachers are expected to assume a new major role as a facilitator in supporting students' learning process and developing students' multiple intelligence and lifelong self learning abilities. Teacher themselves also need to be a lifelong learner, be able to articulate their teaching with the new paradigm of learning, be adaptive and flexible in dealing with a new brand of students comprising different age group, of diverse ethnicity, with a wide range of prior knowledge and background and be conversant with the new technologies which are developing rapidly at an ever increasing speed (Tusi & Cheng 2000). With the support of Information Technology and Networking, teachers are also expected to network and work with peer teachers, students, parents, other experts and the community; so that, the process of teaching and learning can extend beyond the boundaries of one class or the one school to an entire network of local and international learner.

Modern Paradigm	*Traditional Paradigm*
Teacher is the facilitator to support student learning	Teacher is the centre of education
Multiple intelligence teacher	Partially competent Teacher
Individualized Teaching Style	Standard Teaching Style
Teaching is to arise curiosity	Teaching is to transfer knowledge
Teaching is profession to initiate, facilitate and sustain students' self learning and self actualization	Teaching is a disciplinary, delivering, training & socializing process.
Sharing joy with students	Achieving standards in exams.
Networking teaching	Separated Teaching.
Teaching is life long process.	Teaching is transfer and application process.
Teacher is the multiple, local & global source of knowledge	Teacher as the sole source of teaching & knowledge
World class teaching	Site bounded teaching
Unlimited opportunity for teaching.	Limited opportunities for teaching
Teacher with local & international outlook	Teacher with only school experiences
Teacher as a world class & networked teacher	Teacher as a school bounded and separated teacher.

A Model of Teacher Development

The present model (Fig. 8.1) helps a teacher at both initial and in-service level, as effective teaching is essentially concerned with best to bring about the desired pupil learning activities

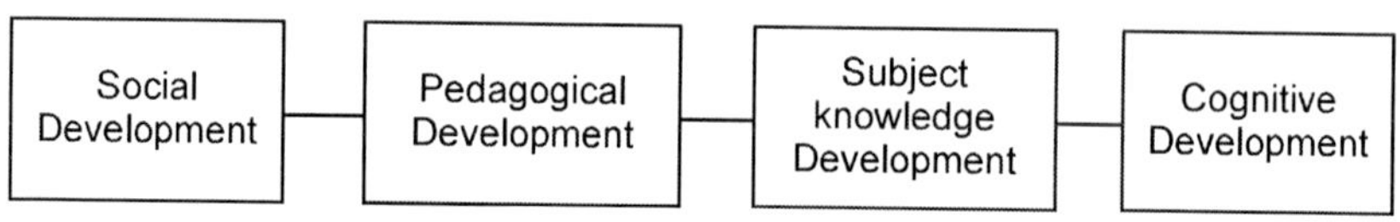

Fig. 8.1: A Model of Teacher Development

The Social Development of Teachers

It involves learning the set of behaviours congruent with environmental demands of that setting. There is substantial evidence that beginning teachers' view, their more experienced colleagues as highly influential in the process of learning to teach. (White & Frederickson, 2000). A competent teacher strives to understand the students in his classes in order to create and sustain a learning community (Richardson 1996) Balance between individual students and groups is a continuous and an unending process on the part of the teacher.

Subject Knowledge Development

The subject matter orientation is a paradigm to understand professional growth. In this perspective, teachers' content knowledge becomes a critical foundation in the practice of teaching and instruction is shaped by what teachers know and do not know about the subjects and they teach (Stiorer & Maybin, 1994).

Teachers' knowledge and understanding of subject knowledge and its application in the classroom can promote more effective passing on of knowledge during the teaching and learning process. Subject knowledge supports teacher to set his short term and long term objectives by creating an encouraging learning environment.

Pedagogical Development of Teacher

Teaching is a thoughtful activity underpinned by knowledge as well as skill. Teaching is a critical awareness of the range of pedagogic possibilities and classroom decision making strategies. Mere content knowledge is likely to be as useless pedagogically as content free skill in teaching (Shulman, 1986). Pedagogy covers a number of aspects of the instruction, most noticeably the teacher interaction with pupils' and. the context, structure, organization of the learning tasks and activities. The competencies of teachers in content and pedagogy can be improved through recurrent training programs, as a teacher should have sufficient understanding about the latest techniques and methods of transaction by renewing his knowledge, methodology and techniques.

Cognitive Development of Teacher

The teacher should visualize present situation where in there is a lot of movement from teaching to learning and hearing to doing. It means more focus should be laid on an individual's capacities and innate abilities. Cognitive development focuses on information processing, conceptual resources, perceptual skills, language learning and other aspects of brain development. If educators are to empower all individuals to learn, they must know and be able to apply information from human development and cognitive science with in their own professional practice. Teacher development programmes should provide opportunities for teachers to learn to increase students' capacity to think, plan, solve problems, set goals and work with focused attention.

New Horizons: Agenda for 21st Century

New Schools for a New Millennium

What we want (according to Art Costa, author of 'The School As A Home for the Mind' 91) are students inspired by whatever talents they have to be able to: 'set goals, establish plans and establish priorities' who can 'generate, hold and apply criteria for assessing the own growth of their own thoughtful behaviour' who can 'take risks, share thinking strategies and venture forth with creative ideas...' 'The School as a Home for The Mind' is a challenging metaphor. 'The best we educational planners can do is to create the conditions for teachers and schools to flourish and get out of their way.' (Theodore Sizer 2009)

We Need a More Informed Vision for the 21st C 'The Best of All Worlds'

For far too long teachers, and the public, have been sidetracked by an either/or mentality about education—'child centered' or 'traditional; whether encourage students to 'learn for themselves' or 'sit them down and teach and test them'. What is needed is to take the best from each 'mindset'. We do need to help students develop a strong sense of autonomy and creativity based around their talents and, as well, we need to help them value the importance of rigor, effort, working in depth and perseverance. When we add new ideas about how students learn we have a powerful philosophy that can be used at all levels losing in the process the problems of transferring between schools.

The Dynamic Role of the Teacher as an Inspirer

Learning needs to be seen as a movement from a position of being a 'novice' to one of being an 'expert'. To achieve such growth requires a master/apprenticeship role between the two parties involved. Teachers to be seen as inspirer need to believe that all students can learn given appropriate tasks, time and help. They need to hold high expectations for all learners with no exceptions. Then, by using their diagnostic skills, they need to assess the current knowledge and skill base of each learner and then negotiate achievable and explicit 'stretch goals' to further each student's ability. Such teacher/coaches are experts in mediating learning even for the most limited students by providing appropriate 'scaffolds', or temporary help, and always in the process encouraging every student to outdo their previous 'personal best'. 'I want you to get excited about who you are, what you have, and what you could still be. I want to inspire you to see that you can go far beyond where you are right now.' Virginia Satire. Figure 8.2 explains the characteristics of the 21st century educators.

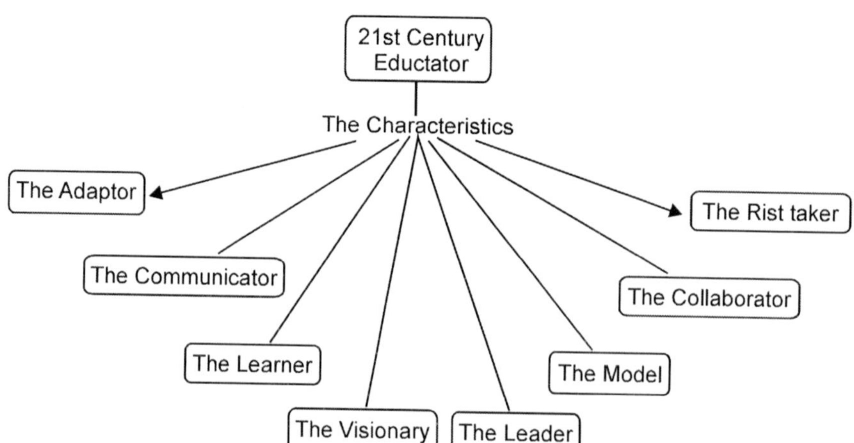

Source: edorigami. Wikispaced/21st century.com.

Fig. 8.2: The 21st Century Educator

All Students Need to Experience Excellence—The Basis for All Learning

Whatever approaches a school uses it will be of little use unless every student gains an appreciation of the need for personal excellence. Too often, schools take on board new ideas about learning, such as multiple intelligences, learning styles, and cooperative learning, before this concept is established. As a result what is often achieved is disappointing. It is important for all students to achieve something beyond their wildest expectations. When students are motivated by interest or relevance and with the assistance of a skilled coach/mentor, this should be the experience of all learners. To achieve such a vision schools would need to cover fewer topics but do them in depth to ensure understanding, aiming for quality rather that quantity. All too often this dedication to doing things well is only to be seen when students undertake out of school or extra curricular activities. Motivation is all about the pride and personal power of doing something really well. Once this quality mindset is accepted there are a range of proven ideas that can be introduced by a skilled teacher. Failing would no longer be seen as an option in such a learning environment.

Learning is about Making Meaning – Constructivism

A constructivist theory, where students 'construct' their own meanings, underpins this future vision of education. This does not exclude the role of expert helper as illustrated by the coaching metaphor. As the Russian educationalist Lev Vygotsky wrote 'What a child can do with help today he/she can do by themselves tomorrow'. A more suitable phrase would be 'co-constructivism. Teachers using a co- constructivist model would first find out (and value) the prior knowledge any student brings to a learning situation. Student's questions would determine the learning pathway but the teacher's role would be to confront their tentative theories and challenge them, expand their knowledge and, in the process, help them develop improved learning strategies. This 'interactive' approach is already the basis of the successful Reading Recovery programmes and is increasingly being used across the curriculum including Multiple Intelligence, Co-operative Learning, Inquiry Learning, Collaborative Learning, and Web Quests etc.

Awareness of the Creative Process to Develop an Appreciation of Reflection and Effort

To achieve quality work in any area the teacher must 'slow the pace' of students work down, not only to introduce a reflective mindset, but also to provide time for the teacher to assist student thinking. Far too often work is spoiled in schools by students rushing in, without even considering what it is they are trying to achieve, with the thought in mind that first finished is always bet!

Students, when they are beginning new tasks, need to be helped through the learning process starting with idea generation and finishing with the idea being realized. An appreciation that in this process, learning can be 'messy' until the idea 'gels' is an important understanding. Students also need to appreciate that, when developing a new skill, it often gets worse before it gets better and that perseverance, practice and effort will be involved. People involved in the creative arts are well aware of these important insights. If these insights are not appreciated, students, particularly those with a 'perfection mindset', can give up and in turn miss out on the excitement of doing something new really well. Shear talent may be enough for a gifted few but for most students, it is important, they learn to value effort, to learn to cope with setbacks (in the process developing resiliency), the need for perseverance and good 'old fashioned' practice.

Creating Powerful, Learners: Learners with Strategies

There are those who believe that being aware of the process of 'how to learn' is now the real content of education. Understanding knowing how to do something is as important as being able to do it—a learner who can articulate his thoughts is a powerful learner. Some practitioners state that it is only when you don't know what to do and then the real thinking begins. The future will be full of 'ill defined' situations requiring intelligent behaviour using 'habits of mind'.

The Importance of Depth Rather than Coverage

The need for in depth powerful learning challenges ('Rich Topics') has already been mentioned. In recent years teachers have been 'encouraged' by a 'flood' of curriculum documents to cover and assess far too many requirements. This has lead to, what one educator (Perkins, 'Smart Schools' 95) calls a 'game of trivial pursuits' leading to 'fragile learning'. What is required is what some have called, the 'Haiku Curriculum—simple and deep'. In the process of working in depth the problem of the 'crowded curriculum' will be solved.

The teacher's role is then to encourage 'deep thinking' about the topics chosen to help students see connections between learning areas. Developing links between Learning Areas is an idea almost impossible in current fragmented traditional secondary schools. The provision of cross curricular powerful learning themes naturally leads to the need to introduce a range of teaching and learning strategies. The best topics, as in the 'real world' will be messy and 'ill-defined' but such generative topics will provide the potential for students to explore a range of traditional disciplines. While planning will still be important much of what will eventuate will be unpredictable and the unexpected developments may well prove to provide the most insight. These ideas reflect discovery in the real world.

The Vexed Issue of Assessment - The Need to Reduce the 'Assessment Frenzy'!

Assessment needs to be determined by what the schools values and then integrate into every learning task. The creative coaching model naturally integrates feedback, both positive and 'suggestive', and negotiates with individual learners specific goals for future improvement. Students in the future will need to be able to self assess their own growth by using agreed criteria. The most important evidence of learning is the student's mindsets, behaviours, dispositions, enthusiasm and positive attitudes towards learning. The best assessments are student demonstrations and performances.

Management—The Lost 'Craft' of Teaching

Classroom management has for too long left to chance. Focused classroom management is a vital element in creating a positive learning environment. Too often, in the rush to cover too many things, teachers are becoming what Mary Hill (University of Waikato) calls 'activity managers rather than teachers!'

Students to learn need safe, predictable classroom environments to encourage them to develop the confidence to take the risks so necessary in any learning. Teachers also need the time to stop and engage in 'focused teaching', so necessary to help all students achieve quality learning. Teachers need to negotiate with students, not only what they are supposed to be doing, but also when, how and why, or students may waste valuable learning time or, worse still, become behavioural problems.

A 'three step learning' format is one way to focus teaching and learning. Each lesson needs to start with an introduction outlining what is going to happen e.g. introducing new vocabulary or relating the lesson back to previous learning. This is followed by focused group work session and concluded with a reflective 'wrap up' session to draw ideas together. Each day should have the same format concluding with a reflective period before students leave for home.

It is a good management idea for the teacher to outline the day's programme and any negotiated class goals and specific group tasks, on the black or white board. This will ensure students have enough information to get on with their tasks independently without interrupting the teachers on procedural matters. Four rotating group tasks are enough to ensure diversity without losing focus. One group task is normally working with the teacher in a focused 'social style' coaching/teaching situation. The other three groups could reflect the three other learning styles: the 'researcher' (perhaps using the computer); the 'active hand on style' doing a practical task; and the 'imaginative/sensitive style'. This of course is a simplification of a complex idea.

If quality work is the aim then students will also need to have the visual and presentation skills required 'scaffold' until they become automatic. The way work is presented in any media, cannot be left to chance. Often students' quality thinking is spoiled by its poor presentation and as well quality presentation/design can 'sell' ideas to others. Schools that have defined these expectations are able to demonstrate to all the quality of their students work. It is all about valuing standards.

Room Environments to Celebrate and Inform

If student have been helped to achieve work of excellence it ought to be displayed with due respect. Displays should reflect, if a primary class, a range of Learning Areas, each with a provocative heading, study questions, in some areas processes and goals outlined, and if necessary, class evaluations. In this way room environments celebrate students' creativity and inform students and visitors. Teachers expert in this area have classrooms with what can be called the 'wow' factor! and other teachers, if they are open to new ideas, can soon learn some simple display principles.

The room, and indeed the total school, should reflect a pride of achievement that can be picked up by even the most casual visitor. Aesthetics is an important and often forgotten aspect, in schools.

Here, an attempt is made to identify the attributes which a teacher of global world should have:

Attributes of the Teachers of the Global World

In the global world, schools have become very crucial to supporting the rapid development of individuals and in local communities, societies and international relations and are expected to perform wide range of new structural, social, political, cultured and educational functions (Cheng 1996). In this connection, teachers in the era of rapid change are often required to take up expanded roles and responsibilities including curriculum- developer, new teacher mentor, staff development facilitator, action researcher, pre service teacher educator, team-leader, decision maker and classroom manager. Here, effort is made to portray the attributes of teachers working with new horizons of the global world:

Skilled and Knowledgeable Practitioners

- Have a deep understanding of their individual content and successfully engages students through a demonstrated passion for the content by connecting it with their lives.
- Continues to be intellectually curious and demonstrates the habits of mind that lead to life long learning about their craft, their students and their context.

- Has the capacity to integrate international context issued and perspectives into a standard based curriculum.
- Uses an inquiry based model of teaching that enables students to actively manipulate ideas in order to construct knowledge, solve problems and develop their own understanding.
- Asks students to analyze and reflect on their own learning.
- Uses multiple forms of assessment to evaluate ongoing student learning, moving students from below grade level to at or above grade—level performance.

Culturally Aware

- Recognize values and respect the broad spectrum of ethnicities and cultures in school community and teach students to collaborate effectively with individuals from different backgrounds.
- Use instructional strategies to understand the contribution of different cultures to Indian life and recognize and draw upon the diverse cultural assets with their classroom.
- Recognize the level of students' literacy in academic and social language and help them build meaningful bridges between the two.

Aware of World Events and Global Dynamics

- Understand and stay current on world event, international issues, and global debates and help students gain understanding through daily interactions.
- Connect their context area to authentic global issues and perspectives.
- Present balanced view points on global issues and assist students in viewing issues from multiple perspectives.

Literate for the 21st Century

- Proficient in and model the essential skills of reading, writing, comprehending, listening and speaking that are necessary for students' learning in their content area.
- Readers with a rich reading life for both work and pleasure.
- Familiar with contemporary culture, its music, art, literature and trends and seek to integrate these in relevant ways into curriculum.
- Able to develop and present information in an articulate and persuasive manner, orally, in writing and through digital media.
- Able and willing to learn to communicate in one or more languages other than English.
- Able to understand and use the arts from its own and other cultures to assist students in learning, expressing ideas and emotions.

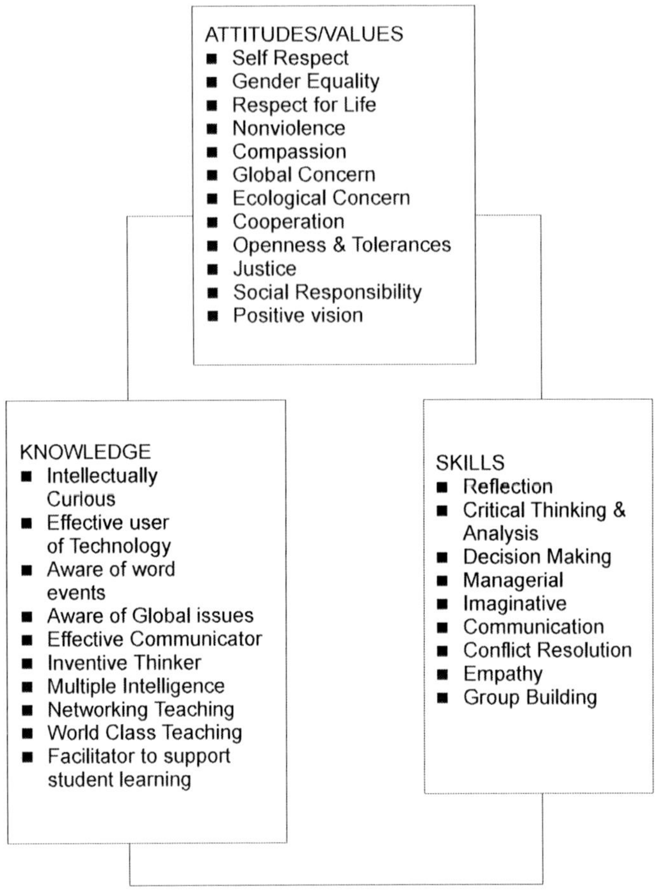

Fig. 8.3: Attitude/Values, Knowledge and Skill as Essential Attributes of Teachers of the Global World

Collaborative Team Members

- Appreciate and respectful of diversity and work effectively with people from other cultures backgrounds and field of expertise.
- Receptive to others perspective, welcome differences in interpretation and judgment.
- Able to revise and expand their own views.
- Committed members of the teaching professional community, participating in on-going professional. development including monitoring lesson study, peer observations, critical friends groups, study groups and collaborating with teachers locally and nationally through the network.

Professionally Responsible and Ethical Citizens

- Are committed to behave ethically towards students and other members of the school community.
- Understand that the decisions made locally and nationally have impact at international level and those international trends and events affect the local and national options.
- Accept responsibilities of global citizenship and make ethical decisions and responsible choices that contribute to the development of a more calm, peaceful and sustainable world.

Effective Users of Technology and Media

- Proficient in the use of essential computer and communications technologies.
- Users of technologies to communicate and work across national and regional boundaries.
- Able to evaluate, critically choose and various forms of media and technology in lesson design and implementation to maximize students' engagement.

Figure 8.3 represents this idea.

Conclusion

To conclude it can be said that Delor's Commission emphasized on the four pillar of education — learning to know, learning to do, learning to be and learning to live together. In the global world, it can be hard to get a grip on the evolving roles of teachers. The role of teacher has grown immensely, as they are now expected to be tech savvy, computer literate and using the legitimate methods of internet research on one hand and be humane, morale developing new axiology, supporter of the feelings to live together on the other hand. In the global world, teachers need to take their roles as both a resource for students and as a guide through the difficulties of life seriously and should strive to foster healthy relationships with their students as the complete focus of education is on producing students who are highly productive, effective communicator, inventive thinkers and masters of technology.

REFERENCES

Beare and Slaughter 1993, *Education for the twenty first century*, London: Routledge.

Cheng Cheong Yin (2001), *Teacher Effectiveness and Teacher Development: Toward a New knowledge Base*, edited by, Magdalera Moching Mok, Kwok Tung Tsui, The Hongkong Institute of Education, Kluwer Academic Publishers.

Cheng, Y.C. (1995). *Function and effectiveness of education* (3rd ed.). Hong Kong: Wide Angle Press.

Cheng, Y.C. and Tsui, K.T. (1996). Total teacher effectiveness: New conception and improvement. *International Journal of Educational Management*, 10(6), 7-17

Csikszentmihaly en.wikipedia.org/wiki/Mihaly_**Csikszentmihalyi.**

Elbow, P. (2004), *Writing First! Educational Leadership*, 62 (2), 8-13.

Goethe www.quotationcafe.com

Piaget J. en.wikiquote.org/wiki/Jean_Piaget

Richardson, V. (1996), The role of attitudes and beliefs in learning to teach in J. Sikula (Eds.), *Handbook of Research on Teacher Education* (2nd ed., pp. 102-119). New York: Macmillan.

Satir V., www.quotationcafe.com

Shulman, L.S. (1986). Those Who understand: Knowledge Growth in Teaching. Educational Researcher, 15(2), 4-14.

Stiorer, B. and Maybin, J. (eds). (1994). *Language, Literacy and Learning in Educational Practice*. Buckingham, England: Open University Press.

Theodore R. Sizer, Leading Education-Reform Advocate, *The New York Times*, By Margalit Fox Published: October 22, 2009

Tsui, K.T., and Cheng, Y.C. (2000). Multi-dimensional teacher performance: An organizational perspective. Paper presented at the 14th International Congress for School Effectiveness and Improvement "Global Networking for Quality Education", 4-8 January 2000, Hong Kong.

White, B., and Frederickson, J. (2000). Metacognitive facilitation: An approach to making scientific inquiry accessible to all. In J. Minstrell and E. van Zee (Eds.). *Inquiring into Inquiry Learning and Teaching in Science*. (pp. 331-370). Washington, DC: American Association for the Advancement of Science.

Whitehead www.auroraproject.com.au/.../2011_10_19_handbook_for_aurora

Wong H. www.quotationcafe.com

9
Researches in Teacher Education: An Analysis

Ramakanta Mohalik

Education is a human right. It is an essential tool for attaining the goal of equality, development and peace. It breaks the vicious line drawn between poverty and illiteracy. Education is an important instrument in bringing out potentialities of human beings while effectiveness of a system of education is mainly dependent upon its teachers. Teacher's performance is the most crucial input in the field of education as teacher is the principal agent for successful implementation of plans and policies. In other words no plan and policies will be successful without effective and quality teacher. The role of the teacher has rightly been emphasized in the Programme of Action (POA) of the National Policy on Education, 1986 that the teacher is the principal means for implementing all educational programmes and of the organization of education. Programme of Action (1992) observed, "Teachers' performance is the most crucial input in the field of education. Whatever policy may be laid down, in the ultimate analysis these have to be interpreted and implemented by teachers as much through their personal example as through teaching learning process". Therefore teacher needs to be educated/trained properly for better discharge of duties and responsibilities.

Teachers' performance is the most crucial input in the field of education. Despite wider aims, comprehensive curriculum, sophisticated equipments, educational policies, different schemes in the field of education will be useless in the absence of competent teachers. Teacher occupies a vital position in teaching learning process. The role of the teachers has been changed from the transmitter of knowledge/information to facilitator of learning. Teacher also has responsibility in community development, social change and reformation and national development. The success of schooling mainly depends on competency, skills and effectiveness of teacher. Consequently, education including teacher education largely remained isolated from the needs and aspirations of the people. During the last five decades, certain efforts have been made to indigenize the system. The gaps, however, are still wide and visible. Various Commissions and Committees appointed by the Central and State Governments in recent decades have invariably emphasized the need for quality teacher education suited to the needs of education system.

Teacher Education Programmes

Teacher Education plays a central role in professional development of teachers. Competencies of professional skill are the heart of the programme of teacher education. Teachers, next to students, constitute the single largest input of the education system. The idea of teaching as everybody's cup of tea has been changed. It is now increasingly accepted that one can't be a good teacher without proper professional orientation. The teacher, in order to discharge his/ her professional duties effectively and efficiently, needs professional preparation. The teachers need to be oriented and equipped properly to play their role most effectively. In order to make teaching effectively and meaningful, every teacher should know not only the subject matter but also the art and science of teaching as well as the latest development in the art of instruction and the instructional field.

Traditionally, the concept of teacher education programmers was identified with the training of teachers for classroom teaching in a face-to-face situation. This programme mainly involves practicing teaching, that is, techniques of imparting knowledge, skills, attitude and also deals with the underlying principles of education and a set of ideas or values which are implicit in the purpose for which knowledge, skills and attitudes are imparted.

Teacher education programme develops awareness among the teachers and teacher trainees regarding the contemporary realities of Indian life and for the realization the national values and goals as enriched in the Constitution of India. In the age of scientific and technological progress, it is essential to enable the teachers to act as agents of modernization, social change and development and transmittance of national thinking and scientific temper through professional programme. A well organized teacher education can help greatly in this regard. Teacher education is of two types: pre-service and In-service. The main purpose of pre-service teacher education is to develop in trainees the abilities, skills and competencies required for a school teacher. In other words it converts a graduate into a teaching professional. The main purpose of in-service teacher education is to update secondary school teachers in latest development in pedagogy, content as well as new syllabus. It is generally conducted on the basis of professional needs of teachers in different school subjects. In some cases, teachers are oriented to new policy of education, National Curriculum Framework etc.

Need of Research in Teacher Education

Today, the system of education needs to respond not only to national, socio-economic and political needs but also anticipate the system which could fulfill the larger goals of human empowerment in the wake of globalization and knowledge explosion. Recognizing this potential of education, empowerment through teacher education has a crucial role to play, which is conceived as an integral part of any system of education. From this point of view, certain initiatives and innovations are necessary in teacher education programmes. Research is something which is concerned with analytical examination of facts and exploring new dimensions of knowledge. It is an effort to promote qualitative improvement of already known and also unknown. Teaching and research are two inseparable components. Research is the measure of standards in a college or university. Research and intellectual creation are necessary to develop a critical innovative approach. Research can increase the quality of future generations.

Therefore, for the development of teacher education and for its upliftment, more research work is necessary. Thousands of research had been conducted on teacher education programme for getting degree as well as for professional development. It seems that some aspects of teacher education was over studied while some are neglected. In this context to analyse researches in teacher education is significant as it would help to identify aspects of teacher education, that needs to be given priority for conducting research.

Teacher Education as a Field of Research

Teacher education is an important area of educational research. It includes research in pre-service teacher education and in-service teacher education. The sixth survey of educational research (1993-2000) listed sub-areas such as admission into teacher training college, pre-service teacher education programme, teacher trainees/educator, affective domain of teacher trainees and outcome of pre-service teacher education under pre-service teacher education and sub-areas such as in-service teacher education programmes and their evaluation, in-service training needs of teachers, higher education-academic staff college etc under in-service teacher education. Some of the latest researches are discussed here.

Basu and Pandey (2012) studied Value Pattern of Teacher Trainees in Relation to Various Demographic Variables. Rajendran, S. and Mary, S.J. (2012) conducted a research study on Correlation between Internal Assessment and External Assessment ofB.Ed. Students. Chavhan, R. and J. Waghmare (2011) worked on Awareness about Education for Peace of B.Ed. Student Teachers. Abdul Saleem, K.P. and Arun, P.K. (2011) conducted a research study on Human Rights Awareness among Teacher Educators. Yadav, S.K. (2011) compared pre-service teacher education programme at secondary stage in Bangladesh, India, Pakistan and Sri Lanka. Nivedita and Yadav, S. (2010) studied Evaluation System in Teacher Education in India with objective to study the Evaluation System in Teacher Education in India. Mehra, V. (2010) conducted study on Pre-service Teacher Education for Emerging Diverse Educational Contexts. Ekambaram, G. and Nagaraja, B.

(2010) conducted a research study entitled An Analysis of Environmental Awareness: The Case of Prospective Teachers. Prasad, D.R. and Vijayalatha, R. (2010) studied Value- Orientation among University B.Ed. Students. Goswami, S. (2009) undertaken study on An Appraisal of Norms and Standards of NCTE Regarding Teacher Education Based on Attitude of Teacher Educators., G.L. (2009) studied Innovative Approaches to the B.Ed. Curriculum in the Universities with objective of the study to analyze the present B Ed curriculum in the universities of Maharashtra. Mushtaq Ahmed, I.P. and Ansari, M.A.A. (2009) conducted study on Practice of Microteaching as a Training Technique in Teacher Education. Begum, A.J. (2009) studied Effect of Self Regulatory Strategies on Enhancing Teaching Competence among B.Ed. Students. Dorai, M. Thambi. and Muthuchamy, I. (2008) conducted study on Impact of Teaching Practice Programme upon the Self-concept of B.Ed. Students. Singh, Gurmit. (2007) worked on Job Satisfaction of Teacher Educators in Relation to their Attitude towards Teaching. Yarriswamy, M.C. (2007) conducted a research study on Individual Need Strength, Locus of Control, Job Involvement and Burnout of Teacher-Educators of Teacher Training Institutes in the State of Karnataka in relation to their Job Satisfaction. Mohalik, R.K. (2007) studied Impact of In-service Teacher Education Programmes on Teacher Effectiveness and Students Achievement in English. Kaur, H. and Meenakshi (2007) conducted study entitled Impact of Teacher Training Programme on B.Ed. Students' Motivity, Attitude towards Teaching and Personality. Zayapragassarazan, Z. and Pughazhendi, S. (2007) studied Perception of B.Ed., Student-teachers towards Teaching Practice Programme. Sudheesh Kumar, P.K. (2007) conducted a research study entitled Developing Reflective Thinking among Pre-service Teachers through Multiple Intelligence Teaching Approach (MITA). Mishra, S.G. (2007) conducted a research study on Teaching Attitude Score a Criterion for Admission in Colleges of Education. Mishra, S.G. (2006)) conducted a study entitled Teaching Attitudes score: A Criterion for Admission in Colleges of Education. Gupta, J. and Ram, S. (2006) researched on Transactional Styles among Prospective Teachers. Thiagarajan, P.A. and Ramesh, R. (2005) conducted a research study on Self-concept of B Ed. Trainees. Gupta, M. and Jain, R. (2005) conducted study on Self-appraisal of their Skills by the Teachers Trained through Formal and Distance Mode: A Comparative Study. Kharlukhi, (Ms) Basansy (2005) conducted a study on Self-concept in relation to some Selected Personality Variables among Teacher Trainees in Meghalaya. Bagga, R. (2005) conducted a research study on Professional Equipment of Social Studies Teachers for Teaching English in Secondary Schools of Punjab. Chakrabarty, A., Bagchi, B., *et al.* (2005) conducted research on assessment of in-service teachers training programmes in five districts of West Bengal.

Critical Reflections

One of the major inputs towards enhancing the quality of teaching and learning in schools as well as the teacher education institution is the extent to which research outputs and the outcomes of innovations are utilized by the system. Researches on teacher education have been and are being conducted in universities, national level institutions and other establishments but their utility for the teacher educator or the classroom teacher remains rather low. Majority of the researches are undertaken to obtain a degree and hence the focus on its possible utility and relevance gets misplaced. Researches must respond to policy issues, curriculum issues, evaluative procedures and practices, training strategies, classroom practices etc. The areas of teacher preparation for children with special needs, gifted children and children from groups with specific cultural, social and economic needs can no longer be ignored. Surveys and studies also need to be encouraged. These may be exploratory or diagnostic in nature. The new initiatives and innovations need to be encouraged and studied. Wherever considered appropriate, these could be brought into the system of teacher education for wider and gainful use.

The analysis of researches on teacher education indicates that many researcher has undertaken study on different sub areas such as awareness of trainees, evaluation of teacher education curriculum, characteristics of trainees and teacher educators—job satisfaction, effectiveness, teaching competency, self concept, accountability etc, evaluation practices, training needs of teachers, effect of teacher education on trainees etc. The sub area that needs more attention is development of affective and psychomotor quality among trainees such as proper attitude, value pattern, and interest for teaching, skills and habits which are necessary for better teacher. More focused research is required on integrating theory and practice, content and pedagogy in teacher education curriculum and transaction. Research is required to study extent of implementation of National Curriculum Framework-2005, Teacher Education Framework by NCTE in teacher education programmes. Research is needed for designing suitable selection procedure for admission into B.Ed courses. Of course, admission test is conducted for admission into the course but its validity is not ascertained. So in-depth research study is required for selecting right candidates having proper aptitude for the teacher training course.

Some of the studies are conducted on different personal, social and psychological characteristic of trainees and educators. Yet no comprehensive result comes out regarding attitude and commitment of trainees to teaching profession. Effectiveness of teacher education programme needs to be analysed deeply. The previous studies judged effectiveness of teacher education in form of perception from trainees and educators. But rigorous studies required on curriculum, courses, practices, the culture in training colleges etc should be given more attention by the researcher. The researcher should provide the fundamental grounds based on the research for effecting changes in teacher education programmes.

It is observed that majority of research study adopted survey/descriptive methods, very few adopted experimental research. So it is required to undertake experimental research in teacher education programmes, assessing effectiveness of different training strategy, methods, modules, textbooks etc for trainees. Also intensive qualitative research is required to analyse different aspects of teacher education. Reflection, a priori thinking, theory building and ethnographic approach can be adopted. It seems that majority of researcher use standardised tools for studying variables, of course a few developed on their own. The self developed tools used for research is in question as investigator may not follow all the process of tool development. A sound background/basic theory behind the use of tools is not visible in the teacher education research.

Population is many a times ambiguously defined. Claims are made for selecting samples by using random sampling techniques but details of claim is presented. In fact, sample is collected by purposive sampling. So validity of research findings is in question. Data are analysed by using quantitative statistical techniques without giving rationale for using it. Findings and conclusions are not always convincing as they are not based on what research had indicated. Sometimes the conclusions and findings give paradoxical result due to improper tools and procedure of data collection.

Conclusion

Indian universities produce more number of researches degrees in education than other universities of the world. Our research in eduction is mainly intended for getting degree, theoretical and not relevant. It is also true for teacher education. Of course, many researchers have been working on teacher education but its effectiveness and utility are less. Universities in developed nations are primarily research universities. Students learn best by researching. We need to make the system of education more innovative and futuristic in order to respond to the changing demands of the society. Sometimes ornamental research is done for the sake of degree acquisition or promotion purpose alone. Researches lack validity and credibility. There is a shortage of systematic and continuous effort. Refocusing on the issue raised in this presentation on quality of teacher education, there is immense need for quality research in this field. Researches, innovations and surveys must become an integral part of the training programmes ofteacher education institutions irrespective of the stages. Thousands of researches had been conducted on teacher education programme. However, a closer look at these studies shows that the impact of present teacher education programme has been studied at the peripheral level and deeper study is needed at social, economic and cultural level. Teacher's contribution to society is also a factor to be studied. It can be said that there is also a need for more comprehensive and sophisticated research and better dissemination of results. These can be used later for the improvement of teacher education programme within the framework of the total education system in the country.

REFERENCES

Behera, L and Basantia, (2005). Evaluation of the Elementary Level Pre-service Teacher Education Syllabus in Orissa. *Indian Educational Review*, July 2005, pp. 96-117.

Bhatt, M.M. (1966). Scheme of Improvement Teacher Training, *Fourth Survey of Research in Education*, NCERT, New Delhi.

Covert, J.R. (1984). The extended practicum, more of the same research in Teacher Education: *International Perspective, Falmer Press*, London.

Devi, Laxmi (1988). Evaluation of the Teacher Education programme in Agra University. *Fourth Survey of Research in Education*, Vol. II, New Delhi: NCERT.

Joshi, J.N. (1997). Teacher Education, Pre-service In-service, *Fifth Survey or Researches in Education, Trend Report*, Vol. I, NCERT, New Delhi.

Mohalik, R.K. (2008). Impact of In-service Teacher Education programmes on Teacher Effectiveness and Students Achievement in English. *Journal of Indian Education*, NCERT, New Delhi.

Mohalik, R.K. (2010). *In-service Teacher Education.* Mahamaya Publishing House, New Delhi.

NCERT, (2000). *Sixth Survey of Educational Research*-1993-2000, Volume-1, NCERT, New Dekhi.

NCERT, (2005). National Curriculum Framework-2005. NCERT, New Delhi.

NCTE (2009), National Curriculum Framework for Teacher Education. *National Council for Teacher Education,* New Delhi.

NCTE (1998), Quality concerns in Secondary Teacher Education. *National Council for Teacher Education,* New Delhi.

NCTE (1998), Curriculum Framework for Quality Teacher Education. *National Council for Teacher Education,* New Delhi.

Sungoh, S.M. (2005). Quality issues in teacher education, *University News*, 43,18,53. AIU, New Delhi.

Singh, L.C. and Malhotra, S.P. (1991). Research in Teacher Education: A Trend Report. In M.B. Buch, *Fourth Survey of Research in Education*, New Delhi, NCERT.

Tisher, P. (1990). One and half decade of Research on Teacher Education in Australia, *Research in Teacher Education International Perspectives*, Falmer Press, London.

Yadav, S.K. (2003). Research Perspectives in teacher education, *University News*, Association of Indian Universities, New Delhi, Vol. 41, No. 22, June, P. 02-08.

10
Crucial Issues and Emerging Concerns in Teacher Education

Sangeeta Barwal

Teachers form the nucleus of any system of education. They are one of the main pillars of the society, responsible for educating young people for different walks of life. No programme of education reform can be implemented without the willing and active cooperation of teachers. Teachers could be the most powerful agents of social regeneration because the whole structure of educational edifice is based upon the teachers. Teacher education is an important area of concern in our educational system. The revitalization and strengthening of the teacher education system is a powerful means for the upliftment of educational standards in the country. It inculcates the necessary pedagogical skill and competencies among the teachers and makes them professionally competent to meet the demands of the society.

The past several decades have been times of widespread change. Teacher education system in India, although basically similar to British structure is influenced, changed and funded by American expectations from teachers. The aspirations of students have been changed after a radical change in structure, economy, social needs and social values. Teacher's responsibilities have been multiplied. Interaction and interactive processes are to be changed in the light of technological advancement in the field of education. There has been an eclectic approach in philosophical and ideological spheres. Objectives of teacher education have been changed from perennial to progressive and ideals of experimental. Old curriculum pattern and methods of teaching education have become obsolete and outmoded. So, reviewing, rethinking and rewriting of objectives, contents and methods of teaching education have become obsolete, outmoded and imperative. Radical reforms of teacher education have become necessary for quality improvement and quality management of 3Ts viz. Teacher, teacher-trainees and teacher educators to meet the demands of the 21st century.

Objectives

Keeping in view the demands of the 21st century the teacher education needs to be restructured to achieve the following objectives:

1. To make the teacher trainees capable of facing the challenges of globalisation in the education sector in 21st century.
2. To enrich teacher trainees with adequate information so that they can solve any problem by using professional skills.
3. To promote social consciousness, accountability and human values in them.
4. To introduce dynamic approach in development of curriculum in place of traditional system.
5. To make the teacher-trainees capable of leading multi-directional teaching programmes and workshops.
6. To make teacher-trainees become skilled teachers and participate in field study or survey works.
7. To make the teacher trainees capable of using information and communication technology, which is a thrust area for elevating standard of education.
8. To make teaching-learning process more interesting by using new technologies while teaching.

Major Issues in Teacher Education

The role of the teacher is changing so fast that no amount of pre-service or in-service teacher education can probably cope with the expectations of the society. The teacher needs to be conceived as a 'change agent' and not as a mere transmitter of knowledge and culture. But is it feasible? There are some contemporary issues in the context of teacher education. Are our teacher preparation programmes competent to inculcate among the trainees the qualities, abilities attitudes, beliefs etc. expected of a good teacher? This is a crucial issue related to teacher education. The meaning and concept of teaching has changed a lot now a day. It is believed today that there is no need for 'teaching'; what we want is learning. Then, how many of our teachers are competent to do this? Can any teacher preparation programme help in this?

The curriculum, content of the course, objectives etc. need thorough overhauling. If we examine the curricular changes at the primary, secondary and tertiary teacher preparation stages, only some additions, deletions have been done and not a drastic change attempted. The courses should be redesigned in such a manner as to enable a teacher-trainee to see clearly how the school can contribute towards the transformation of our society. They should understand their roles in national construction.

The present teacher trainees are aimlessly entering in the teacher education institutions to get certificates, spending leisure time and alluring degree or certificate for marital purposes. Some take this course after booking seats in other countries. Some derive satisfaction by sitting at home and raising families. There are no research studies to reveal the situation.

Even at the M.Phil level, the faculty of education has not much to do now. The foundation of education, techniques of teaching and testing rather that of instruction and evaluation should become an inevitable part of the M.Phil programme. For this, a inter-disciplinarily course has to be encouraged to include adult education, non-formal education, population education as compulsory subjects in the teacher education programmes at all levels. There is need for social sensitivity of socio-cultural, economic issues confronting the present Indian society.

Value erosion among the students and youth are a matter of concern today. There is increased deterioration of respect for teachers in the society. For this, each teacher should be accountable, responsible, disciplined, and have high esteem, satisfaction in the profession and a visionary outlook. Student evaluation should be taken into account by teacher educators and student's self-evaluation should be compared with teacher evaluation.

Policies and Programmes Related to Teacher Education

Educational policies and programme have been reviewed in the light of the goals of national development and priorities set from time to time. The Education Commission (1964-1966) recognized the importance of professional preparation of teacher for the qualitative improvement of education. Attempts to bring qualitative changes in teacher education continued. The parliament and University Grants Commission appointed several committees examining the matter and the first National Policy of Education was brought out in 1968. The National Policy on Education recognized the continuity inseparability of pre- and in-service teacher education and recommended permanent education mechanism for it. This policy was followed Programme of Action (PoA, 1992) which gave details about the concretization of policy into action. The National Commission on Teachers (1983) studied in depth the problems of teachers and the status of teachers in society. Its main recommendations was enhancing the period of training, change in selective procedure of teachers, pedagogy of teacher education, enrichment of the courses, and practical work. The National Council of Teacher Education (NCTE) was set-up by resolution of Government of India in the NCERT which later became a statutory body responsible for the coordination and maintenance of standards in teacher education in 1995. The NCTE came out with a Curriculum framework for Teacher Education in 1998 to provide guidelines for the content and methodology of teacher education. It was a meaningful and purposive effort. The course of teacher education was rehashed with a view to improve teacher education.

Major Shifts in Teacher Education Programme

The learner is seen as an active participant rather than a passive recipient in the process of learning and his/her capabilities and potential are seen not as fixed by dynamic and capable of development through direct self-experience. The curriculum will be designed so as to provide opportunities to directly observe learners at play and work; assignments to help teachers understand learner's questions and observations about natural and social phenomena; insights into children's thinking and learning; and opportunities to listen to children with attention, humor and empathy.

- Learning should be appreciated as a participatory process that takes place in the shared social context of the learner's immediate peers as well as the wider social community or the nation thinkers such as Gandhi, Tagore, Sri Aurobindo, Gijubhai J. Krishnamurthy, Dewey and others are often studies in a piecemeal manner, without the necessary context and without concern about where these ideas emanated from. No wonder they are studied and memorized, but seldom applied, by the very same teacher educators who present these ideas to the trainee teachers. The participatory process is a self-experienced- based process in which the learner constructs his/her knowledge in his/her own ways through absorption, interaction, observation and reflection.
- The major shift is in the teacher's role where he/she assumes a position at the centre stage as a source of knowledge, as custodian and manager of all teaching learning processes, and executer of educational and administrative mandates given through curricula or circulars. Now his/her role needs to be shifted from being a source of knowledge to being a facilitator, of transforming information into knowledge/wisdom, as a supporter in enhancing learning through multiple exposures, encouraging the learner to continuously achieve his/her educational goals.
- Another significant shift is in the concept of knowledge, wherein knowledge is to be taken as a continuum, as generated from experiences in the actual field through observation, verification, and so on. The knowledge component in teacher education is derived from broader areas of the discipline of education and it needs to be represented as such. It means that conscious efforts are needed to represent an explanation from the perspective of education rather than merely specifying theoretical ideas from related disciplines with "implications for education".

- Knowledge in teacher education is multidisciplinary in nature within the context of education. In other words, conceptual inputs in teacher education need to be articulated in such a manner that they describe and explain educational phenomena – actions, tasks, efforts, processes, concepts and events.
- Such a teacher education programme would provide adequate scope for viewing a theoretical understanding and its practical aspects in a more integrated manner rather than as two separate components. It enables the student-teacher and the teacher in the class room to develop a critical sensitivity to field approaches. Thus, once tried out by self and others, it will lead to evolving one's own vision of an ideal setting for learning. Such teachers would be better equipped for creating a learning environment, would try to improve existing conditions rather than merely adjusting to them with the necessary technical knowhow and confidence.
- Another major shift is in understanding the impact of the social context in educative processes.
- Learning is greatly influenced by the social environment/context from which learners and teachers emerge. The social climate of the school and the classroom exert a deep influence on the process of learning and education as a whole. Given this, there is a need to undertake a major shift away from an overwhelming emphasis on the psychological characteristics of the individual learner to his/her social, cultural, economic and political context.
- Different contexts lead to differences in learning. Learning in school is influenced and enhanced by the wider social context outside the school.
- Teacher education programmes need to provide the space of engagement with issues and concerns of contemporary Indian society, its pluralistic nature, and issues of identity gender, equity, livelihood and poverty. This can help teachers in contextualizing education and evolving deeper understanding of the purpose of education and its relationship with society.
- The shift in performance appraisal in the teacher education programme from an annual affair to a continuous feature needs to be recognized. The teacher-educator evaluates the student- teacher's ability to co-operate and collaborate, investigate and integrate, and also appraises written and oral skills, originality in approach and presentation, and so on.
- Several kinds of appraisals take place in the form of self- appraisal, peer-appraisal, teacher's feedback, and formal evaluation at the end of

the year. All appraisals aim at improvement, understanding one's own strengths and weaknesses, understanding what has to be strengthened, and identifying the next goals in the learning process.

- The appraisal mostly will not be given in marks (quantitative), but on a scale (qualitative), where the student's achievement is evaluated as a continuum and he\ she is placed according to his/her performance in various activities.
- In brief, the new vision of teacher education will be more responsive to changes in the school system as it envisages a significant paradigm shift.
- The efforts made by the NCTE are indeed appreciable. The teacher education has been struggling to strengthen its identity. Struggle does not mean degeneration of values and degeneration of institutions. It is true that after persistent struggle there is evident improvement, but, still there is no end to perfection every establishment has noise. There are issues and resolves problems and solutions, puzzles and pathways. Reflections on some of the major issues concerning teacher education in India are discussed in the following sub-sections.

Quality Crisis

There are problems of quality perception, quality scaling and quality differentiations in teacher education. There are wide gaps between expected and actual quality. This gap is widening day by day. There has to be adequate focus on all the systematic parameters—input, process and output. So teacher education programmes need to be reformulated and strengthened, so that the teacher can be an encouraging and human facilitator in teaching learning situations to enable learners to discover their talents, to realize their physical and intellectual potentialities desirable social values to function as responsible citizens.

Brand Inequity

There is public private dichotomy in teacher education. There is a pathetic indifference in public sector institutions and rampant commercialization in private sector. The teacher education degrees conferred by the various universities and institutions are non-comparable. Are TETs, SETs and NETs the solutions? If the inputs and processes are evidently wanting, then how can the quality of the product be ensured.

Overgrowing Establishment

Establishment of overgrown enrolment in most of the teacher education programs. But at the same time there is uneven distribution of the teacher education institutions. Teacher Education regulations, norms and standards, though latest visited during 2009, have further scope for perfection. There is a need to have demand and supply estimates.

Mismatching Teachers

Merit is destroyed due to mismatches between Teacher Educators and Teacher Trainees. Quality teachers can be developed through skilled and competent Teacher Education professionals who have passion for profession. There should be no compromise with the standards and norms.

Poor Integration of Skills

The term Skill has become a misnomer, particularly, in Education. All the skills, such as, Life Skills, Techno-pedagogic skills, Techno-Savvy skills, Info-Savvy skills, Emotional Skills, Human Development skills, Spiritual Skills need to be integrated in Teacher Education.

Incompatible Modes of Education

There is little parity amongst various modes of education, such as, distance mode, e-mode and face-to-face mode. Distance mode is diluted, e-mode is in infancy, whereas, the face-to-face mode is stagnant. There is no network within and amongst the various modes of Teacher Education. These are functioning more or less in isolation.

Philosophers in and Philosophies Out

No Philosophy is of eternal value because each idea is propounded within the limitation of time and space. Since the interplay of space, time and matter changes, it calls for development of new set of theories, which should be identified by examining the fusion of old with the new or discerning a new direction which defies the known patterns. In either case, a new theory is called for to provide guidance to the new developments. Old theories and old philosophies, particularly in Social Sciences, are going obsolete. There is need to build problem specific instantaneous theory.

Mismatch between Demand and Supply

There is imbalance in supply and demand between regions, geographical areas and subject specializations which results into acute unemployment of quality teachers. It is surprising to note that for one vacant post of a teacher there are at least more than thousand applicants. Besides, a number of these professionally trained graduates, postgraduates and doctorate are on a long wait for job and remain unemployed. The situation is becoming more distressful when we find that even the apex level institution such as NCTE has not been able to effectively regulate the demand and supply of the respective seekers of teaching position at school, college and university level education.

Domain Pedagogy Mismatches

There are mismatches between the subject and pedagogy. Subject specific differential pedagogy demands scientific bases.

Identity Crisis

Self disclosure done by the Teacher Education institutions is largely poor. There is faulty identification with Teacher Education. There are non-existent entities. Unique Identifiers need to be worked out.

Rare Innovations

Novel ideas die because of non-incubation. Personalized Teacher Education, Holistic Teacher Education, specialized Teacher Education, and even Integrated Teacher Education are rarely found because we don't have a capacity to tolerate repeated failures arising out of experimentation. One shot success is a fairy tale and not the reality of life. The society and its institutions must have the capacity to tolerate genuine mistakes committed inadvertently during the course of innovation.

Stake Holders Non-alignment

Different parties to education champion their cause by becoming the so called stake holders without having regard to the needs, urges and aspirations of other stake holders. Consequently, the system is unduly stressed, instead of making it resilient enough to deliver man making education. State indifference and displeasure, judicial concern and activism, Privatization and commercialization, Public hope and failure, disregard and disrespect for Education are easily evident.

Little Choice Base

Options are not substitutes for Choice based Education. There are differences amongst, individual, Institutional, State, National, Continental and Global objectives. The issues involved relate to the systematic correction, as well as developing the right attitudes to make it a success. Though we have introduced optional areas in Teacher Education, but the choice is very limited. There is a need to employ CBCS in Teacher Education, which can be realized through e-platforms, and amalgamation of various modes, such as, F2F, Distance and Electronic. Choice base demands plenty of sources and resources. There is a need to introduce super market in Education.

Poor Research Scenario

Research in education is replicate and repetitive devoid of freshness, either of problem or of approach or of methodology. The national agenda for research needs to be developed in alignment with the developmental objectives. A prospective plan for research and innovations should be framed with regional and national developmental priorities. The research Methodology must be compatible with the local problems. There is a need to be innovative. There are mismatches between research trends and problems. Regulatory mechanism to tone up the Research Quality needs to be evolved. There is a need to evolve Research Quality indicators. There is a need to evolve social sciences compatible indigenous Research Methodology. Philosophical and Historical studies are very rare. There is more of quantitative research than qualitative. There is more of descriptive and evaluative research than suggestive. There is more of borrowed methodology than indigenous. Taxonomy of Research needs to be evolved.

Non-Scientific Manpower Planning

There are demand and supply imbalances in Teacher Education. Appreciable attempts have been made for manpower planning. But, the manpower planning still needs to be done more scientifically. It is expected of the various States that these play active role in manpower planning.

Illusive Laboratories

The various laboratories of the Teacher- Education Institutions, namely, Science Lab, Psychology Lab, Guidance and Counseling Lab, Educational Technology Lab, Computer Lab, and Language are either not there or are mostly in very bad states.

Insufficient Practice Teaching

Though a sizable number of innovative approaches of teaching- learning have surfaced, such as, participatory, holistic, activity based, constructivist, interdisciplinary, the practice teaching is largely primitive. Bloom's Taxonomy of Instructional Objectives has become more or less stagnant. There is a need to enhance the taxonomy, by further differentiating and adding domains. The lesson designs ought to be comprehensive of all the domains. There is only a little theory practice nexus. Experimenters, as well as, problems are many, whereas, the labs are wanting.

Over Activism of Distance/Open Universities

Some of the distance and open universities have become over activists in the context of teacher Education. These have a notion that they can open their Teacher Education Extension Centers anywhere. To give birth to infinite is their Right. But, who will rear their babies? Such distance and open universities have resulted into the dilution of Teacher Education.

Rare In-Service and Continuing Teacher Education

Our in-service and continuing Teacher Education is very rare. Most of the IASEs, CTEs and SIE Ts have gone defunct. Refresher courses are largely for name sake. Adequate provisions need to be made for continuous professional development of teachers. There ought to be periodic Teacher Appraisal at all levels. Anyone, anywhere, anytime should have access to learning resources.

Invalid Recognition and Accreditation

There are questions on Recognition of Teacher Education Institutions. There are questions on inputs and processes of teacher education. There are questions even on accreditation of teacher education institutions. Nalanda University was having a much better profile and grade than the highest graded modern universities.

Overhauling Curriculum

The curriculum, content of the course, objectives etc. need thorough overhauling. If we examine the curricular changes at the primary, secondary and tertiary teacher preparation stages, only some additions, deletions have been done and not a drastic change attempted. The courses should be redesigned in such a manner as to enable a teacher-trainee to see clearly how the school can contribute towards the transformation of our society. They should understand their roles in national construction.

Problems of Wastage and Stagnation

The present teacher trainees are aimlessly entering in the teacher education institutions to get certificates, spending leisure time and alluring degree or certificate for marital purposes. Some take this course after booking seats in other countries. Some derive satisfaction by sitting at home and raising families. There are no research studies to reveal the situation. Studies on the wastage and stagnation at the teacher preparation level are, however, in progress, but there is little evidence on the impact of such courses on family life and well-being including have management and rearing.

Erosion of Values

Value erosion among the students and youth are matter of concern today. There is increased deterioration of respect for teachers in the society. For this, each teacher should be accountable, responsible, disciplined, high esteem, satisfaction in the profession and visionary outlook. Student evaluation should be taken into account by teacher educators and student's self-evaluation should be compared with teacher evaluation.

Need for Complementary Structures and Mechanisms

In order to translate the vision of transacting the teacher education programme, it is essential that complementary structures and mechanisms are in place to allow such a transaction all theory courses will need to be in disciplinary in structure and have field based units of study. Likewise, establishing resource centers that enable hands on engagement with concepts and tools of education such as text book, books and other resources in critical to transacting a process based teacher education programme these resource centers are viewed as mechanisms for grounding the education of pre service and in service teachers within immediate classroom contexts, the wider societal context and learner diversity.

Inclusive Education

Inclusive education ensures that access to and conditions of success in education for everybody including those in the margins, either with learning difficulties because of physical or mental disabilities or because of their social position. The aim is to create integrated school setting, providing equal opportunities to children with special abilities, varied social background and diverse learning needs.

Open and Distance Learning

Open and distance learning can be strategically employed in continuing professional development of teachers particularly within a view to overcoming the barriers of physical distance, online support and two way audio- video communications.

Emerging Concerns in Teacher Education

For fulfillment of the above objectives, the major thrust area needs to be emphasized. These major areas identified as new emerging concerns in teacher education are presented below:

- Instead of the traditional 'chalk and talk' method of imparting instruction, teaching method should be aid oriented, scope of maximum interaction during teaching-learning by doing and to develop skill of rationality making teaching-learning process more effective.
- To widen the scope for teacher-student interaction, group discussions, demonstrations, seminars, symposium, fieldtrips, debates, essay competitions, role playing activities may be organized by teacher training institutions by inviting resource persons either from within the institution or from outside. Guest lectures should be arranged and the topic should be related to course curriculum and also has bearing on national issues. After talk the scope for open discussion,

brain storming session must be there. Therefore, the trainee teachers will come out as a dedicated and innovative teacher.

- To make teaching-learning process more effective, the knowledge of information technology in classroom teaching is the thrust area for elevating standard of education. Incorporation of this technology in the course curriculum of teacher education will enable the teacher trainees to develop competency in electronic resources and encourage them to use Internet for improvement of teaching.
- Changes in course duration, weightage in theory, practice teaching, microteaching. Project work, community works were emphasized by a number of researchers. Introduction of two years B.Ed. course and four years integrated course was recommended. It was urged that practice teaching should not be restricted within the sphere of delivery of 25-30 lessons in relevant subject area. Six months internship is to be compulsory in schools after examination. Each school is to provide a certificate after the completion of the internship.
- Keeping in view the developing social needs, a diversified teacher education system has been proposed by a number of educationists. The subject areas of education which are offered as general papers and a few as special papers appear to be inadequate to develop competency in the learners, so that they can apply the concept of E.T. or psychology in the larger social context. Therefore, the relevant diversified areas like guidance & counseling, and educational psychology are to be focused as the key areas of curriculum so that the trainees involved in such teacher education programmes came out as specialist teachers in the concerned branch.
- The preservice teacher education curriculum does not reflect the needs and demands of students and teachers. It needs to be revised and redesigned keeping in view the thrust areas of NCF 2005, and B.Ed. colleges or department of education would not be allowed to continue to get recognition unless it had an attached teaching practices school. The curriculum for teacher education should be developed with coordinated efforts of NCTE, UGC and NCERT.
- The private self-financed teacher training institutions have mushroomed—Most of them with a profit motive, leading to unbalanced expansion and commercialization of teacher education, with some parts of the country facing severe shortage of such institutions while some other areas are having excess number of these institutions. Most of the institutions recruited unqualified teachers with lower salaries, which has serious implications for quality teacher education.
- Teaching of courses through correspondence mode was based on presentation of printed study materials to the enrolled students, personal

contact programme of a few week duration and annual examination at the end of one academic year's students of B.Ed. or M.Ed. courses would have to deliver practice teaching lessons in schools as per arrangement of concerned institutes. Imparting instructions in teacher training programme through distance education mode needs to incorporate the most modern approaches where audio-visual aids and ICT laboratory as the key tools of the teaching learning process in addition to the printed study materials. Creation of scope for teacher student interaction through electronic media is an important feature of this system to satisfy the need for face-to-face interaction among teacher and students as it is the most vital part of teaching-learning process.

- Evaluation and Monitoring should be an integral part of teacher education programme both in pre and in-service training programme to know the strengths, weaknesses and outcomes of the programme. Renovations and experimentation should be promoted for improving the quality of teacher education programmes.
- A regular two-way communication between the trainees and trainers through newsletter, reports, seminars and workshops could be maintained. Visits to the field may be planned.
- Lot of training material is available both with the national and state level institution. It should be distributed/disseminated among teachers and teacher educators for self-learning and their growth. More instructional material should be developed by following the modular approach. It can be used both for self-reading as well as in the training programmes.

Summing Up

The teacher should not only be a communicator but also a mobilizer, motivator and coordinator. It is necessary that the key goals and the priorities be clearly established and defined and then form a machinery through which they may be attained to be designed, in appropriate manner to achieve the goal. Educators in general and teacher educators in particular, are not consulted by the so-called administrator, politicians who have their own wishes and fancies in evolving policies in accordance with their political inclinations. Unless this is changed, education in India cannot deliver the goods expected of it; so it is the case with teacher education. The time has come when reexamination is vitally necessary. We have achieved a great deal in the past decades in the light of recommendations made by different commissions and committees. But the issues and concerns raised above prove that there are some lacunae in our education system, which need deep thinking and action both on planning and implementation level.

REFERENCES

Curriculum Framework for Teacher Education (2005), National Council of Educational Research and Training, New Delhi.

Dash, N. (2000), *Education in India: Problems and Perspectives*, New Delhi, Atlantic Publishers and Distributors.

Singh, R.P. (2006) Teacher Education India Today: The Unanswered Questions. *University News* 44(22).

Arora, G.L. (1998), Educating teacher for the 21st Century, *The Indian Journal for Teacher Education*, 1(1), 15-19.

Abraham, Jessy (2006), Quality in Teacher Education Programmes: Some Suggestion. In Edutracks, *Monthly Scanner of Trends in Educaction*, 5(12).

Pandey, K.P. (2007), Value-based Education: Searching a suitable Paradigm, Anweshika: *Indian Journal of Teacher Education*, Vol. 4, No. 2.

Siddique, M.A. and Bhattacharjee, D.K. (2009). How to prepare A Reflective Teacher? – Needed Reforms in Teacher Education Continuum, Anweshika: *Indian Journal of Teacher Education*. Vol. 6, No. 1.

Singh, R.P. (2005). Teacher Education: Challenges and the Emerging Trends, *University News*, 43(18): 2-8.

Verma, R. (2002). Teachers in the Twenty First Century. *University News*, 40(48), 9-12.

11

Transforming Education: Report of Justice Verma Commission on Teacher Education

Kuldeep Singh Katoch

The main purpose of NCTE is to achieve planned and coordinated development of Teacher Education system throughout the country, regulation and proper maintenance of norms and standards in teacher education system and the matters connected therewith. Keeping in view the recommendations of the Education Commission (1964-66), Government of India through a resolution, set up National Council for Teacher Education (NCTE) in the year 1973 to advise the Central and State Governments on all matters relating to teacher education. Secretarial support to the non-statutory NCTE so set up in 1973 was provided by NCERT. NCTE created nationwide awareness on issues relating to teacher education and developed a "National Framework for Teacher Education Curriculum" in 1978. Regulatory functions like prevention of proliferation of sub-standard teacher education institutions/programmes, maintenance of norms and standards etc. could, however, not be undertaken by the NCTE, it being a non-statutory body. As per recommendations of the National Policy on Education (NPE) 1986 and the Programme of Action (PoA), 1992, a need was felt to upgrade the National Council for Teacher Education, as an autonomous statutory body with a view to giving it necessary capability and powers to regulate institutions of teacher education and to provide guidance to them in the matter of curricula and methods. Accordingly, National Council for Teacher Education (NCTE) Act was passed in the year 1993 and NCTE as an autonomous body with a statutory status came into existence with effect from August 17, 1995.

The NCTE undertakes following functions:

1. Recognise of various teacher training courses based on application submitted by the institutions concerned in the prescribed proforma and along with the requisite documents.
2. Undertake surveys and studies relating to various aspects of teacher education and publish the result thereof;

3. Make recommendations to the Central and State Governments, Universities, University Grants Commission and recognized institutions in the matter of preparation of suitable plans and programmes in the field of teacher education;
4. Co-ordinate and monitor teacher education and its development in the country;
5. Lay down guidelines in respect of minimum qualifications for a person to be employed as a teacher in schools or in recognized institutions;
6. Lay down norms for any specified category of courses or trainings in teacher education, including the minimum eligibility criteria for admission thereof, and the method of selection of candidates, duration of the course, course contents and mode of curriculum;
7. Lay down guidelines for compliance by recognized institutions, for starting new courses or training, and for providing physical and instructional facilities, staffing pattern and staff qualifications;
8. Lay down standards in respect of examinations leading to teacher education qualifications, criteria for admission to such examinations and schemes of courses or training;
9. Lay down guidelines regarding tuition fees and other fees chargeable by recognized institutions;
10. Promote and conduct innovation and research in various areas of teacher education and disseminate the results thereof;
11. Examine and review periodically the implementation of the norms, guidelines and standards laid down by the Council, and to suitably advise the recognized institutions;
12. Evolve suitable performance appraisal systems, norms and mechanisms for enforcing accountability on recognized institutions;
13. Formulate schemes for various levels of teacher education and identify recognized institutions and set up new institutions for teacher development programmes.
14. Take all necessary steps to prevent commercialization of teacher education; and
15. Perform such other functions as may be entrusted to it by the Central Government.

Minister for Human Resource Development Dr. M.M. PallamRaju expressed his views that in a country as diverse and as large as ours, the task of developing national policies while at the same time respecting and incorporating regional aspirations and an inclusive agenda of growth is indeed really challenging. It is in this context that I have always emphasized on a participatory approach in which all of us, be it Central Government or State Governments, academics, autonomous institutions, private sector and all other stakeholders, work together towards a common goal which is empowering the children and youth of India through education and knowledge. I would also like to mention that Planning Commission in its Approach Paper to the XII Five Year Plan has recognized Education as the single most important instrument for social and economic transformation. The Approach Paper mentions that a well educated population, adequately equipped with knowledge and skill is not only essential to support economic growth, but is also a precondition for growth to be inclusive since it is the educated and skilled person who can stand to benefit most from the employment opportunities which growth will provide. Thus, collectively we have to decide policies and programmes for realizing India's human resource potential to its fullest in the education sector, with equity and excellence. I would also like to mention that education should lead to building of an inclusive and fair society. Education in my view should lead to character building of our youth and also inspire them to work towards the task of nation building in addition to their work for employment or self-employment. Keeping in view the present scenario of NCTE regarding its working the Supreme Court of India constituted a high powered commission under the chairmanship of Justice J.S. Verma. The brief report of commission submitted to Supreme Court of India is as under.

Brief Report of Justice J.S. Verma Commission on Teacher Education

The Vision of Teacher Education in India, Quality and Regulatory Perspective (The Report of High-Powered Commission Constituted by SC of India) report highlighted the role of NCTE as per the NCTE Act. There are four Regional Committees of the National Council for Teacher Education (NCTE) – Northern Regional Committee, Jaipur, Western Regional Committee, Bhopal, Eastern Regional Committee, Bhubaneswar, and Southern Regional Committee, Bangalore are empowered under the NCTE Act, 1993 to grant recognition to institutions for conducting programmes on teacher education. In 2008, the Western Regional Committee (WRC) gave recognition to 291 institutions of Maharashtra for starting the Diploma in Education (D.Ed.) programme, in spite of the explicit recommendations of the Government of Maharashtra that the State did not require more D.Ed. institutions due to limited employment opportunities for the graduates of this programme. When the matter came before the Hon'ble Bombay High Court (Nagpur Bench) in a Public Interest Litigation (PIL), after looking into the facts and circumstances of the cases, the High Court quashed the order of the WRC granting recognition to the 291 colleges, vide its order dated 7thJanuary, 2009 on the ground that the recognition had been granted in breach of the directions issued by the Central Government under section 29 of the NCTE Act. Earlier in 2007, the Ministry of Human Resource Development, Government of India, had issued directions under section 29 of the NCTE Act, 1993 to the NCTE which inter alia provided that in respect of cases before the WRC where there was a difference of opinion between the views of the State Government and that of the WRC, such cases should be referred to the NCTE Headquarters. The Hon'ble High Court held that the grant of recognition by the WRC to the 291 colleges was in breach of the Ministry's direction since the Government of Maharashtra had given a categorical general statement that no new teacher education institution offering the D.Ed. programme should be opened in Maharashtra. This was for the reason that the supply of trained elementary teachers was already far in excess of the demand for such teachers in the State. These institutions challenged the decision of the Hon'ble High Court and filed Special Leave Petitions (SLPs) (c) Nos. 4247 and 4248/2009 before the Hon'ble Supreme Court of India. The Hon'ble Supreme Court allowed the institutions, recognized by the WRC to admit students to the D.Ed. course taking the view that the issues raised in these SLPs were of 'considerable public importance'. During the hearing of the SLPs, the Hon'ble Supreme Court vide its order dated 13th May, 2011, appointed a High-Powered Commission under the Chairpersonship of Justice J.S. Verma, former Chief Justice of India, to examine the entire gamut of issues which have a bearing on improving the quality of teacher education as well as improving the regulatory functions of the NCTE.

Terms of Reference of the Commission

The Government of India notified the constitution of a High-Powered Commission and the Terms of Reference vide Notification dated 27th June, 2011, published in the Gazette of India on 28th June, 2011. The Terms of Reference (ToRs) of the Commission are as follows:

- Whether in the context of the provisions of the Right of Children to Free and Compulsory Education Act, 2009 the Regulations on RecognitionNorms and Procedure that lay down the norms and procedure for various teacher education courses which are adopted by the NCTE are adequate or need review.
- Whether further reforms are necessary to improve quality of teacher training and in-service training.
- To review whether the Regulations on Recognition Norms and Procedure, currently in force as laid down by the NCTE are being properly enforced. If not, how to evolve a fair and transparent manner in which these norms and standards may be enforced?
- To review the existing practice of appointment of members to the NCTE and the Regional Committees of NCTE and recommend measures to ensure that a transparent process in which the appointments to the NCTE are undertaken, so that the NCTE discharges its crucial role in providing vision and direction in the functioning of the NCTE.

- To evolve standards and norms for evaluating teacher performance and audit of teachers.
- To review whether the present provisions empowering withdrawal of recognition of institutions are adequate.
- To determine what the methodology should be to examine/enforce quality in teacher training institutions.
- To review whether the 291 institutions in the Western Region qualify to be recognized as Teacher Training Institutions.

Main Recommendations

The Commission submitted its Report to the Hon'ble Supreme Court on 29th August, 2012. The Report is in three Volumes. Volume 1 contain the analysis on the matters covered under the Terms of Reference and is called the main report. The main report of this commission is presented in seven chapters. Chapter 7 contains a summary of the recommendations. Volume 2 contains a report on each of the 291 institutions inspected by the Commission. All the Annexures are in Volume 3. The main recommendations of the Commission are summarized as under:

Quality of Pre-service Teacher Education

- The Commission has noted that 90 per cent of pre-service teacher education institutions are in the non-Government sector, and most of the States of the Eastern and North Eastern Region of the country are facing acute shortage of institutional capacity of teacher preparation in relation to the demand, and have witnessed extremely low contribution of the State Governments. The Commission recommends that the government should increase its capacity for establishing teacher education institutions and increase the institutional capacity of teacher preparation especially in the deficit States.
- Government may explore the possibility of instituting a transparent procedure of pre-entry testing of candidates to the pre-service teacher education programme, keeping in view the local conditions.
- Teacher education should form part of the higher education system. The duration of prgramme of teacher education needs to be enhanced, in keeping with the recommendations of the Kothari Commission (1966), the implementation of which is long overdue.
- It is desirable that new teacher education institutions are located in multi- and inter-disciplinary academic environment. This will have significant implication for the redesign of norms and standards of various teacher education courses specified by the NCTE. This will also have the implication for employment and career progression of

prospective teachers. Existing teacher education institutions may be encouraged to take necessary steps towards attaining academic parity with the new institutions.

- Current teacher education programmes may be re-designed keeping in view the recommendations in the National Curriculum Framework of Teacher Education (NCFTE, 2009) and other relevant material.
- In keeping with the recommendations of the Education Commission, every pre-service teacher education system may have dedicated school attached to it as a laboratory where student teachers get opportunities to experiment with new ideas and hone their capacities and skills to become reflective practitioners.
- There is a need to establish a national level academic body for continual reflection and analysis of teacher education programmes, their norms and standards, development of reading material and faculty development of teacher educators.
- As a matter of policy, the first profession degree/diploma in teacher education should be offered only in face to face mode. Distance Learning programmes and the use of blended learning material may be developed and used for continued profession development of school teachers and teacher educators.
- The institutional capacity should be increased for preparation of teacher educators. There is a need to make the masters in M.Ed. programme, 2 year programme with the provision to branch out for specialization in curriculum and pedagogic studies, foundation studies, management, policy and finance.
- The NCTE would need to develop broad-based norms specifying the qualification of teacher educators which would enable induction of persons with post-graduation degrees in education, science, social sciences, languages and mathematics, along with a professional degree in teacher education or a research degree in education, as teacher educators.
- The idea of creating opportunities for teaching practitioners to teach in teacher education institutions, as visiting faculty, may be explored. Similarly teacher educators could be considered as visiting faculty in schools.
- Faculty development programmes for teacher educators should be institutionalized.
- There is a need for enhanced capacity in promotion of research in education in general, and in teacher education in particular in Universities; creation of an inter University Centre could play a significant role in this regard.

Quality of In-service Teacher Education

- The Government is required to appoint an Expert Group to develop a policy framework for in-service teacher educators in consultation with national and State level institutions, including institutions of higher education, representatives of the State Government and teacher organizations, while taking into account the principles suggested in this Report, and also develop a national action plan for implementation of the policy and guidelines for formulation of State Action Plans.
- All existing teacher training institutions imparting in-service teacher education need to be strengthened. In particular, the decentralized structures of BRCs and CRCs be strengthened with provisions for human and physical resources to enable them to perform effectively. Similarly, the DIETs and SCERTs also require strengthening.
- There is an urgent need to develop comprehensive programmes for continuing professional development of secondary school teachers. Towards this, existing institutional arrangements have to be significantly enhanced, along with strengthening of CTEs and IASEs. Besides some post-graduate colleges and Department of Universities may also function as training centres, especially for secondary school teachers, as well as for educational planners and administrators.

Teacher Performance and Teacher Audit

- The Central Government, in consultation with the State Governments and other stake holders, may develop the framework for assessment of teacher performance, keeping in view the guidelines suggested in this Report.

Strengthening the Regulatory Functions of the NCTE

- The NCTE needs to review the existing norms and standards for the various teacher education programmes and create a Standing Committee for periodic review of curriculum and the norms and standards of the programmes.
- The NCTE should develop comprehensive guidelines for innovative teacher education programme for grant of recognition.
- The NCTE should develop a new framework for undertaking inspection of the recognized institutions, with enhanced focus on process parameters, to ascertain the quality of the institutions, and take appropriate action to improve the overall quality of the teacher education system.
- The NCTE should formulate appropriate regulations for implementing Section17, taking into consideration the guidelines incorporated in this Report.

- The NCTE should set up a Teacher Education Assessment and Accreditation.
- Centre (TEAAC), and constitute a Committee to prepare a comprehensive framework of accreditation, suggested in this Report.
- The NCTE should set up an institutional platform in close coordination and collaboration with State Governments, Universities, UGC, and Distance Education Council (DEC), etc. and take decisions on standards, procedures and quality parameters.
- The NCTE should notify Regulations to govern inspections of teacher education institutions. These should include eligibility conditions for empanelment as inspection team members, composition of an inspection team, time required for conducting inspection, format for obtaining the required information from the concerned institution and submission of the inspection report.
- In order to ensure accountability, it is essential to establish a Vigilance Cell in the NCTE, on priority, which would investigate into any act of misbehaviour and misconduct on part of the various functionaries associated with the NCTE.
- The tenure of the office of the Chairperson and Vice-Chairperson of the NCTE should be raised from 4 years to 5 years and the upper age limit should be raised from 60 years to 65 years.
- The Central Government should develop guidelines regarding the manner of appointment of members of the Council. Further, members of the RegionalCommittee should be appointed by the Council.
- The Commission examined the implications of the ruling of the Supreme Court in the case of NCTE vs. Vaishnav Institute of Technology and Management, dated 12thApril, 2012 and the consequent difficulties in causing inspection under Section 17 of the NCTE. The Commission proposes that Section 17 of the NCTE be suitably amended to enable inspection of institutions, unless the Supreme Court reconsiders its decision.
- Appropriate amendments be made in the Act to provide for the following:
  (a) Empower the Council to issue directions to the Regional Committees on matters of policy and for effective implementation of the Act, which shall be binding on the Regional Committees;
  (b) Empower the Regional Committee to review its order to rectify a mistake apparent from record; and
  (c) Enable the Council to revise an order passed by the Regional Committee under sections 14 and 15 of the Act, either on its own motion or on the basis of information made available, where the Council is satisfied, of reasons to be recorded in writing that

the Regional Committee has granted recognition/permission in contravention of the provisions of the Act, or the Rules and Regulations made there under, and pass appropriate orders, after affording reasonable opportunity to the institution.

- The NCTE should appoint a Task Force to finalise organizational restructuring of the NCTE, and to work out its human resource requirement, as suggested in this Report.
- Recommendations in respect of the 291 institutions offering D.Ed. programme are listed separately in Volume 2 of the Report.

General Recommendations

The above recommendations indicate the trajectory of reform that needs to be taken to reform the existing system of teacher education. The Commission, therefore, recommends the constitution of a Committee to enable the setting up of structural mechanism and processes for instituting each of the recommendations outlined in this Report.

Decision of the Supreme Court

The Supreme Court while hearing the case on 10th October, 2012 decided that the recommendations of the Commission "deserve to be accepted". It has given two months' time to the Central Government and the NCTE to file affidavits indicating the steps proposed to be taken for implementing the recommendations of the Commission.

Suggested Follow-up Action

A. Requiring Immediate Action

- Ministry to constitute an Expert Group to develop a comprehensive policy on in- service teacher education.
- NCTE to recommend action to be taken in respect of the institutions inspected by the Commission.
- NCTE to appoint a Task Force to undertake organizational restructuring.
- Greater investment by Universities in research in teacher education.
- Central Government to propose amendments to the NCTE Act on:
  - (a) Increasing the tenure of Chairperson/Vice-Chairperson, NCTE
  - (b) Empowering the Council to issue directions to Regional Committees
  - (c) Enable powers of review and revision of orders

B. Requiring Action in Short Term

UGC, along with NCTE, to hold a wide ranging consultation to prepare Action Plan to take forward the following recommendations:

- Bringing teacher education under the higher education system;
- Enhancing duration of programme for content enrichment, as recommendedby Kothari Commission and NCFTE, 2009.
- Locating teacher education in multi- and inter-discipline academic environment.
- Increasing duration of programmes for preparation of teacher educators.
- Develop broad based norms for qualification of teacher educators.
- First professional degree only in face-to-face mode.

C. Requiring Action in Short Term by NCTE

- Develop Guidelines for innovative programmes
- Develop Framework for mandatory inspection of all institutions
  a) Prepare Rules enabling mandatory inspection
  b) Develop inspection format
  c) Composition of the inspection team
  d) Training of inspectors
- Prepare Regulations enabling withdrawal of recognition
- Create an institutional platform for close coordination with UGC, Universities, State Governments, etc.
- Constitute a Standing Committee for periodic review of norms and standards, and curriculum
- D. Requiring Action in Medium Term
- NCTE to establish a Teacher Education Assessment and AccreditationCentre
- Establishment of a national level academic body for continued reflection and analysis of teacher education programmes
- Establishment of an Inter-University Centre
- Conduct by Universities of faculty development programmes for teacher educators

E. Requiring Consultation with States

- Pre-entry testing of candidates for admission to teacher education porgrammes
- Increase investment in establishing teacher education institutions
- Develop a framework on school audit and teacher performance
- Strengthen BRCs/CRCs and develop their institutional linkage with the DIETs
- Explore possibility of teacher educators as visiting faculty in schools

Summary/Conclusions

The preface of this Report started with the lines "Fellow citizens, why do you turn and scrap every stone to gather wealth and so little care for your children to whom one day must you relinquish it all?" by Socrates. Then by quoting the words of Mahatma Gandhi that, "Education is the basic tool for development of consciousness and reconstruction of society". By quoting the above said educationist, the Commission would like to highlight that teacher is the only medium to achieve this goal. It was rightly felt by former UGC Chairman Arun Nigavekar that, Teachers are now facilitators; a link between students and a plethora of knowledge. However, this in no way eliminates the good-old, face-to-face method of education. It is a known fact, but, it gets reaffirmed that our teachers in schools and colleges are not equipped to cope with the challenges of 21st century, in which, the complete process of teaching and learning has undergone a tremendous change. The former Chief Justice of India J.S. Verma found that "the assembly line for creating teachers, who impact children's learning process and the country's future, was in tatters and needed heavy investment, both financially and qualitatively." The Committee further reported that, "Around 90 per cent of pre-service teacher education institutions are in the non-government sector, and most of the States of the eastern and north-eastern region of the country are facing acute shortage of institutional capacity of teacher preparation in relation to the demand". This highlights the fact that deficiencies in the poor quality of teacher training programmes are mainly run by private entities. The number of teacher education programmes run by State and Central Governments are very few. The Committee said, "The government should increase its investment for establishing teacher education institutions and increase the institutional capacity of teacher preparation, especially in the deficit states". The Verma Commissions also highlighted that DIETs and SCERTs of the respective States should be required to be strengthened. It is also interesting to observe that the Committee goes back to Kothari Commission's report, submitted in 1966, and shows that the recommendations of the Commission are also yet to be fully implemented. Teacher education should be part of the higher education system. The duration of programme of teacher education needs to be enhanced, in keeping with the recommendations of the Kothari Commission (1966), the implementation of which is long overdue. The Commission also highlighted that, "In keeping with the recommendations of the Kothari Commission, every pre-service teacher education institution may have a dedicated school attached to it as a laboratory where student teachers get opportunities to experiment with new ideas and hone their capacities and skills to become reflective practitioners." We as a nation have categorically failed in this endeavour and it is high time to correct our actions. Education is on concurrent list. The Central Government must create a healthy bridge with the State and create a sense of confidence in the minds of teachers, and other stakeholders through deeds and actions, that we all working together for the betterment of education in our country.

The Justice Verma Committee has also proposed strengthening of regulatory powers and functions of NCTE, which must develop comprehensive guidelines for innovative teacher education programmes. "The NCTE should develop a new framework for undertaking inspection of recognized institutions, with enhanced focus on process parameters, to ascertain the quality of institutions and take appropriate action to improve the overall quality of teacher education system," it said. The government should create a process of assessment and accreditation of teacher education institutions and programmes. The Verma Committee said it inspected 291 institutes which prepared teachers in Maharashtra and found only 34 fit to continue. "There is a need for enhanced investment in promotion of research in education in general, and in teacher education in particular in the universities; creation of an inter-university centre in teacher education could play a significant role in this regard," it said. The Committee said the government needed to appoint an expert group to develop a policy framework for in-service teacher education in consultation with national and state level institutions, including institutions of higher studies."There is an urgent need to develop comprehensive programmes for continuing professional development of secondary school teachers. Towards this, existing institutional arrangements have to be significantly enhanced. Besides, some post-graduate colleges and departments of universities may also function as training centres, especially for secondary school teachers, as well as for educational planners and administrators," it said. The Committee proposed strengthening of regulatory powers and functions of National Council for Teacher Education (NCTE), which must develop comprehensive guidelines for innovative teacher education programmes."The NCTE should develop a new framework for undertaking inspection of recognized institutions, with enhanced focus on process parameters, to ascertain the quality of the institutions, and take appropriate action to improve the overall quality of the teacher education system," it said.

REFERENCES

Arun Nigavekar, Septemer 04 2012, *Investing in Teacher Training Courses.*

Akshaya Mukul, June 25, 2011, Row over HRD notice on NCTE supersession, TNN.

Dhananjay Mahapatra, TNN August 31, 2012, Panel: Assembly Line for Teachers in Tatters,

Government of India, MHRD, Department of School Education and Literacy, Vision of Teacher Education in India, *Quality and Regulatory Perspective*, Vol. 1, August, 2012.

Government of India, MHRD, Department of School Education and Literacy, Vision of Teacher Education in India, *Quality and Regulatory Perspective*, Institution-wise Reports on the Review of 291TEI's Offering D.Ed. in Maharashtra, Vol. 2, August 2012.

Government of India, MHRD, Department of School Education and Literacy, Vision of Teacher Education in India, Quality and Regulatory Perspective, Annexures, Vol. 3, August 2012.

National Council on Educational Research and Training (NCERT). 1988. *National Curriculum for Elementary and Secondary Education: A Framework*. New Delhi, NCERT.

Pranati Panda, *Responsiveness of Teacher Education Curriculum towards Human Rights Education in India.*

Report of Justice Verma Commission on Teacher Education (2012), 60th Meeting of the Central Advisory Board of Education, Agenda Items and Background Notes (1st November), New Delhi.

Times of India, 09 June, 2011, Government all set to take over NCTE.

Times of India, 29 October, 2012 Teacher Education System Usher in Sweeping Reforms.

PART-II

ICT Rejuvenations and Tech-Savvy Teachers

12

Information and Communication Technology (ICT) Initiatives in Teacher Education

Bimal Charan Swain

Information and Communication Technology or ICT represents one of the current applications of technology towards education. With the emphasis on learning and instructional theories to help learners learn, ICT is expected to fulfill some of the needs of learners to function effectively in this world. According to UNESCO (2002), "ICT is a scientific, technological and engineering discipline and management technique used in handling information, Its application and association with social, economical and cultural matters". According to Moursund "ICT includes the full range of computer hardware, computer software and telecommunication facilities. Thus it includes computing devices ranging from hand-held calculator to super computers. It includes the full range of display and projection devices used to view computer output. It includes the local area network and wide area network that allow computer system and people to communicate with each other. It includes digital cameras, computer games, CDs, DVDs, Cell phones, telecommunications satellites and fiber optics. It includes computerized machinery and computerized robots."

ICT in Teacher Education

The face of the classroom is changing. The teacher education institutions should prepare in-service teachers to keep up with the technology utility in the classroom. ICT is not only an essential tool for teachers in their day to day, but it also offers them opportunities for their own professional development. ICT use brings the change in the pedagogy, shift in the perspective about learning, shift in teaching-learning paradigm. In conventional teaching, most of the time is consumed in in-put output and less time is left for process. But, in teaching with the ICT, the input and output time is reduced and process time is increased. When the process time increases the time of students activities, discussion, correlation with other subjects, brain storming, learning etc., we get more time to process phase (Dahiya, 2005).

ICTs can be used firstly to enhance richness and quality of teacher education in the classroom and secondly to distribute own developed multimedia resources to others through distributed learning as well as flexible learning. In either case, the selection to technological tools will depend on costs, technology infrastructure, learner access to the technology, the support personnel and facilities available to create digitized knowledge resources and individuals (Dahiya, 2005).

Four Theme Frameworks for Teacher Education

UNESCO (2002) has projected a holistic framework taking into consideration four supportive themes viz. Context and Culture, Leadership and Vision, Lifelong Learning and Planning and Management of Change. The framework of competencies is encircled by four supportive themes. The curriculum framework also suggests that each teacher is allowed to interpret the framework within his or her context and personal approach to pedagogy, which is always related to the subject discipline or content area, rather than to the technology itself (Ranjan and Naimur, 2011, as reported by Swamy, 2012).

Context and Culture identifies the culture and other contextual factors that must be considered in infusing technology into the teacher education curriculum. It includes the use of technology in culturally appropriate ways and the development of respect for multiple cultures and contexts, which need to be taught and modelled by teachers. Leadership and vision are essential for the successful planning and implementation of technology into teacher education and require both leadership and support from the administration of the teacher institutions. Lifelong learning acknowledges that learning does not stop after school. Planning and Management of change signifies the importance of careful planning and effective management of the change process (Ranjan and Naimur, 2011, as reported by Swamy, 2012).

Pre-Service Teacher Education and ICT Use

In order to introduce ICT in pre-service teacher education, a number of methods and strategies are suggested. Many of these strategies employ commonly used productivity tools such as word processing, data base, spread sheet and browser applications. Additional strategies that are multipurpose in application may also be used to help teacher trainees to quickly develop technology-rich lesson plans for their practice teaching.

Key Components for Planning the Curriculum

Four important components must be considered while introducing ICT in any educational organization.

(a) Leadership and vision
(b) Context and culture

(c) Planning and management of change
(d) Lifelong learning (Kamat, 2005).

Basic Principles for Development of Effective ICT Teacher Education

The Society for Information Technology and Teacher Education (SITE, 2002) has identified basic principles for development of effective ICT teacher education. They are:

- Technology should be infused into the entire teacher education programme.
- Technology should be introduced in context.
- Students should experience innovative technology supported learning environments in their teacher education programme.

ICT Content in Teacher Education Programmes

Four phases are conducted to implementation of ICT content in teacher education programmes. The phases are:

i. ICT Literacy (Such as general software applications like Microsoft Office Word, Power Point, Excel, know your computer, computer operating system, computer – input, output, storage devices and functions).
ii. The effective and efficient use of ICT hardware and software for teaching, learning activities.
iii. Pedagogy based ICT use (Integration of ICT in subject content, teaching, on line support, networking and management.
iv. Adoption of best innovative practices in the use of ICT.

ICT Helps Teachers

ICT helps teachers in the following ways:

- ICT helps teachers in preparation for teaching.
- With the help of ICT, teachers can have access with institutions and universities, UGC, NCERT, NAAC, and NCTE etc.
- ICT helps teachers to interact with students.
- ICT enables the teachers to have access to online libraries, journals, and research for individual learning.
- ICT enables to give feedback and testing objectively and fast without biases.

UNESCO Guidelines (2002) for introducing ICT in Teacher Education are worth mentioning here. They would help the Teacher Education Colleges and organizations to plan the introduction of ICT properly.

- When planning curriculum, be sure it is congruent with the educational vision, the culture and context of each region both locally and globally. Develop the vision and standards in stages starting with a core that can be expanded into a set of standards, implemented with ICTs for the preparation and continuing professional development of teachers.
- The ICT curriculum should facilitate change toward a more inclusive approach that promotes positive and supportive interdependence between teachers and students, while maintaining individual accountability and autonomy.

One can draw from Jung's (2000) experience and state that the success of the ICT integration lies in the inclusion of certain strategies like:

- Providing a short compulsory course that focuses on hands on ICT experience at the pre-service teacher training programme. That is to say the focus needs to be on successfully applying ICT skills to achieve pedagogical objectives rather than teaching the ICT skills in isolation.
- Providing an advanced level course for interested students who can develop more advanced ICT based pedagogical skills.,
- ICT should be used to teach all subject matter areas at the pre-service level so that the pre-service teachers are able to get hands on experience.
- The curriculum of the teacher education programme needs to provide flexibility so as to provide opportunity for students teachers to develop various ICT infused instructional material.

Researches on ICT in Teacher Education

A few studies on the use of ICT in teacher education/teaching learning process is described below.

Leong (1995) in his study found that by using ICT materials and strategies, teachers can be indirectly made aware of research findings and intervention strategies to develop and strengthen the cognitive structure of students and clarify their meanings. Goodwyn *et al.* (1997) in their study "The future curriculum in English and IT" reported that student teachers of English had a positive and committed attitude towards the use of ICT in current and future literacy curriculum. Jorrett (1998) in the study on "Integrating technology into middle school mathematics" found the benefits of using ICT were: motivation, communication skill, problem solving, building basic skills, curriculum development, and creation of authentic learning experiences. Williams *et al.* (2000) in a study on "Integrating Information and communication Technology in professional practice of primary and secondary teachers in Scottish Schools" reported that there is need for an increase in the availability of "helpdesk" and formal technical support systems; training for school technicians and mechanisms to support knowledge sharing among teachers. Otieno (2008) in a study on, "A framework for evaluating ICT use in Teacher Education: A Case Study of Primary Teacher Training in Kenya" found that ICT develops the General Knowledge of teachers, it develops the capacity to introduce a lesson using the ICT and increases the interest of students by using computer technology in classroom situation. Verma (2010) found that innovative use of ICT in teaching learning can stimulate dynamic learning environments. Swamy (2012) in a study found that ICT has not been included as core course at the B.Ed. level in the colleges but fundamentals of computer knowledge were included in the curriculum. All the respondents reported that ICT was not included as compulsory core course. Swain (2012) in a study on the availability and use of ICT in secondary schools found that more than 50 per cent of teachers used ICT in teaching-learning process.

Issues related to the ICT in Teacher Education

Laferriere and Breuleux (2002) raise many issues related to the ICT in Teacher Education. Some of them are:

- ICT as mere Technology or a Catalyst of Change?
- ICTs as a subject matter or as tools for bearing a broad variety of subject matter?
- ICTs as time consuming or time saver?
- ICTs belonging in the lab or in the Computer?
- Face to face or on – line interaction?
- ICTs as information source or communication tool?

While planning to introduce ICT, one has to resolve them.

To conclude, a classroom is a different place from what is used to be. The black board and chalk is being supported by Computers, Video-Cassette players, tape recorders and radios. The infusion of ICT into the teacher education programme will help the future teachers cope with the paradigm shift in learning.

REFERENCES

Dahiya, S.S. (2005). "ICT Enabled Teacher Education", *Universities News*, Vol. 43, No. 18.

Dewal, O.S. (1997). "Educational Technology", in *Fifth Survey of Educational Research (1988-92). Trend Report. Volume I.* New Delhi: National Council of Educational Research and Training.

Goodwyn, A. *et al.* (1997). "The Future Curriculum in English and IT. How Teachers and Student Teachers view the Relationship?", *Journal of Information Technology for Teacher Education*, Vol. 6, No. 3, pp. 227-240.

Government of India, Ministry of Human Resource Development (2007). *Annual Report. 2006-07*. New Delhi: Ministry of Human Resource Development.

Jarrett, D. (1989). "Integrating Technology into Middle School Mathematics, It's Just Good Teaching." Northwest Regional Education Laboratory. *http://www.nwrel.org/msei/book.6 pdf.*

Jung, I. (2000). "Singapore: Pre-service Teacher Training in Technology Use", *Technologia*, November/December.

Kamt, V. (2005). "ICT in Teacher Education", *University News*, Vol. 43, No. 18.

Kumar, S.K. (2002). "Information Technology and Teacher Education", *Edutracks*, Vol. I, No. 10, pp. 16-18.

Leong, Y.P. (1995)." Institutional Mediation in Mathematics and Science", *Paper Presented at the International Conference on Computers in Education. ICCE, Singapore*.

NCTE, (1996). *Curriculum Framework for Teacher Education*. New Delhi: Government of India.

NCTE (2002). *ICT Initiatives of the NCTE. Discussion Document*. New Delhi: National Council for Teacher Education.

Ranjan, N and Naimur, R. (2011). "Role of Teacher in enhancing Learning Achievement of Children and Emphasis on Teacher Skill Development, Knowledge Building and ICT." *www.dhsekerala. gov.in*

Sandholtz, J.; Ringstaff, C and Dwyer, D. (1997). *Teaching with Technology*, New York: Teachers College Press.

Satyanarayan, B. *et al.* (1998). *Information Technology: Issues and Trends*. New Delhi: Como Publications.

Swain, B.C. (2012). "Availability and Use of Information and Communication Technology in Secondary Schools." *Ambikeya Journal of Education* (Communicated).

Swamy, R.N. (2012). "Integrating ICT in Teacher Education: An Inevitable Step Towards Improving the Quality of Education," *University News*, Vol. 50, No. 6, pp. 1-6.

UNESCO (2002). *Information and Communication Technologies in Teacher Education, A Planning Guide*. Paris: UNESCO.

Williams, D. *et al.* (2002). Integrating Information and Communication Technology in Professional Practice: An analysis of Teachers' Need Based on a Survey of Primary and Secondary Teachers in Scottish Schools, *Journal of Information and Technology for Teacher Education*, Vol. 9, No. 2, pp. 167-182.

13

Prospective Scenario of Teaching Profession in Techno-Savvy World

Sangeeta Solanki and ***Shri Kant Dwivedi***

The evolution of education and its future has been tackled from various perspectives varying from technology enhanced learning and personal digital spaces, schools reforms and revision of curricula, amongst many others. The role of teachers for the future of education plays a major role in such discourse. Increasing computational power and the emergence of the Internet has had a great impact on the way teachers are doing their jobs. Teachers in India believe that Information and Communications Technology (ICT) have improved their teaching and they claim to combine various modes of ICT as resources for their teaching. However, in many ways, teachers are caught with one foot in the future and another one in past. On the one hand, developments of technological tools and the vast take-up of such applications imply that teachers need to keep abreast of technology developments, in order to keep up with their students' knowledge of new technologies, while on the other, most teachers still have to work in school environments where policies are outdated and curricula no longer cover the skills required for today's societies. Moreover, while teachers are major stakeholders in the education field, they are rarely consulted for foresight research on the future of learning.

The unprecedented opportunities brought about by networking tools are enabling teachers to network and collaborate with other teachers from anywhere, at any time. Such development in the profession of teachers is a significant aspect which cannot be ignored when discussing the future of education. Teachers tend to feel isolated in their own schools and are often confined to a single school experience. Tight timetables and overloaded curricula do not allow them much time to explore innovative pedagogies. Various literatures in education have explored a vast array of research addressing teachers' professional development. Recently, we observe some focus on alternative approaches of addressing professional development, through the study of networks. A survey conducted in the US found that teachers believe that collaborative professional development activities, such as networking with other teachers outside school, is more effective and helpful as professional development than traditional forms of training. Similarly, the report suggest that involvement in a "professional development network" ranks high as regards the perceived impact on teachers' professional development and participation in informal dialogue has a moderate or high level of impact on their professional development.

Key Issues in Future Teacher Education Networking

Prospective Role of the Teachers

The important role of teachers as major stakeholders in shaping the future of learning is also highlighted in various studies. As learning becomes more personalised, the one-size-fits-all teaching method is becoming more and more outdated. Teachers will be prepared to design learning experiences which reflect the growing importance attributed to innovation and creativity in our societies. They also must be prepared to adapt their teaching practices to a rapidly changing global society. A call for action designed for the redefinition of teacher education highlights that teachers should become able to enable students to maximise the potential of their formal and informal learning. Teachers should also be ready to facilitate learning in multiple modalities: embracing a greater diversity of spaces, times, resources, media and methods for learning, as well as 21st century environments which are synchronous and asynchronous, face-to-face and virtual, local and global. The role of teachers will evolve and become closer to that of mentors. The emergence of open content has resulted in a vast array of education material posted online to be shared for free. Openness, sharing and collaboration are having a profound shift on the way students study and learn and on the way teachers teach and learn. Teachers will need to work as effective members of learning teams, made up of novice and accomplished educators, students and subject matter experts which will turn schools into hubs of networked learning ecology. Simulations can be used as a method of training prospective teachers to encounter and respond to difficult situations in collaboration with colleagues.

Teacher-Training

Teacher training is a major aspect of education. Teacher training has been recognised as key element for the creation of an effective "knowledge triangle" which consists of education, research and innovation (Council of the European Union, 2010). In a recent study on creativity and innovation in school, teacher training has been highlighted as a major area where more efforts and improvement should be addressed in educational policies. Teacher training must go beyond the present paradigm of teacher preparation. Prospective teachers need to experience a wide array of learning environments: observe how students learn in non-school environments, how learning takes place in formal and informal contexts, how students engage in socially networked informal learning and how they collaborate between themselves. Unfortunately, diverse policy contexts and a lack of shared vision among stakeholders are limiting the reinvention of teacher education.

The Role of Schools

The role of schools as the major source of knowledge transmission has for a long period of time been taken for granted. Schools became so important in our societies that political intervention has made school attendance obligatory in countries in the East. However, recent developments of education suggest that as education can take place anywhere, the role of schools continues to evolve. The traditional link of learning with specific spaces, such as classrooms, is becoming de-linked as time and place constraints for connectivity are abolished. Increasingly, information is stored outside school servers and acceptance and adoption of cloud-based applications and services is changing the way information is conceptualised in education.

These changes have led to the discussion on de-institutionalisation of schooling in different future scenarios, as learning is taking place inside school, outside school, at home and online. For instance, in one scenario, the development of learning networks and powerful ICT solutions are created as alternatives to the public school sector which is no longer able to deliver learning tailored to individual needs. However, schools remain an important institution in other future scenarios, as they are seen as instrumental in maintaining social capital. In more recent studies, it has been argued that schools need to be repositioned within the emerging learning landscape, both in terms of new formats and strategies for learning, as well as offering relevant, effective and relevant learning experiences.

Schools have to be situated within the context of the future labour market requirements, so as to be flexible in responding to individual's learners needs. The role of schools shall be to guide students in selecting learning opportunities which best fit their lifestyle; to monitor progress; and to manage assessment, certification and accreditation mechanism. Controlling of costs from schools will also bring about the development of new models to serve students, such as providing open content through the network.

Re-Skilling of Teaching Competencies

Literature on the future of learning has also brought to the limelight the issue of re-skilling. The future of education will be influenced by a need for new skills which are "generic, transversal and cross-cutting", through which learners will be able to benefit as part of their lifelong learning path. There is a need of a major shift from knowledge to competencies, namely: problem-solving, reflection, creativity, critical thinking, learning to learn, risk-taking, collaboration and entrepreneurship. In addition to these competencies, in a world where information is everywhere, mentoring and preparing students to be able to assess credibility of information and make sense of it should be high on the education agenda.

It can also be said that learning will become more active and hence, there should be more skills focusing on learning by doing and through interaction and collaboration with others. These changes also mean that teachers will need to be able to re-skill their competencies, so as to keep updated with changes and be able to respond to fast changing working environment. In parallel, school policies need to better align learning objectives with societal needs mainly because in the future societies will be more intercultural and students need to become better active citizens.

Formal and Informal Learning

Another observable trend in terms of how education will evolve is the shift between formal and informal learning. It has been recognised that education mechanisms will have to be developed to better identify and assess informal skills. With the emergence of innovative technologies, individual learners are becoming more and more empowered. Learning is no longer confined to the classroom. While digital media literacy is on the increase, as an alternative to the lack of formal training, as yet, we are far from seeing digital media literacy as the norm. Discourse on the future of learning is also grounded on the idea that learning should be a continuous activity and not only bounded to educational institutions. Lifelong learning should span from pre-school to post-retirement. A major component of learning takes place at the work place, in non-formal contexts and during leisure time. The trends and challenges listed above demonstrate that some major changes are taking place in education. Predictions on the future of education challenge current settings and propose various horizontal changes that need to take place in order to enhance education. In the next sections, consultations with teachers are presented, as a way of understanding how teachers perceive and view current trends and challenges and what they believe should be done.

Development of New Technologies

Various studies demonstrate that a major driver influencing the future of education is the increasing development of new technologies and their appropriation in everyday life. It is difficult to think on the future of learning environments without ICT at the forefront or at the background. Portable applications (such as laptops and mobile phones) and new communication applications (such as collaborative and social networking sites) are empowering users to access information from anywhere at any time. Technological applications are not only facilitating access, but have also amplified diversity of resources; they allow users to connect through online content and they have become models of collaboration. In the future, learning is expected to be supported by flexible and dynamic virtual environments and by a range of tools which facilitate learning within and outside school. Research suggests that teachers envisage a shift in education to complex digital competencies juxtaposing with new communication skills, such as 24×7 online connection and management of different online identities. Another aspect in relation to the future of learning is personalisation of learning. Learners will be able to choose their own learning paths encompassing different types of content (such as mobile, videos, social media tools etc). It is predicted that learning analytics which refers to a group of tools which will allow teachers to monitor student engagement, performance and progress will also be part of the future of learning. Within such a context, attainment of digital competences, that is, the competence to efficiently, confidently and critically use the technologies of the future in an efficient and targeted way becomes a priority.

Teachers' Network: Support and A Mentor

Networks developed by prospective teachers can act as a form of support and mentoring during their careers and also as a means to access new research-based teaching practices and resources. Networks have been proposed to be an organisational answer to the diversity and complexity of educational needs. The expectations of the potential of networks Teachers' Lifelong Learning Network is often exaggerated; networks can have an important role in education in providing a structure for teachers' professional development and in integrating the diverse and fragmented lifelong learning landscape. Moreover, they provide platforms where resources can be shared; hence reducing teachers' workloads as teachers do not need to create resources from scratch. To our knowledge, the potential of teachers' networks is somehow still missing in the discourse addressing the future of education. Social learning networks can support teachers' competence building, by identifying drivers and barriers for lifelong professional development of networked teachers, mechanisms for disseminating practices and innovations within and across networks, and innovating new peer-learning approaches within India-wide teacher networking platform.

Unless we plan strategically for the future of teacher education, we will be unable to deal with teachers' future needs. While 21st century might seem a long way ahead in the future, and the future can be changed by unexpected interventions, we have to keep in mind that children starting schools in 2011 will be finishing their obligatory schooling or entering higher education in 2020-2025. Various studies demonstrate that a major driver influencing the future of education is the increasing development of new technologies and their appropriation in everyday life in most of the societies. When innovative educator Will Richardson speaks to audiences he often asks how many people belong to social networks (aside from dating sites)? About 10 per cent of hands go up depending on the audience. He follows that with how many people teach through MySpace or Face book? Usually no hands are raised. These are good questions and when I've been in the audience I put my hand up only half way because while I do have a MySpace account, I don't really use it at all, so I almost feel like I'm cheating. MySpace just isn't a place for me, even though I want it to be if for no reason other than to be more in touch with the digital natives. The reality for innovative educators though, is if we don't quickly find value in what we are doing, we don't pay it much attention. Although I see myself as an innovative educator, and wish I was more active in MySpace, and even taught it...I wasn't more active and don't teach it because I wasn't a deeply involved or experienced online social networker.

Innovative Educators Participation in Social Networks: Five Reasons

1. ***Connecting to Digital Natives***: We need to be deeply knowledgeable about the power of tools such as these that our students are using without us. If we know and can talk from experience about how we use social networks responsibly and effectively, we gain credibility with our students.
2. ***Digital Natives***: As a social network participant, innovative educators can share their site and refer to how it affects their learning often with students. This enables students to know that they do have something in common with their teachers and see smart ways their teachers are using their networks.
3. ***Interacting with Digital Natives:*** One of my favourite quotes is we need to replicate in the classroom the world in which our students are living. After getting some experience, innovative educators can create social networks for their students to participate in and can then actually "teach" social networks and help students make connections between what they are doing in an educational social network and how these lessons can be transferred to their personal social network interactions.
4. ***Developing Your Personal Learning Network:*** A social network is a great place to begin and develop your own personal learning network of colleagues with whom you can connect, share, and learn from anytime and anywhere.
5. ***Share Your Own Reason:*** How do you see social networking being used to enhance innovative educating? Share your ideas by commenting on this post.

How to Network: Some Techniques

How and how well teachers are prepared for teaching is a critical indicator of education quality. Preparing teachers for the challenges of a changing world means equipping them with subject-specific expertise, effective and innovative teaching practices, an understanding of technology and the ability to work collaboratively with other teachers, members of the community and parents. Synthesized lessons learned and best practice from successful and sustainable teacher training and ongoing teacher professional development initiatives utilizing ICTs to meet these and related challenges in developing countries are not well documented.

i. Set up Appointments with Other Schools *(A Crafty way to network with a Specific School)*

Let's say that you work in a pretty bad school. For whatever reason, you don't like our school, and you know about specific districts that you'd love to work for. Maybe the pay is higher, the students generally more motivated, the commute is less, whatever the reason, you have reasons to want to be at a specific district. A great way to get your foot in the door at another school and to network with them is to set up a formal visit with the school. If you're a Math teacher, run the idea by your supervisor and tell him/he that you've heard great things about what that other district is doing (you need to have some specific reason to want to visit). Your supervisor might want to set up the visit or will just tell you to try to set up the visit. If so, contact the appropriate supervisor at the other district to set up the meeting. Again, you'll have to have some specific reasons for the visit—pretty easy to come up with some reasons, as I've done this trick before.

ii. Attend Conferences *(Slow but the potential connection).*

People usually don't want to go to an education-conference. I'm just not the conference type; personally, I'd rather read a book on teaching. That said, some of the best contacts that I've made have been from attending 1 day teaching workshops. These are great! Usually, you'll meet people of the same discipline so you'll easily be able to talk shop and at the end exchange information. After the conference is over, just decide which of the contacts you want to keep networking with. If you meet someone from a district you'd like to work for, and then definitely keep in touch—this should be easy since you'll probably teach the same discipline. That said, you should probably try to keep in touch with as many people as you can. Don't write someone off just because they don't work where you want to work. Remember teachers move from school to school; maybe in a few years, the seemingly undesirable contact will be working at your dream school!

iii. Online Teacher Networking.

This last feature was not available for our teachers few decades ago. Nowadays, it is possible to meet teachers in a variety of ways. There are online teacher forums and even a fully fledged teacher community, where you can post a profile, chat with other teachers and much more. Also, don't forget about LinkedIn. If you don't know what LinkedIn is, it's kind of like Face Book but for job seekers. It was designed for people who want to network. You can post a resume and meet other people of the same profession. I know a few people who have landed interviews from LinkedIn. Here is the figure that shows the ways how a teacher can set up network with other teachers.

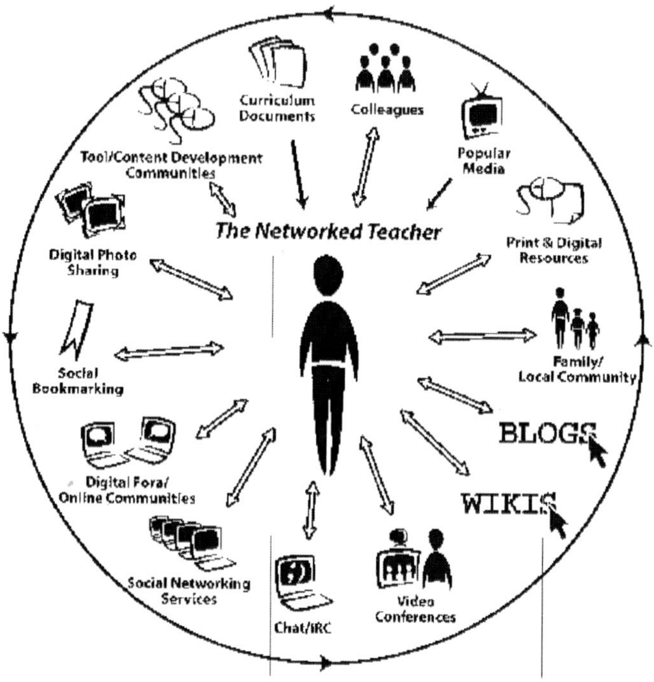

Conclusion

Since young people will likely to continue to be at the forefront of technological change, Net Genres will continue to have a lot to teach educators about evolving technology. Yet educators must not abdicate their role as authorities directing the learning experiences of their students. Our research observes the existence of a fine line: Educators should continue to find ways to exploit the skills students develop outside of class without accommodating the habits of instant gratification and shallow thinking. To be human is to learn, and we learn from good teachers. The current education system does not teach students how to learn; Today's digital and computer technologies allow us to remedy this by giving us the tools to teach Net Generation not just what to learn but how to learn. To conclude we must say that teachers in the digital age should use new strategies to transform theory into practice. There is wide recognition that teacher education must change to meet the needs of 21st Century learners. The scenario of teaching profession in techno-savvy world should involve following competencies on the part of the teacher:

- Facilitate and inspire student learning and creativity so that all students achieve in the global society.
- Be global educators.
- Work with their students to create new learning opportunities.
- Enable students to maximize the potential of their formal and informal learning experiences.
- Use the full range of digital-age learning tools to improve student engagement and achievement.
- Use student data to support student learning and programme improvement.
- Be life-long learners.

REFERENCES

Ala-Mutka, K. (2009). The impact of social computing on the EU information society and economy. In Y. Punie, W. Lusoli, C. Centeno, G. Misuraca and D. Broster (Eds.). Seville: European Commission—Joint Research Centre - Institute for Prospective Technological Studies.

Ala-Mutka, K., Redecker, C., Punie, Y., Ferrari, A., Cachia, R., and Centeno, C. (2010). The future of learning: European Teachers' Visions: Report on a foresight consultation at the 2010 eTwinning Conference, Seville, 5-7 February 2010. Seville: Institute for Prospective Technological Studies, Joint Research Centre, European Commission.

Bartlett, M. 2005. Generation X? So old school. The emphasis now is on the 'Millennials.' *Credit Union Journal*, May 9.

Bienzle, H., Gelabert, E., Jutte, W., Kolyva, K., Meyer, N., and Tilkin, G. (2007). The Art of Networking. European Networks in Education. Retrieved from http://www.networksin-education.eu/fileadmin/images/downloads/art_EN.pdf

Bonamici, A., D. Hutto, D. Smith, and J. Ward. 2005. The "Next Generation": Implications for libraries and higher education. http://www.orbiscascade.org/council/c0510/Frye.ppt (accessed March 26, 2007).

Bugeja, M.J. 2006. Facing the Facebook. *The Chronicle of Higher Education*, January 27.http://chronicle.com/jobs/2006/01/2006012301c.htm (accessed March 26, 2007).

Cachia, R., Ferrari, A., Ala-Mutka, K., and Punie, Y. (2010). Creative Learning and Innovative Teaching: Final Report on the Study on Creativity and Innovation in Educationin the EU Member States (No. EUR 24675). Seville: European Commission - Joint Research Centre -Institute for Prospective Technological Studies.

Cagnin, C., and Keenan, M. (2008). Positioning Future-Oriented Technology Analysis. In C.H. Cagnin, M. Keenan, R. Johnston, F. Scapolo and R. Barré (Eds.), *Future-oriented technology analysis: strategic intelligence for an innovative economy* (pp. viii, 169 p.). Spain; London: Springer.

Calde, S., Goodwin, K., and Reimann, R. (2002). SHS Orcas: The first integrated information system for long-term healthcare facility management. Paper presented at the Conference on Human Factors and Computing Systems, Case studies of the CHI2002/AIGA Experience Design Forum., New York.

Caroll, T., and Resta, P. (2010). Redefining teacher education for digital-age learners. Summit report from the Invitational Summit on Redefining Teacher Education for Digital-Age Learners.

Council of the European Union. (2010). 2010 joint progress report of the Council and the Commission on the implementation of the 'Education and Training 2010 work programme'. Official Journal of the European Union, C117/111.

Crawley, C., Gerhard, P., Gilleran, A., and Joyce, A. (2010). eTwinning 2.0. Building the community for schools in Europe. Retrieved from http://ec.europa.eu/education/pub/pdf/school/et10_en.pdf

Crawley, C., Gilleran, A., Scimeca, S., Vuorikari, R., and Wastiau, P. (2009). Beyond School Projects, A report on eTwinning 2008-2009. Retrieved from http://resources.eun.org/etwinning/25/EN_eTwinning_165x230_Report.pdf

Day, P. 2007. Back to school for business schools. Works in progress. BBC News Business. http://news.bbc.co.uk/2/hi/business/6406965.stm (accessed March 26, 2007).

Dodge, B. 2001. Some thoughts about Webquests. The WebQuest Page. http://webquest.sdsu.edu/about_webquests.html (accessed March 26, 2007).

Enrollment Management Report. 2005. Use emerging technologies to recruit today's millennial students. December 1.

Glenn, J.M. 2000. Teaching the Net Generation. Business Education Forum 54 (3): 6-14.

Hay, L.E. 2000. Educating the Net Generation. *The Social Administrator* 57 (54): 6-10.

Gatt, S., Pereira Cunha, M.F., and Costa, M. (2009). Networking School Teachers to Promote Better Practice in the Teaching of Science across Europe. *European Journal of Education*, 44(4), 493-506.

Hofman, R.H., and Dijkstra, B.J. (2010). Effective teacher professionalization in networks? [doi: DOI: 10.1016/j.tate.2009.10.046]. *Teaching and Teacher Education*, 26(4), 1031-1040.

Johnson, L., Adams, S., and Haywood, K. (2011). *The NMC Horizon Repot: 2011* K-12 Edition. Austin, Texas: The New Media Consortium.

14
Integrating ICT in Professional Development of Teacher Educators

Ranjan Kumar Rout

Education for All and *Knowledge Society* agendas are challenging the institutional and human resource capacity of education systems around the world. The pressure to provide access and a quality education to learners taking part in 21st Century knowledge -based societies and economies is immense. Teachers and teacher educators are the pivotal agents in the drive to transform education systems through Teacher Professional Development (TPD) strategy. Many educators, business and industry representatives and government leaders believe that creating a paradigm shift in views of learning, coupled by applications of new information technologies, can play a key role in renewing educational systems to bring them into alignment with the needs of a Knowledge Society for All. Shafika (2006) defines *Teacher Professional Development (TPD)* as 'a systematized, initial and continuous, coherent and modular process of professional development of educators in accordance with professional competency standards and frameworks'. Teacher professional development would also include training in the adaptation to the evolution of change of the profession of teachers and managers of education systems. The integration of ICT in teacher professional development according to Perraton *et al.* (2001, cited in Anderson and Glen 2003) involves two sets of activities or roles:

> One is training teachers to *learn about ICT* and its use in teaching as computers are introduced to schools.... The other role of ICT is as a means of providing teacher education, either as a *core* or main component of a programme, or playing a *supplementary* role within it (emphasis added) (*ibid*: 5).

Now the question arises as to who can provide ICT training to the teachers and how the professional development of teacher is possible? Probably the answer is the 'teacher educators', who has the expertise and who is well versed with ICT. In this regard the Professional Development of Teacher Educators is a must. But, due to the more structured and time bound professional development programmes, many teacher educators are not able to take part in the traditional; 'time-in-a-seat' structured faculty development program. Professional development within an online community of learners can bring teachers, parents, community members and administrators together through the training, support and communication links necessary for their continued growth of knowledge.

Who is a Teacher Educator?

Winter Conference Standards Clinic New Orleans, LA February, 2008 suggested standards (nine parameters) for teacher educators which helped to distinguish the role of teacher educators from the role of other professionals in the education of teachers. Presentations about the Association of Teacher Educators (ATE) Standards for Teacher Educators have always generated intense discussions that begin with a broad interpretation of the term. For example, everyone agrees that the college instructors who teach content courses for prospective elementary teachers have a high level of influence on what those future teachers will do in teaching those disciplines to young children. Subsequent discussion then distinguishes the role of this individual from the university professor who engages the future teacher in planning and implementing instruction in the classroom. The content instructor is not expected to research in the field of teaching, conduct workshops for teachers on how to teach, or attend ATE conventions. A simple definition of *teacher educator* is anyone who educates teachers. Such a definition is too general to be useful in establishing standards for teacher educators. Moreover, it diminishes the professionalism of teacher educators and impedes the profession in distinguishing highly qualified teacher educators from others who contribute to the education of teachers. The purpose of the Standards is to promote more effective practice by these teacher educators. For the purposes associated with the ATE standards, teacher educators are identified as those educators who provide formal instruction or conduct research and development for educating prospective and practicing teachers. Teacher educators provide the professional education component of pre-service programmes and the staff development component of in-service programs.

Changing Role of Teacher Educators in the 21st Century

In the past, the teacher educators were required to enable the teacher trainees with multifarious teaching skills. But practically it was not cent-percent possible in the part of the teacher educators. With the advent of science and technology, the teacher educators were supposed to assume that they will achieve their goal. But their ignorance on technological knowledge and skill made them handicapped in achieving their goal. Realizing the importance of technology, the International Society for Technology Education has re-released its educational technology standards/skills for teachers. Some of these skills are: finding and managing recourses, publishing on the web, connecting with colleagues, students, parents, and local and global communities. The teacher educators must be proficient in these skills in order to model good practices for their students and help students include these skills for learning. To equip teacher educators with these skills, professional development of teacher educators is a must. But, the quality of professional development depends on the extent of ICT integration in teacher education programmes.

Need of Professional Development of Teacher Educators

Professional development, is a broader sense, refers to the development of a person in his/her professional role. More specifically, "Teacher development is the professional growth a teacher achieves as a result of gaining increased experience and examining his/her teaching systematically." (Glatthorn, 1995, p. 41). Professional development includes formal experiences (such as attending workshops and professional meetings, mentoring etc.) and informal experiences (such as reading professional publications, watching television documentaries related to an academic discipline etc.). (Ganser, 2000). In a nut shell, professional development programme for teacher educators seeks to equip the teacher educators with the following skills:

- ***Updated Content Knowledge***: Teacher educators will develop and update their content knowledge through attending professional development programmes.
- ***Development of Pedagogical Skills***: Teacher educators will attain the desired level of instructional skill and learner characteristics, which are required to systematically design and deliver instructions.
- ***Development of Assessment Competencies***: As assessment is an integral part of teaching learning process professional development programme develop assessment skills among the teacher educators.
- ***Equip with Technological Skills***: Teacher educators will develop the ability to use appropriate instructional technology for information management, communication and instructions.
- ***Development of Professional Ethics***: Similarly, PD programme also assists the teacher educators to practise their role effectively and efficiently.

Rationale of Integration of ICT for Professional Development of Teacher Educators

How much and how well teachers are prepared for teaching is a critical indicator of quality teachers as well as quality education. Preparing teachers for the challenges of a changing world means equipping them with subject-specific expertise, effective and innovative teaching practices, developing an understanding of technology and the ability to work collaboratively with other teachers, members of the community and parents. Basically the advancement of science and technology in teaching-learning process makes the process more contextual, learner-centric, and innovative.

In a nut shell, integration of ICT for professional development of teacher educators serve the following purposes:

- Successful integration of ICTs into teacher education programmes
- Empower teacher educators to develop their knowledge and skills actively and experimentally, in a variety of learning environments, both individually and collaboratively.
- Include a variety of learning strategies, encompassing direct instruction, drill and practice, deduction, induction, and sharing.
- Provides an authentic learning environment so that teacher educators engage themselves in concrete tasks within realistic scenarios.
- Emphasize ways that technology can facilitate and enhance teachers' professional lives.
- Encourage teacher educators to be mentors, tutors, and guides in teaching-learning process.
- Develop teacher educators' skills in learning how to learn.
- Promote cooperative and collaborative learning.
- Be sensitive to the culture and diversity of teachers as learners, using a multifaceted approach to respond to different learning styles, opportunities, environments, and starting points.
- Enable learning independent of time and place.

Integration of ICT and Teacher Education

The most critical factor in the successful integration of ICTs into teacher education is the extent to which the teacher educators have the knowledge and skills for modeling the use of ICTs in their own teaching practices. To enable them to develop these skills requires a well conceive and sustained programme of professional development. Countries that have initiated efforts to infuse ICTs into teacher education have found four professional development strategies helpful in successful technology integration.

- First, professional development needs to focus on teaching and learning rather than on hardware and software. It should be designed by first considering what student teachers are expected to know and be able to do in a specific discipline, and then infusing ICTs into the learning process so that acquiring the knowledge and skills is more efficient.

- Second, professional development is practically useless unless leaders and teacher educators are provided with access to technology resources and have the time and support—when needed—to apply the new knowledge and skills that they have learned. A just-in-time approach to professional development is a model that works well. In this approach, professional development is provided to teacher educators when they have a need or opportunity to use a specific technology tool or application to enhance learning.
- Third, professional development in the use of ICTs is not a one-time activity. To keep current with new developments means that professional development in ICTs must be an ongoing process.
- Fourth, professional development starts by providing ICT competencies to a small group of teaching staff. Perhaps this group will have volunteered or demonstrated that they have basic ICT competencies for personal use, or have expressed personal interest in using ICTs in their teaching. Working with this small group allows the professional development staff to determine the specific interests and needs of the teacher educators and what works best in the professional development process.

Professional development may be provided to other small groups of faculty, thus expanding and refining the professional development efforts. The most important criterion for effective professional development is to tailor it to the learning needs and skill levels of individual teaching staff within a faculty. This suggests that, ideally, an institution should be based on availability of resources, and provided a variety of options for professional development of faculty.

Professional Development Stages for ICT

Teachers and teacher educators develop ICT Competence through different stages. Those who are fluent with technology may not appreciate how difficult it is for technology novices to appropriate ICTs into their professional practice. Teacher educators often find this task even more difficult than teachers do, because they typically have higher levels of content and pedagogical expertise that must be respected. Teacher educators, because they have to work in multiple contexts—both the home institution and the field where students are placed to observe and practice teaching—may also be more influenced by the absence of the essential conditions for ICTs in teacher education. In the beginning of professional development stages for ICT, each individual is required to be aware ofICT applications, and the appropriate response at this stage is to provide information about a relevant application of ICTs and appropriate ways that it may be used in the individual's current professional personal concerns.

Teacher educators then explore the use of the application. They need support to put this ICT application into practice in a timely manner and to reflect on its effectiveness. Only after teacher educators have gone through these stages are they able to adapt their practice to make better use of ICTs, and then move toward the final stage to become innovators and modelers of excellent practice for their students and colleagues.

The advent of ICTs provides the opportunity to engage in this process from a new perspective and to model processes of learning for colleagues and students. It is acceptable for teacher educators to adopt only those aspects of ICTs that are relevant to their practice, but they must first be allowed to explore the range of possibilities, so that they and their students may become critically aware of, and competent in, diverse ICT applications. Of course, any teacher educator will continually strive to be responsive to developments and innovations in education within and beyond his discipline. To understand the strategies of professional development it is important to understand how they are embedded in the broader context of the planning and implementation of ICTs in teacher education. Teacher educators need to develop competence in the core themes of: pedagogy, collaboration, and networking, technical competence, and social issues. This needs to be done within the local and global cultural contexts of: lifelong learning, leadership and vision, and planning and management of change.

Frameworks for Integration of ICT for Professional Development of Teacher Educators

Collis and Moonen, 2001 (cited in Davis and Kirschner, 2003) elaborate on the goals of professional *learning about ICT* as centered on learning *how to use ICT* and learning *with ICT*. When learning *how to use ICT*, the instructional focus is on the use of products in or outside the classroom. In learning *with ICT*, instruction is presented and distributed primarily through 'web environments or with systems offering an integrated range of tools to support learning and communication' (*ibid.* 128). Davis and Kirschner, (2003) clarify the distinction between the role of ICT as a *core* and a *complementary (supplementary)* technology for professional learning settings. A *core technology* role refers to 'the principle way of organizing the learning experience'. In contrast, a *complementary technology* role is 'optional serving a valuable function but able to be compensated for via the core technology if so needed, or dropped altogether if not functioning or feasible' (*ibid*: 128).

A synthesis of the two dimensions of ICT integration combining the roles and activity sets is presented in Figure 14.1.

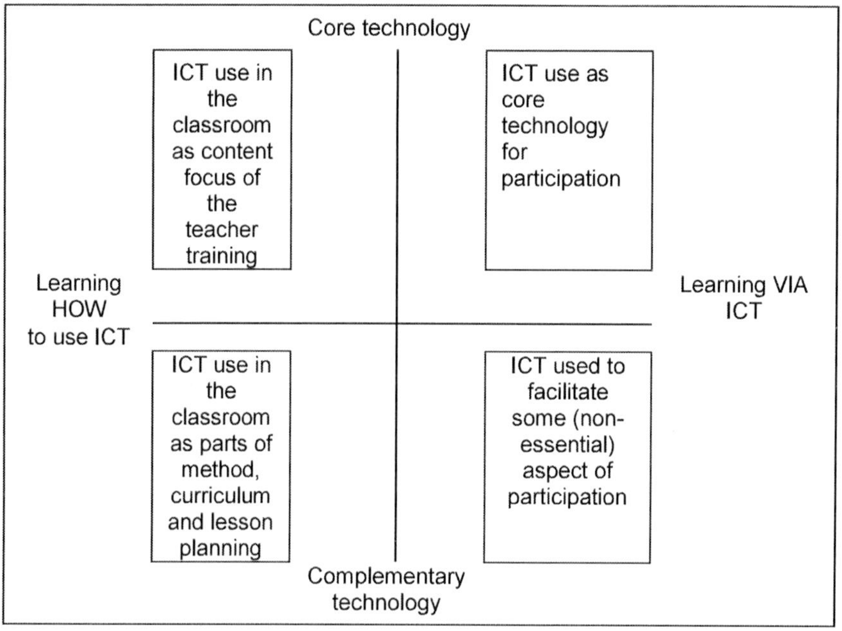

Fig. 14.1: Two dimensions of *ICT integration* in Teacher Professional Development

Source: Collis and Moonen 2001, cited in Kirschner and Davis, 2003.

Frameworks of Integration of ICT: An Institutional Perspective

Pulkinnen (2009) explains that ICT is more a process than a tool, and in the context of ICT innovations, 'ICT innovation is more a new process to be developed than a technology (a tool) to be applied' (ibid. online). Benchmarking ICT innovation in TPD programmes in a meaningful way would require institutions to articulate clearly the new process around which the benchmarks will cohere. Jochems, van Merrienboer and Koper (2004 cited in Robertson, 2008) propose that a new process for ICT integration needs to address organizational, technological and pedagogical perspectives. The benchmarks of an institutional technology management plan can be independently developed from the benchmarks of the management plan for teaching and learning. If an institution is unable to establish a coherent relational approach to technology integration that is driven by its policy and vision definition (Table 14.1), ICT planning activities may often overlook the needs of students and teachers (Ellis and Moore, 2006).

Table 14.1: Three Approaches for ICT Integration in Teacher Professional Development

Policy and Vision	Technology Literacy	Knowledge Deepening	Knowledge Creation
Curriculum & Assessment	Basic Knowledge	Knowledge Application	21st Century Skills
Pedagogy	Integrate Technology	Complex Problem Solving	Self Management
ICT	Basic Tools	Complex Tools	Pervasive Technology
Organization & Administration	Standard Classroom	Collaborative Groups	Learning Organizations
Teacher Professional Development	Digital Literacy	Manage & Guide	Teacher as model Learner

Source: UNESCO 2008c

The UNESCO (2008c) Information and Communication Technology—Competency Standards for Teacher's (ICT-CST) project attempts to bridge both mainstream and ICT specialist domains in a holistic framework for a modular continuum of ICT integration in all TPD programmes—moving from *technology literacy*, through to *knowledge deepening* to *knowledge creation* purposes which develop increasing capacity for teacher empowerment in the utilization of ICT as a tool to enhance the quality of learning (Fig. 14.1).

Approaches to Integration of ICT for Professional Development of Teacher Educators

For successful integration of ICT in teacher education programmes, the teacher educators must understand the following approaches and their applications in their day to day life professional activities. These activities require practical ICT integration skills in the part of teacher educators.

1. ***Online Course:*** The courses which are completely taught via Internet are called as online courses. These courses are useful for both on-campus and off campus learners. The very strong point of online course is that students can take anytime at any place. To produce online course material a teacher educator required to first assembling and writing contents, then produce in internet with the help of content development software.
2. ***Online Journals (Cyber Journals):*** Theoretically, a journal is a personal story or diary. So it offers people a place to document their

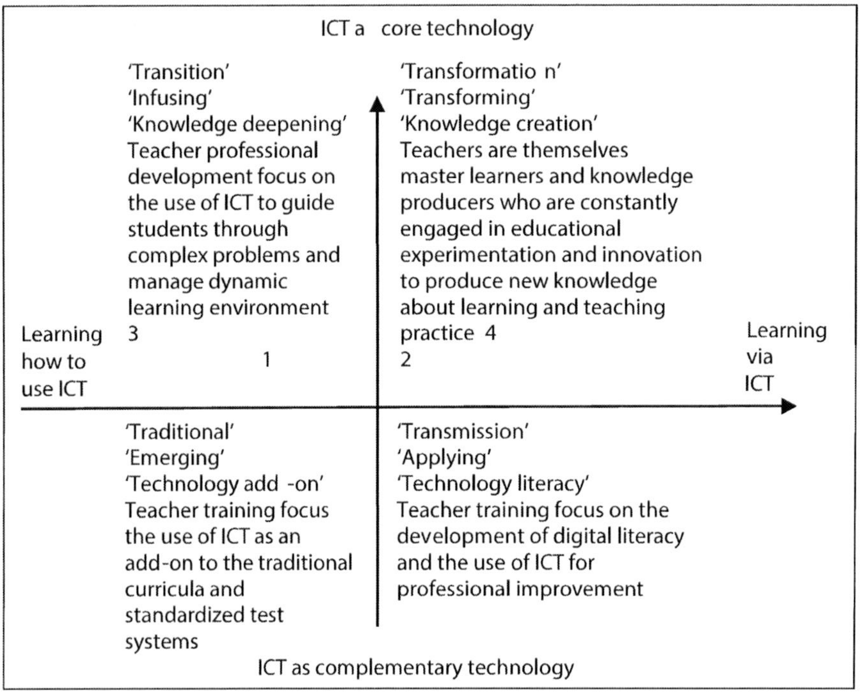

Fig. 14.2: A consolidated continuum of approaches for ICT Integration in Teacher Professional Development

lives. One of the largest online journals is Diarist.net established in 1998, available at www.diarist.net. One can check many online journals through the links i.e. http://www.aiims.edu/aiims/library/Listofjournal.htm.

3. ***E-books and E- libraries:*** Through Digital Library our knowledge becomes globalized and we can access any book in the form of e-book. Electronic books offer creative possibilities for expanding access as well as changing learning behaviour and academic research. In an e-book content can always be accessible, regardless of time or place, to be read on PCs or on portable book-readers. Books here never go out of print, and new editions can be easily created. One can carry several titles at once on a portable reader and, over the time build a personal library. Features such as full text searching, changeable font size, mark-up, citation creation, and note taking will enhance usability. Print text can be integrated with multi-dimensional objects, sound, and film to create a whole new kind of monographic work.

4. ***Web2.0 Tools:*** Web2.0 refers to the so-called second generation of Web based communities. The term Web 2.0 is commonly associated with web applications that facilitate interactive information sharing interoperability, user- centered design, and collaboration on the World Wide Web. A Web 2.0 site allows its users to interact with other users or to change website content, in contrast to non-interactive websites where users are limited to the passive viewing of information that is provided to them. Web 2.0 technologies are created around the idea that the people who access and consume the web content should not passively absorb what's available; rather, they should be active contributors. These are Web-based utilities and technology tools that focus on social, collaborative, user driven content and applications which facilitate a more socially connected Web. The Web provides access to resources of information, encourages meaningful interactions with content; and brings people together to challenge, support, or respond to each other. There are a number of Web-based services and applications that demonstrate the foundations of the Web 2.0 concept, and they are already being used to a certain extent in education. These are not really technologies as such, but services (or user processes) built using the building blocks of the technologies and open standards that underpin the Internet and the Web. These include blogs, wikis, multimedia sharing services, content syndication, podcasting and content tagging services. Details list of some web 2.0 technologies along with its description and example are given below.
   - *Wiki:* Wiki is a piece of server software that allows users to freely create and edit web page content using any Web browser and are often used to create collaborative websites. The examples of wikis with URL are: Wikispace - www. Wikispaces.com; Twiki – http://twiki.org/; Wetpaint - http://www. Wet paint.com/.
   - *Blog*: A blog is a type of website, usually maintained by and individual with regular entries of commentary. The examples of blogs with URL are: Edublog http://edublogs.org/; Twitter – http://twitter.com/; Wordpress http://wordpress. org/; Livejournal http://www.livejournal.com/
   - *Podcast/Vodcast*: A podcast is a series of digital media files, usually either digital audio or video, distributed over the internet for playback on a mobile device or a personal computer. Example, Gcast - http://www.gcast.com; Podbean - http://podbean.com/; Gabcast - http://gabcast.com/index.php.
   - *Document and multimedia Sharing*: Online facility to create, edit and share documents, graphics, presentation and multimedia for collaboration. Examples of document and multimedia sharing

are: Teachertube – www.teachertube.com; Schooltube - http://www.schooltube.com/; Scribd – http://www.scribd.com; You-tube, Slideshare, Flickr.

- *Web Conferencing*: Web conferencing is used to conduct live meetings, training, or presentations in which each participants connected to other participants via the internet. Yugma, Palbee, ivist, webex are the examples of web conferencing.
- *E-mail/news Groups*: Make it easy for groups to hold conversations and share files using email and the web for public discussions, and secure private groups for team collaboration. Examples, Tgethr, e-mail collaboration, e-pals, yahoo groups etc.
- *Social Networking:* A social network focuses on building online communities of people who are able to share interests, build on-line profiles, share information, pictures, blog entries, music clips, etc. Examples, Orkud, bing, classroom 2.0, Google wave etc.
- *Social bookmarking:* Social bookmarking is the practice of saving bookmarks to a web site and 'tagging' them with keywords and is a popular way to store, classify, share and search links. Examples, Stumbleupon, Delicious, Buzka etc.

5. ***Online Faculty Exchange Programme:*** To enable the faculties to acquire new information and skills, to bring to their home institutions a general awareness of different environments which are relevant to their teaching areas, and to expand experiences with the objective of improving their professional expertise, online faulty exchange programme help a lot.
6. ***Webinar:*** The term webinar stands for Web-based seminar. A webinar is a presentation, lecture, workshop or seminar that is transmitted over the web. The key feature of a webinar is its interactive elements- the ability to give, receive and discuss information. Contrast with web-cast, in which the data transmission is one way and does not allow interaction between presenter and audience.
7. ***Teleconference:*** A teleconference is a meeting or conference held via a telephone or network connection between participants in remote cities or work sites. It involves the exchange of audio, video, and data among participants. Similarly, the term teleconference can also refer to a live event that is transmitted via satellite to various locations. Email is a common example of a computer teleconference.
8. ***Online Research Guidance:*** This interactive guide helps the user to locate records that may contain ancestral information, and provides details on where to find them.

9. ***Online Learning:*** Online Learning allows for flexibility of access, from anywhere and usually at anytime. Essentially it allows participants to collapse time and space. The learning materials for online learning are designed properly with learners need and learning focus. Hence online learning have high authenticity (i.e. facilitate students to learn in the context of workplace), high interactivity, and collaboration.
10. ***Online Community:*** Online Community is a gate way to keep people coming back to your Web site. Community consists of forums, chat rooms, calendars, and other tools. It helps the readers return to your site again and again.
11. ***E- Tutoring:*** E- Tutoring refers to the process of tutoring within an online virtual environment or networked environment where teachers and learners are separated by time and space. In the context of education it involves the use of learning management system or virtual learning environment such as Moodle, Sakai, WebCT Blackboard etc.
12. ***Electronics Teaching Portfolio:*** An Electronic Portfolio uses multimedia technology allowing students/teachers to collect and organize portfolio artifact in many media types (audi, video, graphics, text) with hypermedia links connecting that evidence to the appropriate standards.

Conclusion

ICT integration is a comprehensive process of applying the emerging technologies to the educational processes to improve all aspects of education in general and teacher education in particular. Its success in teacher education programme depends not only on the availability of technologies, but also heavily on the professional development of teacher educators and their skills to use ICT. In this paper the need of ICT for Professional development of Teacher Educators, ICT integration frameworks, and different approaches to ICT integration are highlighted by the author to equip them with appropriate teaching learning skills through techno-pedagogical knowledge. It ultimately helps to achieve the goal of educational access for all in the 21st century.

REFERENCES

Anderson, J. and Glen. A, (2003). *Building Capacity of Teachers/Facilitators in Technology-Pedagogy Integration for Improved Teaching and Learning* [Online]. Available from UNESCO Bangkok at: http://www.unescobkk.org/fileadmin/user_upload/ict/e-books/ICT Buidling_Capacity/BuildingCapacity.pdf [Accessed 9 April 2012]

Ellis, R.A. and Moore, R.P. 2006. Learning through benchmarking: Developing a relational prospective approach to benchmarking ICT in Learning and Teaching.

Higher Education [Online]. 51 pp. 351-371. Available from: Academic Search Premier http://www.library.dcu.ie/Eresources/databases-az.htm [Accessed 26 August 2012]

Ganser, T. (2000). An ambitious vision of professional development for teacher. *NASSP bulletin*, 84 (618), pp. 16-12.

Glatthorn, A. (1995). *Teacher development*. Anderson, L. (Ed.), International encyclopedia of teaching and teacher education (second edition). London: Pergamon press.http://www. teachersn.com/general/ict-for-teacher-education.html: *ICT for Teacher Education*. [Accessed on 1st August 2012].

Kirschner, P. and Davis, N. (2003). Pedagogic benchmarks for information and communications technology in teacher education. *Technology, Pedagogy and Education* [Online]. 12(1) pp. 125–147. Available from Academic Search Premier http://www.library.dcu.ie/Eresources/databases-az.htm [Accessed 15 April 2012]

Mishra, D.C., and Mohanty, R.R., (2010). *Professional Development and ICT: Constructivist Perspective*. Package on ICT Mediated Constructivist Learning for the Professional Development of Teacher Educators: RIE (NCERT), Bhubaneswar.

Pulkkinen, J. (2009). Preliminary Conclusions and the Way Forward. *IN: UN Global Alliance for ICT and Development Expert Group Web-Forum*. 11 March 2009 [Online]. Available from GAID at: http://un-gaid.ning.com/forum/topics/preliminary-conclusions-and-1 [Accessed 28 September 2009]

Robertson, I. 2008. Sustainable e-learning, activity theory and professional development. IN: *Proceedings ascilite Melbourne 2008, November 30 – December 3* [Online]. Available from: http://www.ascilite.org.au/conferences/melbourne08/procs/index.htm [Accessed 06 January 2012]

Shafika, (2006). *Towards a GeSCI Initiative on Teacher Professional Development in Africa*. Dublin: GeSCI

UNESCO, (2008b). ICT Competency Standards for Teachers: Policy Framework [Online]. Available from UNESCO at: http://cst.unesco-ci.org/sites/projects/cst/The% 20Standards/ICT-CST-Policy%20Framework.pdf [Accessed 11 April 2012]

UNESCO, (2008c). ICT Competency Standards for Teachers: Implementation Guidelines [Online]. Available from UNESCO at: http://unesdoc.unesco. org/images/0015/001562/156209E.pdf [Accessed 11 April 2012]

15
Blended Learning in Teacher Education: A Viable Option

Sonal Chabra and ***Chetna Bajwa***

Since independence India has been a witness to considerable progress in school education through several efforts. Two major developments in the recent years have been the political recognition of Universalisation of Elementary Education (UEE) as a legitimate demand and the State commitment towards UEE in the form of the Right of Children to Free and Compulsory Education Act, 2009. Besides continuous efforts like Operation Blackboard (OBB) 1986, and the District Primary Education Programme (DPEP) 1995, SSA in 2002 and RMSA in the current decade have increased the demand manifold for qualified school teachers both at elementary and secondary level. Besides, there is a backlog of untrained teachers in the system, which also has to be tackled with. The teacher education programme in the country has to address the need of supplying well qualified and professionally trained teachers in larger numbers in the coming future. Given the problems of inadequate quality in most schools due to poor infrastructure and insufficient and poorly equipped teachers, the need for addressing the professional education of teachers acquires great importance.

All these factors in combination with the market forces have also led to a large scale mushrooming of teacher education institutions and programmes across the country. The number of courses offered at different stages – pre-primary, elementary and secondary – face-to-face and distance modes of teacher education; programmes of M.Ed, face-to-face and distance modes, C.P.Ed., B.P.Ed. and M.P. Ed. have increased from 3,489 courses in 3,199 institutions in March, 2004 to a whopping 14,428 courses in 11,861 institutions in March 2009. The student intake has likewise increased from 2,74,072 to 10,96,673 during this period (NCFTE, 2009). This expansion has inadvertently come with a disregard to the quality parameters.

It is both at pre-service and in-service level, that the education of teachers is a major area of concern. Since both public and private institutions are engaged in the process of pre-service teacher education, there needs to be improved and differently regulated mechanisms. Similarly, systems for in-service training require expansion and major reform that allow for greater flexibility. Besides there are other curricular and programme concerns like wide variation in the status of teachers and the need for teachers at different levels of school education across the country. All this makes it imperative to develop a broad framework that can address some of the crucial issues common to teacher education across different levels. Amongst this discussion of the concerns and issues, is needed a mention of the necessity of the different approaches to be evolved to educate a large number of teachers in a qualitative manner. Blended learning approach can be one such option for trained and skilled teacher workforce. At this juncture it is essential to understand the nature of blended learning and its dynamics in the teacher education programme in Indian settings.

Blended Learning

E-learning, on-line learning and blended learning are terms that have penetrated the system and in a way have changed the face of traditional teaching. Though they have been interchangeably used at several points, however, they mean different things. Blended Learning in simple words is a combination of multiple approaches to learning. Blended learning can be accomplished through the use of 'blended' virtual and physical resources. A typical example of this would be a combination of technology-based materials and face-to-face sessions used together to deliver instruction. In different contexts, different definitions have been proposed to explain the concept. Purnima Valiathan (2002) has defined blended learning as the term "used to describe a solution that combines several different delivery methods, such as collaboration software, Web-based courses, Electronic Performance Support System (EPSS) and knowledge management practices. Blended Learning also is used to describe learning that mixes various event-based activities, including face-to-face classrooms, live e-learning and self-paced learning".As per the words of Graham, C.R. (2005) blended learning is a blending of different learning methods, techniques and resources and applying them in an interactively meaningful learning environment. Researchers have developed the following definition for Blended Learning in higher education: "Blended Learning is learning that is facilitated by the effective combination of different modes of delivery, models of teaching and styles of learning, and founded on transparent communication amongst all parties involved with a course".

Blended learning combines face-to-face learning with on-line learning with a goal to provide the most efficient and effective instructional experience by combining several delivery modalities. Here teacher or lecturer uses multimedia teaching objects to improve his teaching efficiency so that better learner differentiation may be applied. Using the teaching objects which constitute the backbone of class activities, the conducting lecturer prepares the students, then plays the animated tutor like teaching objects and assesses students' understanding via a range of online activities or exercises. It should not be myopically seen as reshaping an enhancing the traditional classroom or about making e-learning more acceptable. It recognizes the strengths of integrating verbal and text-based communication and creates a unique fusion of synchronous and asynchronous, direct and mediated modes of communication in that the proportion of face-to-face and online learning activities may vary considerably.

Blended learning is not an addition that simply builds another expensive educational layer. It is the thoughtful fusion of face-to-face and online learning experiences. The basic principle is that face-to-face oral communication and online written communication are optimally integrated such that the strengths of each are blended into a unique learning experience congruent with the context and intended educational purpose. Most important, blended learning is a fundamental redesign that transforms the structure of, and approach to, teaching and learning.

In essence, it can be said that blended learning has to be viewed as a planned combination of online learning and face-to-face instruction using a variety of learning resources. Its basic assumption is to open the educational mind to a full range of possibilities. It must be based on a sound understanding of the learning environments, communication characteristics, requirements of various disciplines and resources available. There have been discrete efforts in Indian setting where the blended learning approach has been successfully used. Yeshwantrao Chavan Maharashtra Open University offers e-B.Ed (as the course is referred to) as a pioneering effort in teacher education. Through a distributed classroom, on-line workshops and interviews, podcast of lectures, blogs, discussion forums and whiteboards, along with face-to-face interaction is being used in this course.

***Potential Constituents of a Blended Learning Approach*:** The notion of blending is nothing new. Good classroom teachers have always blended their methods; reading, writing, lecture, discussion, practice and projects, to name just a few, are all part of an effective blend. As has already been discussed, blended learning arrangements tend to combine an electronic learning component with some form of human intervention; the constituents may vary in different settings. As is clear, the medium is not limited to technology and can include:

- Stand-alone, Asynchronous, or Synchronous online learning/training
- Performance support tools (knowledge management tools)
- Traditional classroom, Labs, or other 'hands-on' experiences
- Reading assignments, CD-ROM or other self-paced learning
- Teletraining/Telelearning, or Other media

In the Table 15.1, there are are different types of learning that may be used:

Table 15.1: Types of Learning

Live face-to-face (formal) * Instructor-led classroom * Workshops * Coaching/mentoring * On-the-job (OTJ) training	**Live face-to-face (informal)** * Collegial connections * Work teams * Role modeling
Virtual collaboration/synchronous * Live e-learning classes * E-mentoring	**Virtual collaboration/asynchronous** * Email * Online bulletin boards * Listservs * Online communities
Self-paced learning * Web learning modules * Online resource links * Simulations * Scenarios * Video and audio CD/DVDs * Online self-assessments * Workbooks	**Performance support** * Help systems * Print job aids * Knowledge databases * Documentation * Performance/decision support tools

Source: Strategies for Building Blended Learning by Allison Rossett, Felicia Douglis, and Rebecca V. Frazee.

Some of these have been discussed below owing to their newness as a learning resource:

- *Video/DVD* - Blended learning can include technology as common place today as using a video/DVD clip, segment, or movie. Videos used in classroom settings, regardless who produced them, can be educational, promotional, training, event, and evaluative.
- *Virtual Field Trips* - Blended learning Virtual Field Trips can be used in any number of ways to serve a variety of educational goals. Using blended learning through the virtual fieldtrip is a wonderful opportunity. The virtual fieldtrip experience is an excellent model of a teaching strategy that was not possible before the advent of computers in the classroom.
- *Interactive Websites* - Blended learning often includes the use of interactive websites. The use of interactive web sites requires computer and internet access in the learning situation. These sites provide another opportunity for teachers to use technology in their classroom, thus promoting blended learning. Interactive websites can be utilized within the class for those students who do not have internet access and can give other students the opportunity to expand knowledge if access is available privately.

- *Websites for Teachers* - Classroom websites help facilitate the creation of a blended learning environment. Teachers use classroom websites to post assignments, receive homework submissions, administer tests, and post grades and classroom policies. Teachers also use classroom websites as the medium to link to blended learning sites such as external websites, videos, software, graphics, audio feeds, and virtual field trips.
- *Course Management Systems* - The use of a Course Management System (CMS) can assist a teacher when he or she is creating a blended learning environment in the classroom. In addition to using a classroom website to communicate and administer classroom activities (as described in the previous section), a CMS can better assess student work, share course content and help develop a community among the teacher, students, and parents. A CMS allows for the administration of blended activities into the classroom through various tools included with the software.
- *Synchronous and Asynchronous Discussions* - Blended learning combines technology with face to face instruction. Synchronous and asynchronous discussions are both types of internet communication that can be utilized in blended learning to fulfill the technology requirement. Both synchronous and asynchronous discussions utilize the internet to provide forums for use by the classroom teacher to either give instructions or facilitate conversation among students that would normally take place in a classroom setting. Asynchronous and synchronous discussions can be teacher or student led and can be guided by a pre-set format or take place in a more open setting, just like a classroom discussion. While both synchronous and asynchronous discussions have advantages and disadvantages, their use together in a blended learning situation is critical to the development of the online learning community.
- *Blogs* - Blog is a term coined for the combination of two words, web and log. As part of a blended learning project, it is an asynchronous form of online discussion. A blog is a publicly accessible website which contains a journal or diary of sorts. Anyone can initiate a blog either as a part of another website or personal web page or a blog can stand alone. The author of the blog can choose to write in this journal as she pleases with no filters or censorship. Blogs span a wide variety of topics. There are reportedly over 11 million blogs on the web. Blogs offer a forum for many people to state their opinions or comment on other's opinions. Blogs could provide a great medium to enhance student writing through the use of technology.

The success of a blend largely depends on the right mix of the elements. A good blend would provide optimum role of live interaction. It is essential to provide a good support and training model and should keep the cultural components in mind. A successful blend would strike the right balance between innovations and mass utility. Some of the basic factors which should be considered in identifying the blend are:

- Course instructional goals
- Student profile
- Hours of learning/training
- Teacher experience and teaching style
- Cultural dimensions
- Resource availability
- Budgetary requirement for training implementation

Advantages of Blended Learning for Teacher Education Programmes

Blended learning, the design approach whereby both face-to-face and online learning are made better by the presence of other, offers the possibility of retaining traditional values of teacher education while meeting the demands and needs of the twenty first century. The blended-learning approach attempts to improve the effectiveness and efficiency of learning by combining different instruction design methods and delivery modes. All levels of education have been researched with blended learning, from the elementary school grades up to graduate school and all have shown positive results. Blended learning, if used in teacher education would offer the following advantages:

- One clear advantage of blended learning in education is its connection with differentiated instruction. Differentiated instruction involves "custom-designing instruction based on student needs." In differentiated instruction, educators look at students' learning styles, interests, and abilities. Once these factors have been determined, educators decide which curriculum content, learning activities, products, and learning environments will best serve those individual students' needs. Blended learning can fit into a number of these areas. By using blended learning, educators are definitely altering the learning environment when students work collaboratively in learning communities online, for example. Teachers could also add relevant curriculum content that would be unavailable or difficult to comprehend outside the internet. Learning activities and products can also be changed to use technologies in a classroom that uses blended learning. This becomes essential for a teacher education course like B.Ed where the entry level of pupil teachers is very different owing to their different educational backgrounds.

- Another advantage of blended learning is pacing and attendance. Blended learning classrooms offer the possibility of study whenever the pupil teacher chooses to do so. If a pupil teacher is absent, she/he may view some of the missed materials at the same time the rest of the class does, even though the pupil-teacher cannot be physically present in the classroom. This would help pupil teacher stay on track and not fall behind, which is especially helpful for pupil teachers with prolonged sicknesses or injuries that prevent them from attending colleges. These "self-study modules" also allow learners to review certain content at any time for help in understanding a concept or to work ahead for those pupil teachers who learn at a faster pace.
- Because of the ability of pupil teachers to self-pace, there is a higher completion rate for pupil teachers in blended learning classrooms than for those in strictly distance learning situations. This self-pacing allows for the engagement of every learner in the classroom at any given time. Pupil teachers also see that the learning involved becomes a process, not individual learning events. This revelation allows for an increased application of the learning done in the classroom by the prospective teachers.
- Different researches make it clear that using blended learning in education improves the teaching and learning done in a given course. Educators want to teach in a way that best reaches all of their pupil teachers. If blended learning accomplishes this, then more teachers will begin to use these methods. When teachers begin to explore blended learning and the resources that can be found through the internet and other technologies, they can structure their classroom in a way that best suits their teaching style and their students' learning styles.
- Blended learning approach provides room for the development of autonomy, self-efficacy and individual organisational skills since it gives scope for self-regulated learning. Blended learning can offer good opportunities to foster self-regulated skills (Dettori, 2007). The mentioned skills are essential to be acquired by any prospective teacher for their future roles.
- Teacher educators that have been teaching for numerous years may be stuck in their traditional teaching methods. Blended learning offers possibilities for teacher educators to use technology literate which in turn limits what they can do with technology. The prospective teachers if exposed, and trained would use blended learning in their post training classrooms successfully. The teachers may use a variety of teaching styles, but without technology the students are being cheated out of what they need to be successful in today's world. Proper teacher training is the only way teachers and students will get the best of both worlds.

Besides it offers pedagogical richness and ease of revision of the curriculum. The time has come to reject the dualistic thinking that seems to demand choosing between conventional face-to-face and online learning, a dualism that is no longer tenable theoretically and practically. There is a better approach. With the increasing awareness and adoption of the Internet and communication technology to connect learners, a more sensible way forward would be to better understand the potential of these technologies and how they might be integrated with the best of face-to-face learning environment. Sonkambl, C. and Pagare, P. (2010) in their work found that blended learning represents a real opportunity to create learning experience that can provide the right place for each and every individual in school and universities and even at home, it can be truly universal, crossing global boundaries and bringing groups of learners together through different cultural settings become one of the most significant development of the 21st century.

Challenges in Blended Learning in Teacher Education Setting

With the emerging new technologies, the teaching profession is evolving from an emphasis on teacher-centered, lecture-based instruction to student-centered, interactive learning environments. The teacher education indeed needs to prepare the teachers for the same. However, the adoption of blended learning approach in teacher education in India has to face some challenges such as the following:

1. ***Managing Instructional Complexity*:** In blended learning, the teacher educator has a wider choice of delivery mediums to combine. With that wider choice also comes greater complexity and pressure owing, to the variety of combinations of technology and possibly the lack of patterns to follow for that particular mix. In other words, finding the 'right' blend is the first challenge.
2. ***Managing the Roles and Responsibilities*:** Unlike traditional classroom learning in which there usually is a single teacher, in blended learning there may be multiple individuals, each taking a modality or role in the blend. Up front clarification of teacher and assistant roles is essential for success and the reduction of potential conflict and learner confusion.
3. ***Creating a Seamless Learning Experience:*** Good communications among different teachers and careful planning is another important element in the success of blended learning. It would be essential to maintain regular communication between the teachers and assistants communicate with one another throughout the instruction, not just before the course. Similarly, arranging learning objects to ensure each

segment reinforces the previously acquired knowledge or skill and introduces new concepts seamlessly in spite of the different modality of delivery.

4. ***Meeting Expectations:*** Management of expectations is also important for teachers and learners to realistically perceive the benefits and work to be performed during the training or course.
5. ***Managing Costs:*** Blended learning offers great flexibility and great effectiveness as it can chose the best medium for every objective; however, the challenge is to make the blend not only effective but also cost-efficient. The technological resource requirements to use such an approach are extensive, and would escalate the costs. Though in the long run it may prove to be cost-effective, the initial expenditure is a challenge in India where we do not have any stipulated budget for Teacher Education in the country's Annual Budget and otherwise also have limited resources at hand.
6. **Adapting the Culture to Accept Blended Learning Environments:** Limited technological skills and a negative attitude towards new technology among both the teacher educators and the pupil teachers is a big challenge for the successful adoption of the blended learning approach. One of the most difficult challenges of transforming a traditional class into a blended learning classroom requires a shift in an educator's teaching paradigm. Teachers and learners both would need to be accustoming with the different modalities.

The interest in blended learning can also be attributed to the advances and proliferation of communication technology in most segments of the society-advances that have not seen the same degree of uptake in the teacher education classroom. Although this is changing, there is still a lack of understanding how best to use technology to advance the goals of teacher education in terms of engaging pupil teachers in critical thinking and discourse.

Implications for Teacher Education Programmes

Blended learning is not something which is very new. What needs to be accepted is its potential to help fundamentally redesign the learning experiences in ways that can enhance the traditional values of teacher education in India.

Adopting Blended learning cannot be a one-shot affair. A lot of planning needs to be done before that. Some of the implications for teacher education classrooms are:

1. ***Restructuring the class:*** Instead of preparing the necessary materials for the off-line setting of a traditional classroom, the blended

learning teacher now must also organize and maintain the on-line, virtual classroom. The time, planning, and organization needed to restructure a blended classroom requires the educator to, in essence, plan and organize a class in two settings, which complement each other in terms of scheduling, content, lesson flow, and organization.

2. ***Training:*** Both the teachers and the pupil teachers would need to be trained to enhance their technological capabilities.
3. ***Administration:*** Organization of the syllabus, arranging the required resources, distributing/collecting material, and scheduling duties among teachers and assistants and likewise would comprise the additional administrative responsibilities on the institution.
4. ***Creative assessment:*** The adoption of the blended learning approach would necessitate different mechanisms of assessment like providing regular feedback, tracking student progress, and testing opportunities, which would need to developed.
5. ***Availability of technology:*** The availability of different modes of technology, say for example uninterrupted internet access, and servers with better capacity among others would need to be made.

Maximizing success in a blended learning initiative requires a planned and well-supported approach that includes a theory-based instructional model, high quality faculty development, course development assistance, learner support and ongoing formative and summative assessment.

Conclusion

There has been little fundamental change with regard to how we approach teaching and learning in teacher education, yet there is increasing dissatisfaction among the students, faculty and society at large with the quality of learning experience. Although the technological changes in the society have been unrelenting, technological innovation in teacher education has been largely restricted to administration. The technological innovations need to be applied to address the issue of access, and convenience as well as to address the relevance and quality of the learning experience. Blended learning is one potent solution which represents a shift in instructional strategy. The goal of blended learning is to use technology as a tool for learning and to promote a discovery-based approach to online learning. It is also intended to help students become "anytime, anywhere" lifelong learners. Keeping abreast of the technology is a challenge for teachers as well. The teacher needs to participate in ongoing professional development, read the latest research, and share ideas with other teachers. Blended learning can provide opportunities for teacher education at both pre-service and in-service levels.

REFERENCES

Allison Rossett, Felicia Douglis, and Rebecca V. Frazee (2003) *Strategies for Building Blended Learning,* http://www.learningcircuits.org/2003/jul2003/rossett.htm

Garrison, D.R. and Vaughan, N.D. (2008) *Blended learning in higher education: Framework, principles and guidelines,* John Wiley and Sons: USA.

Mohansundaram, K. and Kumaran, D. (2001). Web-based instruction: An innovative teaching strategy, *University News*, Vol. 39, No. 47, pp. 8-11.

Sonkambl, C. and Pagare, P. (2010). Use of blended learning approach in teacher education. In Z. Abas *et al.* (Eds.), *Proceedings of Global Learn Asia Pacific 2010* (pp. 3978-3981). AACE.

Talawar, M.S. and Pradeep Kumar, T. (2009). Podcasting: A new trend of web-based technology in education, *University News*, Vol. 47, No. 30, pp. 13-15.

Valiathan, P. (2002). "*Blended learning models*", ASTD Learning circuits, 2002 http://www.learningcircuits.org/

ACCESSED WEBSITES REFERRED

http://www.learningcircuits.org/

http://www.grayharriman.com/blended learning.htm

http://www.e-learningcentre.co.uk/eclipse/Resources/blended.htm

16
Role of ICT for Capacity Building of Teachers: An Analysis

Rajalakshmi Das

In recent decades information revolution is the major factor affecting the nation's economic growth. Globalization and democratization of information has made possible the access information to every one and everywhere. Though there is an abundance of information and good infrastructure, there is a lack of awareness as regards the optimum utilization of created information. There is an imbalance between the emphasis given to infrastructure development and enhancing human capability as these are critical components of any good information management systems. The institution or individuals who have access to information and can process that information effectively will have a competitive edge over others. According to Ives and Jarvenpaa (1993) "information requirements must be met by stitching together human skills and expertise with the threads of information and communication technology".

Capacity Building: The Concept

Capacity building of teachers is a complex function of economic, social and institutional factors. It is a way for groups or organizations to increase their ability to contribute. Capacity building involves expansion of human potential, enhancement of human functioning, widening range of activities and development of understanding and insight into the matters the teachers deal with and enabling them to make their thinking and belief operational. Capacity development is the "process by which individuals, groups, organizations, institutions, and societies develop abilities (individually or collectively) to perform function, solve problems and set and achieve objectives" (Ballantyne *et al.*).

Capacity building of teachers refers to the organization of all such programmes and activities and making provisional conditions that help the teachers to be capable of actualizing their thoughts and vision, operation of their ideas, conducting themselves in desired manner. Capacity building is a process of helping the teachers to develop in them (i) the capacity to understand their roles and responsibilities (cognitive) and (ii) the capacity to perform their duties and functions (functional) (Tripathy, 2005). It is an ongoing process to go along with regular activities of professional life. Accountability and participation of teachers in teaching, research, tutoring students and steering institutional affairs by the teachers shall be ensured to achieve quality and excellence. Teachers are required to update themselves to discharge their duties to meet the demands of students. Teachers have to place themselves at appropriate level to have command over the students. Capacity building programmes empower institutions and teachers to (i) assess their own information needs (ii) set their own priorities and (iii) build their own information system. Capacity building is not focusing on the people working in one particular organization but intends to the development of capacities of different people working in the same origination who share a same concern.

Levels of Capacity Building

Capacity building can take place at all levels of an organization or community and the major players in this process are as follows:

- **(i)** ***Information Producers:*** Scientific and technical personnel, database producers, consultants, writers and composers.
- **(ii)** ***Information Processors:*** Administrators and managers, policy formulators, decision makers and also the people in power. They sell the ideas to their peers and one often becomes the capacity builder himself.
- **(iii)** ***Information Custodians and Distributors:*** Professionals involved in knowledge transfer, such as educators, teachers, librarians and communication and media personnel.
- **(iv)** ***Ultimate beneficiaries:*** The users. They have to be involved in the process (Lim –1999).

Process of Capacity Building

Process of capacity building includes the following:

- **(i)** ***Potential Development:*** It deals with development of knowledge, understanding, vision, skills, competencies etc.
- **(ii)** ***Attitude Promotion:*** It deals with development of willingness, motivation, arousal of need for status and recognition, ego and integrative need, self actualization need etc. and

(iii) ***Infrastructure Building*** for creation of conditions that facilitate operation and functionality (Tripathy, 2005).

Aspects of Capacity Building

Capacity building is entirely dependent on the sustainable development of the institution. Administrative and Academic developments are two important aspects of capacity building. Teachers have a positive role to play in formulation of processes of modernization in admission procedure, examination affairs and office record-keeping system, as a part of capacity building exercise to keep pace with the modern office management system.

As a part of academic capacity building, the teachers need to play an important role for developing classroom teaching, its methods, as well as developing teaching materials and updating laboratories for enhancing skill components (Bhattacharya, 2005). Students' progression is another important constituent for capacity building. It needs constant monitoring by teachers about the performance of students in the class and also in different examinations and class tests. Progression of students also depends on their participation in societal activities and the teachers have a role to play for motivating the students for such activities.

An institution's capacity building can be enhanced through inter activity and linkages among faculties of other institutions. In this changing world, networking and connectivity through inter activity is the prime need of the hour for capacity building. In this context, UGC's initiative of networking of libraries of Universities and colleges may be of great help.

Need for Capacity Building of Teachers

Application of information technology and changing role of media will offer more interaction and would cater to various styles of learning and improving efficiency. With the impact of globalization, privatization, liberalization, integration of world economy and world education, e-learning world with networking through internet, emerging technological revolution and growth of inter connectedness, education of 21st century will take its new shapes in terms of objectives, content, methods of learning and management of learning. Therefore the shift in teachers will be as teachers from seeing themselves as users of knowledge to stimulators of knowledge. Certain capacities are required to be built among the teachers for enabling them to face the challenges in the real world, in their professional career and also facilitate their participation in the task of national development. The capacity of accumulation, assimilation and management of knowledge and information, the capacity of research or enquiry, the capacity for creativity and innovation—particularly the creative transfer of knowledge, the capacity to use high technology, the capacity for leadership are required.

Education system around the world are under increasing pressure to use the Information and Communication Technologies (ICTs) to reach students the knowledge and skills they need in the 21st century. The UNESCO World Education Report (1998) 'Teachers and Teaching in a changing world' describes the radical implications the new information and communication technologies have for conventional teaching and learning. It predicts the transformation of the teaching-learning process and the way teachers and learners gain access to knowledge and information. If future citizens are to maximize the power of ICT, teachers, the curriculum and the schools are critical elements because it is the school's responsibility to teach students the essentials of the accepted content knowledge, essential skills to utilize ICT and the attitude and abilities to become life long learners. The following essential conditions must be met in order to effectively harness the power of ICT to improve learning:

- Students and teachers must have access to digital technologies and the Internet in their classrooms, schools and teacher education institutions.
- High quality, meaningful and culturally responsive digital content must be available for teachers and learners.
- Teachers must have knowledge and skills to use the new digital tools and resources to help all students achieve high academic standards (UNESCO, 2002).

Role of ICT for Capacity Building of Teachers

ICT can play a tremendous role in the capacity building of teachers as follows:

- Development of website for each subject.
- Preparation of CD by eminent teachers for building further capacity.
- Developing digital Library.
- Organization of video conferences among the teachers.
- Teachers can conduct surveys with online medium.
- Providing the disciplinary knowledge about the subject as well as interdisciplinary research.
- Appropriate methods like training and impact assessment should form a part of the training. This would enrich capacity building and lead to greater utilization of expertise and knowledge.
- Capacity building can be accomplished by mutually beneficial inter-personal relationships. Networks of professionals, free exchange and mobilization of information, establishment of centre of excellence are excellent strategies for building capability.

- Introducing ICT tools such as Internet, e-books, software, e-content etc. in the curriculum and enhancing knowledge through the use of them.
- Implementation of adequate strategies for teachers such as proper interaction with students by use of ICT tools, use of journals or research in classroom learning, proper planning and organization of instructional design etc.
- Proper management of classroom learning through the use of ICT tools.
- Proper evaluation of learning and adequate feedback programme for teachers.
- Diagnostic and remedial teaching through video conferencing.
- Organization of sufficient in-service training programmes for teachers relating to the ICT in teaching and learning.
- Organizing seminars and workshops on ICT based instructions etc.

Conclusion

UNESCO has taken concrete steps for using ICT for capacity building. UNESCO highlighted ICT portal for teachers, which provides a gateway to Internet resources and websites for the teachers to enhance their teaching. UNESCO envisions that the ICT programme will result in an educational environment involving enriched curricula, resource sharing, quality multimedia material and a cadre of teachers who are competent in facilitating better learning with ICT. To conclude, the role of the teacher is now changed from being an instructor to a constructor, facilitator or creator of learning situation. Such role of a teacher can easily be played when he gets competencies in the skill of his teaching and acquiring knowledge and building his capacities.

REFERENCES

Ballantyne, P., Labelle, R. and Rudgard, S. Information and Knowledge Management: Challenges for Capacity Builders. (Policy Management Brief No. 11.) Retrieved from http://w.w.w. one world. org/ecdpm/pmb/bll-gb. htm.

Bhattacharya, A. (2005). The role of teachers in developing capacity building; in R.N. Roy (Ed.) Proceedings of national seminar on capacity building of teachers and role of teachers' organizations, Cuttack: I.G. Women's College.

Byadgi, G.G. and Karisiddappa, C.R. (2004). Information empowerment and capacity building in IT era. *University News,* 42(22).

Ives, B., Jarvenpaa, S.L. (1993). Competing with information: empowering knowledge networks with information technology. Institute of Information Studies. The Knowledge Economy: The Nature of Information in the 21st Century, The Aspen Institute, Queenstown, MD.

Lim, E. (1999). "Human resource development for the information society" in Asian libraries. 8(5).

Tripathy, S. (2005). Capacity building of teachers and role of teachers organizations", in r.n. Roy (ed.) Proceedings of the national seminar on capacity building of teachers and role of teachers' organizations, Cuttack: I.G. Women's college.

UNESCO (2002). Information and communication technologies" in Teacher Education – a Planning Guide, Paris.

PART-III

Professional Developments, Curricular Issues and Frameworks for Implementation

17

Teacher Education Curriculum Reforms and Its Effectiveness

Peeyush Kumar Garg

Teachers are the greatest assets of any educational system of any country in the World. They stand for the transmission of various knowledge, skills and values. They are accepted as the backbone of our educational system. Teacher quality is, therefore, crucial and has been globally accepted to be significantly associated with the quality of education in general and student's learning outcomes in particular. The Education Commission (1964-66) of India accepted this influence of teachers in powerful words, "No system can rise above the status of its teacher…" Similar sentiments have been expressed by UNESCO report on *Teacher and Educational Quality: Monitoring Global Needs for 2015 (2006).* The European Commission Report 'Communication on Teacher Education' (2007) in the very beginning observes 'research shows that teacher quality is significantly and positively correlated with pupil attainment and it is the most important within school aspect explaining student's performance (40, p. 3). Teachers help in shaping and reshaping the society and determine the quality of life in the community and the nation. Experiences of various countries reveal that the most effective way to develop good teachers in a dynamic and changing environment is to begin with a well developed pre-service teacher education programme and continue with career long learning opportunities. Each society, therefore, makes some provision for pre-service education and continuous professional development of teachers in order to help them contribute in the growth of the society. There is ample empirical research evidence to suggest that student's achievement is significantly related to the professional preparation of teachers (Darling- Hammond, 2000a; Ferguson, 1991a; Goldhabar and Brewer, 2000).

The organization of teacher education in any system can be visualized at two levels. At the first level, the positioning of teacher education determines its nature. Teaching is a multifaceted and specialized activity, and therefore, is housed in single purpose Institutions in majority of countries around the world. The *second* level is the structure of curriculum i.e., what should be taught and how it should be taught? At this level, Schulman's (1987) conceptualization of teacher's knowledge provides the base of teacher education curriculum structure. According to Schulman (1987) a teacher should possess subject content knowledge, general pedagogical knowledge and the knowledge of educational contexts and goals; and should be able to use this knowledge creatively to deal with ever changing classroom situations. If we analyse teacher education systems in different countries from this perspective we will find majority of teacher education reform efforts centered on reforming the knowledge base of teachers and similarities can be observed in teacher education curriculum across various societies.

Policy for Teacher Education Curriculum Reform

The National Policy of Education (NPE, 1986) reflects this commitment by considering pre-service and in-service teacher education as a continuous process and two ends of a continuum. An analysis of the recommendations of various commissions, Committees and the Education Policy of India reveals the efforts of policy planners to bring qualitative improvement in teacher education system along with quantitative expansion of the facilities. Efforts have been made to make teacher education curricula responsive to the contextual needs of emerging Society, and break the isolation of teacher education institutions. In fact, the first two decades of the post independence period are characterized by significant efforts to break away from the colonial legacy, and modernize the teacher education curriculum along with the school curriculum. The concern for quality improvement of teacher education had been the top priority for educational planners which is reflected in the concerns expressed, and recommendations made by various Commissions and Committees appointed by the Government of India from time to time since independence.

The University Education Commission (1948), Secondary Education Commission (1953), Chattopadhyay Committee Report (1983-85), Acharya Ramamurthy Committee Report (1990) and several Seminars and study groups that were set up to discuss improvements in elementary and secondary teacher education from time to time expressed concern over the poor quality of teacher education and its isolation from both the main stream of university life and the ground realities of schools. These Commissions stressed on the need for flexibility and strongly felt that the whole teacher education programme needs to be remodeled to strike more balance between the theory and practice and assessment of student's performance. One of the important effort towards bringing qualitative improvement in education in general and teacher education in particular is the recommendations of Education Commission (1964-66).

This was the first Commission in the post independent India which comprehensively worked with all stages of education from pre-primary to higher level including the vocational and technical education etc. The Commission stated, "The essence of programme of teacher education is quality and in its absence, teacher education becomes, not only a financial waste but a source of overall deterioration in educational standards" (Para. 4.13; p. 72). Accepting that the existing teacher education programmes are largely divorced from the realities of schools, it recommended reorientation of subject knowledge; vitalization of professional studies and to root the entire curriculum in Indian conditions; development of special courses and programmes; and revision and improvement of curricula. The Commission stressed that the prospective teachers need courses which will help them to build up a proper perspective of life, of our cultural heritage, and, of problems and aspirations of the nation as well as of human culture, and civilization in general" (Para. 4.29; p. 75). It also emphasized the need for teacher education to be brought into the mainstream academic life (Para 4.04; p. 68) of universities and relate the curriculum closely to the teacher's responsibilities and to Indian conditions, problems and studies (Para. 4. 31; p. 75).

Later on, a Committee known as the Prof. Yash Pal Committee (1993), appointed to analyse the academic burden on students and unsatisfactory quality of learning expressed concern over the poor quality of teacher preparation programmes in the country which leads to unsatisfactory quality of learning in schools. This Committee also suggested restructuring of the course content of teacher education programmes to ensure its relevance to the changing needs of school education, longer duration of training, emphasis on self-learning and independent thinking and making whole teacher education programme more practicum-oriented (p. 26-27).

All these Commissions, Committees, and study groups expressed concern over the irrelevance of teacher education programme. However, in reality even after five decades the observation made by the Education Commission (1964-66) in this context that "Vitality and realism are lacking in the curriculum and programme of work which continue to be largely traditional with disregard for the present day need and objectives" (Para. 4 02; p. 68) remains relevant, though, a number of policy initiatives have been taken by the government, from time to time, to modernize and bring qualitative improvement in teacher education curriculum of the country.

National Curriculum Frameworks for Teacher Education (NCFTE)

Teacher development is considered as the continuous process of developing and maintaining professional competence in teachers through pre-service, induction training, in-service training and on-going professional development programmes. Pre-service is the first step in the ladder of developing professionalism in teachers that is in turn dependent on the professional preparation of teachers through well designed education courses suited to the needs of contemporary educational system.

Consequently, with changes in the curriculum framework for school education we find subsequent efforts to adjust the teacher preparation curricula accordingly. The first comprehensive attempt was made in 1978 with the publication "Teacher Education Curriculum: A Framework' by the National Council for Teacher education (NCTE), a non-statutory body located in the National Council of Educational Research and Training (NCERT). Major recommendations of this Framework included:

- Relevance of the curriculum to the personal and social needs of children and schools; as well as aspirations of people and ideology of nation.
- Flexibility within the framework of acceptable national goals and values. The Framework suggested that 'flexibility is urgently required not only to break the barriers between the stage wise teacher education programmes, but also, between different disciplines'. Flexibility for relevance, mobility and continuing education was emphasized.
- Interdisciplinary and integrated approach in teacher education curriculum should be so designed that integration among theory courses takes place, and this integrated pedagogical understanding flows into the skill dominated areas of methodology of teaching various subjects as well as into the attitude-building areas of work experience, health, physical and recreational education, along with social service.
- Task-oriented teacher education. Teacher education must be treated as an "exercise of training a teacher for handling a variety of tasks inside and outside the classroom."
- Reform in practice teaching. The framework suggested that student teachers should be put through a series of simulating, microteaching situations before being pushed into actual classrooms.
- Semester system was suggested to replace the yearwise course.
- Evaluation system to be made more reliable and valid.
- Promotion of research and experimentation in teacher education Institutions (Pp. 4-12).

On the lines of Kothari Commission, the Framework (1978) emphasized pre-practice teaching activities including simulated teaching and model lessons delivered by teacher educators, actual teaching through block teaching approach instead of delivering one lesson per day, and post teaching follow up by taking up related practical work in evaluation etc. Therefore, the duration of practice teaching was considerably increased. A significant feature of this framework was the conceptualization of paper—'teacher and education in emerging Indian society' replacing philosophical and sociological foundations of education, and the space provided for core training and skill developing programme. Another significant attempt to bring qualitative improvement and professionalize teacher education curricula was made in 1988.

The Curriculum Framework of 1988, developed against the backdrop of the National Policy on Education (1986), has significant implications for strengthening and restructuring the curricula of all the stages of teacher education. The changing role of teacher had been strongly emphasized in this framework as "The Future teacher will be a competent professional and a skilled teacher as always has been expected, but this will now mean that he will also need to be an effective communicator, a designer and user of learning resources, a learning facilitator, and active participant in community life".

The course content included:

(i) ***Foundation Courses***, emphasizing mainly the philosophical and social perspectives, and psychological bases of education at the stage concerned;
(ii) ***Stage-Relevant Specializations***, emphasizing understanding of the professional functions of the teacher in a general way relevant to the stage and competencies and skills of teaching relevant school subjects.
(iii) ***Field Work or Practicum***, emphasizing application of theory in classroom teaching and in the practical activities involving students, parents and the community.

With the establishment of the National Council for Teacher Education (NCTE) as a statutory body by an Act of Parliament in 1993, another 'Curriculum Framework for Quality Teacher Education' was bought out in 1998. While the 1978 Teacher Education Curriculum Framework was developed on the backdrop of 1975 school education curriculum reform, and 1988 framework on the backdrop of NPE1986, the 1998 Framework for teacher education preceded School Curriculum Framework which was developed by the National Council of Educational Research and Training (NCERT) in 2000. This framework (1998) tried to address and reflect on the changing international scenario as the result of globalization, privatisation, and communication technology etc.

In a major departure from earlier frameworks it accepted *commitment, competence, and performance* as guiding principles in developing curricula and programmes for teacher preparation. Teacher education curriculum responding to the regional needs of community, culture-specificity in pedagogy, and preparing teacher as life long learner had been stressed in this Framework. The trend analysis of teacher education curriculum in terms of content, duration transactional methodology and evaluation systems proposed by these frameworks reveals the efforts of curriculum planners to address the contemporary needs of Indian education system. While the 1978 Teacher Education Curriculum Framework stressed an explicit task-oriented approach, and reduction of theoretical component from teacher education curriculum, the 1988 Framework emphasized the need to incorporate and accommodate technological advances and knowhow, and indicated towards the changing role of teacher as an effective communicator, a designer, and user of learning resources, a learning facilitator, and an active participant in community life. The 1998 Framework provided a futuristic, dynamic and forward looking perspective in teacher education curriculum while reinforcing the indigenous culture and identity of the nation.

However, in spite of three curriculum frameworks, and recommendation of National Policy on Education (NPE, 1986) for complete overhauling of teacher education programmes (Para 9.4; p. 44) the teacher education system of the country is often criticized for its quality. In 1985, an important document '*The Challenges of Education,*' which preceded the NPE (1986) made the statement: "We are on the threshold of development of new technologies likely to revolutionize teaching in classroom. But unfortunately the process of updating the curricula of teacher education has been very slow. Much of the teacher education is irrelevant even to contemporary requirements leave alone those of the future. We, therefore, face a paradox of having better books, and research but progressively more indifferent Teachers". (p. 54). The situation has not changed much even today. The changes suggested by these curriculum frameworks have not been fully implemented at the ground level. We have yet to evolve our own context specific content and pedagogy. Consequently, the whole teacher education curricula is heavily loaded with western psychological, philosophical and sociological theories and information, many of which have become outdated and discarded even by the western countries. For example the teacher education system heavily relies on behaviourist theories and theorists like Pavlov, Thorndike, Skinner, Gagne, and Tyler etc., while the western teacher education system has moved towards the constructivist approach long back.

Even the Model Curriculum (2001) developed by the University Grants Commission (UGC) had very little new ideas to offer. This Model Curriculum banks mainly on the four major traditional schools of philosophy—idealism, naturalism, pragmatism and realism that continued to dominated the teacher education curricula. Teacher education curriculum is expected to develop dispositions among teachers to discharge their duties effectively. It fails to develop an understanding among the students about education as independent discipline in itself and it does inter linkages with various cognate disciplines.

This split between the classroom realities a teacher has to face and the teacher education programmes he/she receives also finds an expression in the *World*

Bank Report (1997) as "in India teachers need but do not receive-preparation for teaching in the situation that two thirds of them have to face: multi grade class-rooms with many first generation learners who attend school irregularly". Similar concerns have been expressed by Raina (1999) "teacher training programmes in India have remained procrustean, offering the same menu to all without slightest regard for varying cultural and physical settings. They remained unresponsive to vast cultural, linguistic, regional and geographical diversity".

Teachers in the existing socio-cultural context of the country need to be logical and reflective because of increasing racial, ethical, and cultural and linguistic diversities in the society which demands broadminded citizens. Teacher education curriculum, therefore need to be planned and organized to develop the spirit of inquiry, initiative, scientific temper, conceptual clarity and linguistic skills through rigorous practice teaching which has so far remained a neglected area of teacher preparation.

The National Curriculum Framework for Teacher Education, 2009 (NCFTE, 2009)

A major effort to rejuvenate teacher education towards modernization and contextualization has been made in 2009 through the National Curriculum Framework for Teacher Education (2009). During recent years the epistemology of learning has undergone a major change; i.e., learning does not involve discovering the reality, but constructing the reality. Knowledge and cognitions are to be constructed and affects are to be felt. Emphasis has, now, shifted towards constructivist approach of learning. Learning is also perceived as an integral part of learner's physical, social, and cultural contexts.

The whole pedagogical approach of teacher education programme, therefore, needs to be reoriented from traditional behaviourist to constructivist discourses. The National Curriculum Framework for Teacher Education (2009) developed by NCTE tries to ensure that teacher education courses are reoriented to align with the epistemological shift envisaged in the NCF 2005 and develop teachers as facilitators of learning. It includes the contexts, concerns and visions of teacher education which calls for preparing teachers for learning society, empowering teachers in learning to learn, and making teacher education liberal, humanistic and responsive to the to the demands of inclusive education. It has tried to incorporate the changing school contexts and demands in the light of recently implemented Right to Education Act (RTE, 2009), issue of academic burden of students, and universalisation of secondary education that have implication for teacher education. The major concerns addressed by this framework include inclusive education, ensuring equitable and sustainable development, utilising community knowledge in education, and integration of ICT and e-learning in the curriculum of teacher education which is in tune with the thrust of NCF 2005 and the needs of contemporary Indian society.

Therefore, the traditional approach to teacher preparation based on philosophical, sociological and psychological orientation of courses has given way to 'carefully crafted curriculum design that draws upon theoretical and empirical knowledge as well as student teachers' 'Experiential Knowledge' (NCFTE 2009, p. 24). Three broad curricular areas identified by this framework are: (A) *Foundations of Education* which includes courses under three rubrics, namely, Learner Studies, Contemporary Studies and Educational Studies; (B) *Curriculum and Pedagogy* including Curriculum Studies and Pedagogic Studies; and (C) *School Internship*, leading to the development of a broad repertoire of perspective, professional capacities, teacher sensibilities and skills (NCFTE 2009, p. 24). An attempt has been made through this curriculum framework to not only address the issues, concerns and pedagogical shifts visualized by NCF 2005, but, also organize the entire teacher education curriculum as an organic and integrated whole.

This Framework envisages a two year teacher preparation programme along with the four year integrated teacher education courses.

Conclusion

To conclude, any effective teacher education curriculum calls for systematic task analysis of teachers at various levels and inclusion of relevant contents, which alone can infuse confidence among the would be teachers to negotiate the school curriculum in classroom. The present teacher education programme is inadequate to meet the challenges of diverse Indian social, cultural, economic and present contexts and the paradigm shift envisaged in the NCF 2005. The pedagogic reform from this perspective need to invest on building teachers' capacity to act as autonomous reflective groups of professionals who are sensitive to their social mandate and to the professional ethics and to the needs of heterogeneous groups of learners. The National Curriculum Framework for Teacher Education, (2009) promises to translate the vision into reality and prepare humanistic and reflective teachers that has the potential to develop more professional teachers and improve the quality of education.

REFERENCES

Darling-Hammond, L. (2000a): Standard Setting in Teaching: Changes in licensing, certification and assessment. In V. Richardson (Ed), *Handbook of Research on Teaching, (4th Ed, pp. 751-776))*. Washington DC: American Educational Research Association.

Ferguson, R.F. (1991a): Paying for Public Education: New evidence on how and why money matters. *Harvard Journal of Legislation*, 28(1), pp. 1-35.

Gold Haber, D.D.; and Brewer, D.J. (2000): Does teacher certification matters? High School teacher certification status and student achievement. *Educational Evaluation and Policy Analysis,* 22 (2), pp. 129-145.

Ministry of Human Resource Development (MHRD (993): *Learning Without Burden*, Prof. Yash Pal Committee Report. New Delhi: India.

MHRD (1985). *Challenges of Education.* New Delhi. Govt. of India.

MHRD (1986). *National Policy on Education*, New Delhi. Govt. of India.

Ministry of Education (1948-49). *Report of the University Education Commission.* New Delhi, Government of India.

Ministry of Education (1953). *Report of the Secondary (1952-53)*, New Delhi: Government of India.

Ministry of Education (1966): *Education and National Development: Report of the Commission (1964-66).* New Delhi, Government of India.

National Commission on Teachers-1 (1983-85): *Teacher and Society*. Delhi: Government of India Press.

National Council for Teacher Education (1998): *Curriculum Framework for Quality Teacher Education*, New Delhi: NCTE.

NCERT (1978): *Teacher Education Curriculum a Framework.* New Delhi: NCERT.

NCTE (1988): *National Curriculum Framework for Teacher Education*, New Delhi: NCERT.

Raina, V.K. (1995): Teacher Educators in India: In search of an Identify. *Journal of Teacher Education*, No. (46), pp. 45-52.

Raina, V.K. (1999): Indigenizing Teacher Education in Developing Countries: The Indian Context. *Prospects*, Vol. Xxiv (1) p. 5-25.

Shotton. J. R.1 (1997) No Master high or low: Challenging the Pedagogy of the Oppressed in Ved Prakash (ed.) *Teacher Empowerment and School Effectiveness at Primary Stage*, NCERT, New Delhi.

Shulman, I.S. (1987): Knowledge and Teaching: Foundations of New Reforms. *Harvard Educational Review*, 57(1), pp. 4-14.

World Bank, (1997). *Primary Education in India.* Washington DC: The World Bank.

18

Professional Development of Teachers and Improvement in Quality of Education

Sabita Mishra

Teacher is the central of whole educational programme of a nation. No educational programme can be successful without proper education of teachers. Even the best system is bound to fail without good teachers. The quality of education in a society depends upon quality of teachers, and quality of teachers in turn depends upon education teachers themselves have had. Teachers must be provided with best possible professional education and training. Kothari Commission (1964-66) has rightly acknowledged that of all the different factors which influence the quality of education and its contribution to national development; the quality, the competence and character of teachers are undoubtedly the most significant. Nothing is more important than securing a sufficient supply ofhigh quality recruits to the teaching profession, providing them with best professional preparation and creating satisfactory conditions of work in which they can be fully effective. Professional development of teachers becomes a necessary input for the improvement of overall quality of education.

Professional Development: Concept

Professional development refers to various activities that enhance professional career growth. Such activities include individual development, continuing education and in service education as well as curriculum writing, peer-collaboration, study groups and peer coaching or mentoring. Fullan (1991). states that the sum total of formal and informal learning experiences throughout one's career from preservice teacher education to retirement. The term professional development is used to refer to the process through which teachers attain higher professional competence and expand their understanding of self, role, context and career. It is any kind of experience that helps teachers engage into widening their knowledge, appreciation, skills and understanding of their work inline with goals, values of the institutions and the interests and needs of teachers.

Professional development is the driving force which helps to bring much change in the area of teaching and learning. As in any other profession, it is vital that teachers keep up-to-date with the most current topics, thinking and research in their field. This in turn supports them in their life long learning. It is a worldwide experience that professional development is the key determining factor for improved student performance. Effective professional experiences are designed to help teachers in a better understanding of teaching and learning. "To be effective, professional development must provide teachers with a way to directly apply what they learn to their teaching." (Resnic, 2005). Rudduck, (1991) refers to the professional development of the teacher as the teachers' ability to maintain the curiosity of the class; to identify significant interests in the teaching and learning processes; to value and seek dialogue with experienced colleagues as a source of support in the analysis of situations.

Professional development is a process, which can be either individual or collective. It contributes to the development of various professional competencies by means of a variety of formal and informal experiences. Professional development plays an essential role in successful education reform and serves as a bridge between where prospective and experienced teachers are now and where they will need to meet the future challenges of guiding students in achieving higher standards of learning and development.

Need of Professional Development for Teachers

At present, expansion of knowledge in all fields of learning is taking place at a very rapid pace. Each and every day new developments, new facts, new theories, and new methodologies are being evolved. It is obvious that the knowledge, skills and competencies which is attained by the teachers at their pre and initial service period are never sufficient for their whole professional career. They need to go for continuous professional updating by various trainings and programmes to maintain the competence. Now, teacher is expected to play multiple roles than he played in earlier. A teacher, besides being an expert helper of student learning, has to be a community leader, adult educator, local developer etc. The present day teacher, instead of being an instructor or task-master, has to be an expert in various fields of life. In order to be capable, the teachers have to face all the changing situations. Programme of professional development is given importance for all teachers.

Globalization brings many challenges and diverse opportunities for people: the economic and societal changes are creating new demands and pressures on schools, teachers and students. Thus, the role and activity of teachers are considered as the most significant in the education system. In this context, the education of teachers assumes crucial significance in equipping them with appropriate professional skills and competencies to discharge their expected roles with greater efficiency and effectiveness. Professional development of teachers is not one shot, one size fits all event; rather it is an ongoing learning process in which teachers engage themselves out of their zeal and interest to learn how best to perform their teaching and to satisfy the learning needs of their students.

Teachers should be provided with common skills, and assisted to become adaptive to the changes as they participate in planning at instructional level, otherwise a new curriculum would have the least worthwhile impact. According to Fullun, M. (1990) "Teachers of today and tomorrow need to do much more learning on the job, or parallel with it—where they can constantly test out, refine and get feedback on the improvements they make." This assertion puts an urgent call for professional development of teachers. The following facts emphasize the need for professional development of teachers. These are to:

- maintain ethical behaviour in his relations with fellow teachers and educational associations;
- maintain membership in key professional organizations relevant to his subject or area of specialty;
- keep abreast of subject matter by study of books, periodicals, newspapers and other sources concerned with his field;
- utilize films, TV and radio as a means of keeping abreast of new and advanced knowledge in his field;
- attend conferences, workshops, seminars etc. to broaden his knowledge; and to
- use ICT in teaching learning process.

Need of Professional Development for Teachers: Commissions and Committees

No doubt, for the professional development of teachers, professional training of the teachers is one of the basic requirements. Different Commissions and Committees have suggested various programmes for the professional development of teachers to improve them in particular and the whole education system in general.

Secondary Education Commission (1952-53) states that the most important factor in the contemplated educational reconstruction is the teacher, his personal qualities, his educational qualifications, his professional training and the place he occupies in the school as well as in the community.

Education Commission (1964-66) recommends that a sound programme of professional education of teachers is essential for the qualitative improvement of education. Investment in teacher education can yield very rich dividends because the financial resources required are small when measured against the resulting improvements in the education of the millions. The Commission suggests that for the professional preparation of teachers of higher education, orientation is necessary, especially of newly appointed teachers. The commission recommends that the orientation course should be organized for the new staff in every university.

National Policy on Education (NPE, 1986) proposes:

- To organize specially designed orientation programme for all entrance lecturers.
- Organize refresher courses for all the teachers at least once in five years.
- To organize orientation programme for the teachers.
- To encourage teachers to participate in workshop, seminar, conference and symposia etc.

The Mehrotra Committee suggests that for three to four weeks duration orientation programme for the newly appointed teachers, the emphasis should be laid on the methodologies of teaching in the concerned subject. Ramamurti Committee (1990) recommends that there should be one year training after recruitment of the teachers for their professional development.

Yashpal Committee (2009) suggests that it is necessary to enhance the quality of teacher education within higher education. For this it is necessary to develop full-fledged orientation programmes for newly recruited teachers in colleges and universities.

Quality of Education and Teacher

Quality is the real key to development. Quality generally refers to the degree of excellence. In the educational context, quality is seen as a complex issue as education is concerned with human beings.

Quality of education acts as a significant factor in the process of development of nations. The development of nation rests on the shoulders of teachers because they shape the future generations. Thus, the quality of teachers directly depends on the quality of teacher education. The efficiency of an educational system depends largely on the efficiency of its teachers. Infrastructure, equipment, curricula, books and teaching methods are no doubt important for quality of education. Besides these factors, teacher is the most vital and supreme in the education system. It is no exaggeration to state that a spacious building, costly equipment and sound syllabus will serve some useful purpose only when there are teachers who are fully aware and dedicated to the profession. They should give importance to their attitude, personalities, and characters as the builders of nation. Effective teacher education can only enhance quality of teacher as well as education.

Determinants of Teacher's Quality

Teacher's quality can be determined from various aspects. These are described as follows:

Teacher Effectiveness

i. Personal characteristics of teachers

Teacher effectiveness is concerned with personal characteristics of teachers. It is related with his qualification, intelligence, confidence, trustworthiness, analytical and conceptual thinking, drive for improvement, flexibility, accountability, love for children, passion for learning and so on.

ii. Pedagogical content knowledge

Teacher should acquire pedagogical content knowledge. This refers to deep knowledge about the content and structure of a subject matter. Teachers with more pedagogical content knowledge display a broad repertoire of teaching strategies for creating cognitive stimulating learning situations.

iii. Self-efficacy of Teacher

Self-efficacy, influences students towards learning, even if they are not motivated towards learning. More efficacious teachers have more commitment. They believe in innovation, use more communicative based strategies and thus influence students' learning experiences and academic outcomes. Ross (1994), reports that teachers with high self-efficacy are more likely to learn and use new approaches and strategies for teaching and provide special assistance to low achieving students. Teachers who have high sense of self-efficacy are more creative in their work.

iv. Commitment

Commitment is an important component of teacher effectiveness. It leads the teacher to effective achievement. Commitment is an attitude—a psychological frame of mind which motivates people to work towards certain goals. Teachers' commitment includes commitment to one's self, to one's students, to one's organisation and society as a whole. The impact of teachers on their students is subtle and long lasting. It is therefore necessary that teachers should be committed, contented and devoted to their noble profession.

Teaching Effectiveness

Teaching effectiveness deals with the teaching process. Teaching is a complex endeavour, involving classroom management, lesson preparation and organisation of teaching and learning activities, creating and maintaining a certain climate, evaluation and feedback. Brophy, (2001) advocated 12 principles of effective teaching. These are: supportive classroom climate, opportunity to learn, curricular alignment, establishing learning orientations, coherent content, thoughtful discourse, practice and application activities, scaffolding students task engagement, strategy teaching, co-operative learning, goal-oriented assessment, and achievement expectations.

Academic qualification, subject matter knowledge, pedagogy and teaching skill are important factors in determining teachers' effectiveness and teaching efficiency. A knowledgeable teacher without motivation and dedication to teaching cannot provide quality education. The quality of teaching is not only governed by the knowledge, skill and competence of teachers but also their enthusiasm and commitment in teaching. When a teacher is motivated and loves the teaching profession, the students not only learn the content taught by the teacher, they may also be motivated towards learning (Czubaj, 1996). Teachers who are dedicated and committed to teaching might facilitate school based innovations or reformations that are meant to benefit students' learning and development. In fact, teachers' commitment and engagement has been identified as one of the most critical factors in the success of education (Nais, 1981).

Promoting Professional Development of Teachers and Enhancing Quality of Education: Some Suggestions

Since teachers are expected to perform multiple roles in the present time, their continuous professional development becomes inevitable. The following suggestions deserve attention for professional development of teachers:

Academic Development

Teachers should make efforts and manage time for their academic development, increasing and updating their subject-matter knowledge. They must enroll themselves for M.Phil and Ph.D. programmes. They should do coursework revision of notes, adding new materials, referring to latest books and journals. They should develop the habit of regular reading of professional journals and periodicals. Teachers should maintain a good personal library at home and make a regular use of internet to provide adequate knowledge and information to students.

Life-long Learner

Teacher must continue his learning throughout his life. Teachers need to be aware of new ideas, to refine decisionmaking skills and to become more effective in integrating theory to practice. A teacher has to ensure that whatever a student learns, he must learn for himself. Colleges and universities offering teacher education programme need to give priority to purchase latest books and subscribe to research journals to serve the teacher in updating his knowledge. Library should be equipped with internet and other modern facilities.

Use of ICT

The role of the teacher has been multiplied as instructor, constructor, creator, and facilitator of learning situations. The teacher training programmes can not be successful if the teaching pedagogy is not properly matched with the emerging learning environment. Information technology has created opportunities for better education. The teacher should be aware of ICT programmes. But, our teachers are still uncomfortable with the use of latest tools of technology; such as e-learning, use of computers, e-mail, OHPs, etc. They should be trained to use the technological innovations that are readily available. Effective use of information and communication technologies in teacher education institutions can ensure qualitative teaching and bring a change in the pedagogy and a shift in the teaching-learning paradigm.

Participation in Seminar/Conference/Workshop

Teacher must keep himself abreast of current developments. He should find a forum to exchange ideas and share suggestions with the peers. This interaction will enable him to enhance his knowledge. Teacher should regularly participate in conferences, seminars and workshops to expose his academic knowledge.

Self Study

Self study is another effort to develop professional skills of teachers. Every teacher must carry out self study for his own professional needs, interest and teaching responsibilities. Self learning helps to upgrade the competencies and skills of teachers. A competent teacher must be familiar with the day to day improvement of modern knowledge and technology. Self-learning is to be pursued by teachers through books, journals, audio-visual aids and sources of electronic medias. A successful and dynamic teacher is always a self-directed and self-motivated learner throughout his career.

Exposure to Innovations

In order to bring excellence in imparting knowledge, teachers should get exposed to innovations. The innovations in various teaching institutions can be compiled and disseminated among teachers. There is a need to develop linkage with other teacher education institutions all over the world for meaningful interaction and sharing for development.

In-service Training Programmes

Knowledge explosion in every discipline is the main source of development. The teacher has to continuously update his/her knowledge in his/her field of expertise. In-service training programme is more valuable for the teachers. It is an organized need based continuing programme. For school teachers, in-service programmes are offered by CTEs, DIETs, SCERT. For college and university teachers, orientation, and refresher like courses are offered by Academic Staff Colleges (ASCs). These courses provide opportunities to the teachers to keep themselves abreast of latest advances in their fields. College Development Councils of universities should plan a variety of need-based in-service programmes for teachers.

Soft Skills Development

Teachers should be well equipped to understand and interact with students and also help them in understanding and interacting with others. In spite of possessing sufficient knowledge of content and teaching skills, they cannot be good teachers unless they have soft skills—interpersonal qualities, caring attitude towards students in terms of feelings, interests and values. Teachers acquire these life skills through a teacher education programme that helps to lead better personal life and to make their classroom teaching more effective.

Conducting Research Activity

Teachers should undertake research activity on pertinent issues of the society. Research activities will involve them in exploring ideas and creating new knowledge. This will definitely upgrade their competence. Moreover, with growing experience and knowledge, the teacher develops insight into educational process. He should spread his thoughts widely through articles/research papers for development of society.

Value Oriented Teacher Education

Quality of education can be enhanced through value oriented teacher education. Deterioration of values is a world wide phenomenon. In the present context, certain values need to be redefined and reinstalled. Values such as democracy and human rights must be understood as basic fundamentals of quality education. Teachers must teach about values not just through the substantive content of their teaching, but also by using teaching methods which will integrate democracy, interaction, equality, respect and cooperation as parts of the work in institutions. While imparting values, teachers must be role models for students.

Developing Teaching Competency

To provide the best education, teacher should be necessarily equipped with skills and competencies. However enlightened the aims of education, updated the equipment, and efficient the management, unless the teacher is competent, the whole system of education collapses gradually. Therefore, the best way to provide quality education is to empower teachers with required competencies. The teacher should be properly enlightened, educated through proper training and be made to develop sense of responsibility and love towards his profession.

For the 21st century, teachers are required to address several challenges, such as the need to educate an increasingly diverse student population, teaching through ICT, to function well and to create new organizations etc. The paradigm shift in professional development suggests a change in emphasis from transmission of knowledge to experimental learning; from reliance on existing research findings to examining one's own teaching practice; from individual focus to collaborative learning and from mimicking best practice to problem-focused learning (Loucks-Horsley, 1998). The diverse demands on 21st century education create new roles for teachers in their classrooms. The following points describe the roles of teachers for enhancing quality of education.

Leadership Role of Teachers

Teachers take leadership for the development of students as well as institution. Teachers work collaboratively with other personel of the institution to create a professional learning community. They actively participate in and advocate for decision making structures in education and government that take advantages of the expertise of teachers. Teachers advocate for positive change in policies and practices affecting students' learning. They participate in the implementation of initiatives to improve the education of students.

Creation of Suitable Environment by Teachers

Teachers encourage an environment that is inviting, respectful, supportive, inclusive and flexible. They appreciate the differences and value the contributions of each student in the learning environment by building positive and appropriate relationships. Teachers with the support of specialists meet the special needs of all students. Through inclusion and other models of effective practice, they should ensure students to meet their needs.

Teachers' Content Knowledge

Teachers develop and apply strategies to make the curriculum need based and relevant for all students and provide a balanced curriculum. Teachers bring a richness and depth of understanding to their classrooms by knowing their subjects beyond the content they are expected to teach and by directing students' natural curiosity into an interest in learning. Teachers understand how the teaching of the content relates to other disciplines in order to deepen understanding and connect learning for students. They should promote global awareness and its relevance to the subjects they teach. Teachers incorporate life skills in their teaching deliberately and strategically to help students lead to a better quality life in future. These skills include leadership, ethics, accountability, adaptability, personal productivity, personal responsibility, people skills, self direction and social responsibility.

Teachers as Facilitators of Learning

Teachers' first and foremost duty is to understand well the psychology of students and to design instructions as per their needs. That must be constantly monitored and modified to enhance learning. Teachers choose the methods and techniques that are most effective in meeting the needs of their students and help the students to use technology to maximize their learning. Teachers help students in developing their critical thinking and problem-solving skills. They should help students work in teams and develop leadership qualities.

Reflection of Teacher on Practice

Teachers actively investigate and develop new ideas that improves teaching and learning. They adopt their practice based on research and data to meet the necessities of their students. High quality professional development of teacher reflects on better educational practices for improvement in quality of education.

Conclusion

In the present learning age, professional development is very essential for all teachers. It improves the quality and excellence of teacher in all walks of life. Continuous professional development is essential to increase teachers' competency, knowledge, skills, attitude and confidence by which they can improve the quality of education. Government, universities, colleges of teacher education and other organizations need to take initiatives for professional development of teachers which will enable them to create best educated individuals to cope effectively with fast emerging challenges of the century.

REFERENCES

Brophy, J. (2001). Genetic Aspect of Effective Teaching, In Wang, M.C. and Walberg, H.J. *Tomorrow's Teachers.* MC Cutchan Publishing Company.

Czubaj, C.A. (1996). Maintaining Teacher Motivation. *Education,* 116(3): 372-376.

Dash, M. (2004). *Education in India-Problems and Prospective.* New Delhi: Atlantic Publishers.

Fullan, M. (1990). Staff Development Innovation and Institutional Development, In B. Joyce,(Ed.), *School Culture Through Staff Development,* Virginia: ASCD.

Fullan, M. and Steigelbauer, S. (1991). *The New Meaning of Educational Change*, New York: Teachers College Press.

Govt. of India, Ministry of Education (1952-53). *Secondary Education Commission-1952-53.* New Delhi: Ministry of Education.

Govt. of India, Ministry of Education (1964-66*). Kothari Commission-1964-66.* New Delhi: Ministry of Education.

Govt. of India, Ministry of Human Resource Development (1986). *National Policy on Education-1986.* New Delhi: Ministry of Human Resource Development.

Govt. of India, Dept. of Education (1990). *Ramamurti Committee-1990,* New Delhi: Dept. of Education.

Govt. of India, Ministry of Human Resource Development (2009). *Yashpal Committee-2009.* New Delhi: Ministry of Human Resource Development.

Loucks-Horsley, S. *et al.* (1998). *Designing Professional for Teachers of Science and Mathematics*. Thousand OAKS, CA: Corwin Press.

Nais, J. (1981). Commitment and Motivation in Primary School Teachers. *Educational Review,* 33(3), 181-190.

NCTE. (1998). *Policy Perspectives in Teacher Education Critique and Documentation* 1998. New Delhi: National Council for Teacher Education.

Resnick, L.B. (2005). Teaching Teachers: Professional Development to Improve Student Achievement, *Research Points*, 3(1), 12-18.

Ross, J.A. (1994). The Impact of an In-service to Promote Cooperative Learning on the Stability of Teacher Efficacy. *Teaching and Teacher Education*, 10, 381-384.

Rudduck, J. (1991). *Innovation and Change*. Milton Keynes: Open University.

19

Professional Ethics, Professionalism and Teacher-Educators in 21st Century

Dillip Kumar Khuntia and Laxmidhar Behera

The NPE (1986) and its revised version (1992) observe that the status of teacher reflects the socio-cultural ethos of society and no people can rise above the level of its teachers. Thus, with more active, influential, resourceful and competent teacher, the more is the possibility of effective and useful the process of education. The ironic words of Gurudev Tagore are worth mentioning in this context: "only he can teach who can love". The greatest teachers of men have been lovers of man. The real teaching is a gift. To run the system of education effectively, it is essential to have a standard reservoir of teachers. Within the sphere of education, the responsibility to develop well-equipped teacher is assigned to the sub system of Teacher Education. A weak programme of teacher education is a national calamity. In this era of value erosion, value degradation and value degeneration there is an urgent and immediate need of value regeneration and resurrection. Unless and until there is resettlement of theory and practice there would be no hope. There is the need of eyeing upon professional ethics, professionalism and role of teacher-educators in the scenario of teacher education.

Professional Ethics: What and Why?

In the term professional ethics, the word "ethics" adds to the professional obligations that a professional abides by. Every profession, in order to regulate its terms, conditions, norms and quality of service rendered, habits own professional ethics as different from general ethics. The National Assessment and Accreditation Council [NAAC], The International Network for Quality Assurance Agencies in Higher Education [INQAAHE] strongly advocated the encouragement and consideration of good practices as one of the parameters of quality education. Academic Staff colleges run orientation and refresher courses for college and university teachers. Whatever may be proposed, planned or executed for quality control and quality management, there is still a rethinking about the vital importance of professional ethics as set and fixed by different organizations and professional bodies. The think tank should rediscover the perennial and essential values to reset again for fulfilling the purpose of nation building and to live in peace and harmony.

Professional Ethics and Teacher-Educators: Tri-Directional Application

Let us have a glance over the three directional ways and means in which to note the application of professional ethics.

(a) Dedication of the Teacher-Educator to his/her Subject Matter

Teaching is a vocation—A sacred vocation but not a vacation job. Teaching involves in making a move from teaching to learning or learning to teaching. Teacher is the first learner. A teacher-educator should go to the class room directly from the library involving in continuous scanning of the available related knowledge, skimming the same and scouting in the class room. Each teacher-educator should have mastery over the subject matter he/she has to teach.

(b) Relationship between the Teacher-Educator and Pupil-Teacher

The relationship between the teacher and taught is well reflected in the Upanishad saying-

Sahanavavatu- Let us live together;

Sahanau Bhunaktu- Let us participate and rejoice together in the learning process;

Sahaveeryam Karvavavahi- Let us acquire knowledge together;

Tejaswina Vadheetamasthu- Let our education become dynamic, flexible and vibrant one;

Mavidwishavahai- Let not hatred divide us.

There should prevail a cordial relationship between the two. The teacher-educator should be the motivator factor and he/she should inspire the pupil-teacher to follow the lines of the lighted path.

(c) Relationship between the teacher-educator and his/her colleagues-

There should prevail a caring and sharing attitude among them along with the line of co-operation and understanding. They should stand for each others' painstaking periods and find solutions to come out of that.

Professional Preparation of Teacher-Educators: National Curriculum Framework for Teacher Education, 2009

In chapter six under the heading of preparing Teacher-Educators it has been noted that the education and training of a prospective teacher will be effective to the extent that it has been delivered by teacher-educators who are competent and professionally equipped for the job. The quality of pedagogical inputs in teacher-education programmes and the manner in which they are transacted to realize their intended objectives depend largely on the professional competence of teacher-educators.

Professionalism in Teaching: Role of Teacher-Educators

Good teachers are now rarely found in academic institutions. Some teachers feel nervous about their profession. Some others concentrate on research. Few regard teaching as a noble vocation. This scenario must change, Oscar Wilde once said, "Nothing worth teaching can be taught and all that is taught is not worth teaching." Teaching is a demanding occupation. It is rarely a dream job and most of the time it is a nightmare. Teaching may be a fascinating experience but few teachers actually know how to teach. Brilliant students do not necessarily become brilliant teachers. Teaching is really a tough job. Teaching is a skill that can be learned and teachers need to ensure adherence to fair play while teaching. Teacher professionalism contains the essential characteristics such as competence, performance, conduct, which reflect the educator's goals, abilities, and standards and directly impact the effectiveness of teaching through the development of these qualities. Professionalism, therefore, implies professional preparation of teachers and their professional development through pre-service and continuous in-service training programmes.

Quality Process Norms for Teacher Education System

In this crucial period, there is a need for the Teacher-Educators to change their role to improve the quality of teacher training, because Teacher-Educators are bearer of knowledge and knowledge to be developed by pupils through the learning experiences; from executors of teaching procedures recommended by others to designers or adaptors of such procedures; and from being isolated individuals in their classrooms to being co-worker collaborating in the improvement of teaching and learning, Teacher-Educators' role will be changed from teacher to knowledge workers, consultants and counsellors. Teacher-Educators should internalize their changing role and make them ready for this change. When Teacher-Educators accept their changing role, there is need to adopt according the changing world: hence teacher-educators have to empower themselves to do justice with the would-be teachers or future students and to try hard to increase the quality of their teacher learning.

In the fast changing scenario of global world, there is a need for creating a learning society on the four pillars of education. The whole world is shrinking to a global Village due to the faster change in information and communication technology. There is a felt need to think globally and to act locally. We have to live together through working together. It is the role of the Teacher-Educators to prepare future teachers to be life-long learners and educational workers to create a learning society. Teacher-educators are responsible for producing quality teachers. Harvey (1993) and Atwood (2007) point out that quality process tend to focus on 'core' aspects of education such as learning, teaching and course organization. In other words, teacher educators' way of organizing theoretical framework, practical sessions and skill development programme affect the future teachers. The activities suggested during training are carried to the classroom teaching in the schools.

Teacher-Educators have never taken the aspect of professionalism very seriously. They have been criticizing the process of teacher education rather than providing answer to problems faced by them. However, NCTE was established in 1993 by the Act of parliament to give the tinge of professionalism to teacher preparation programme. Unfortunately, instead of mending the system, it caused some damage to the programme of teacher education. An obvious reason was lack of insight on the part of Teacher-Educators to provide a good model of teacher education. Till date they have not been able to envision a good model of teacher programme.

The Teacher-Educators have much to contribute to the development of quality amongst the teachers. It is high time, they understood their role rather than simply criticize the system in the name of NCTE. If they don't contribute, they will move from the current marginalized states to the one of irrelevance. They will have to respond at both conceptual/empirical and pedagogical levels (Liston *et al.* 2008).

- The first and foremost thing is that they will have to accept the existing realities of the world. Privatization has entered educational system and they cannot deny it at any cost. A large number of men and women aspire to get degree or diplomas in teacher education to join teaching or jobs similar to teaching. The existing teacher colleges or the university departments of education cannot accommodate all the aspirants. The nation at such a juncture will have to depend on private participation in education system of the country. Teacher-Educators should start devising the knowledge akin to the discipline of education.
- Secondly Teacher-Educators should envision functions other than teaching by making education degree/diploma broadbased with respect to changing times. The teacher-educators should be competent enough to handle the children with special needs. The curriculum of teacher education should comprise specializations like public relationship, parent counseling, behaviour therapy, developing E-learning material etc.

- Thirdly, the Teacher-Educators will have to develop on specialized skills that add quality to the professional functioning. Such skills mean having hard, technical expertise along with softer interpersonal capabilities. Skills of quality teaching and quality assessment are most desired. Quality teaching skills involve the process of making students work hard and become independent learner.. Similarly the teacher trainees have to be trained in quality assessment procedure.
- Fourthly, the Teacher-Educators will have to organize their research as per the needs of the society and the market forces. Liston et at. (2008) in his editorial pointed out that "Teacher quality research emerges from different conceptual lenses, some less familiar to education (e.g. labour economics). It is important to grasp varied theories of action implied and to analyze assumptions and values in different research designs." To put it in simpler words, it connotes that research process and research problems in education should be such that these solve societal problems from different angles.. The Teacher-Educators need to get all essential knowledge to take up the issue and find workable solutions. After all it is the Teacher-Educators who teach about the nature of the child and work directly in the field.
- Fifthly, as a whole, nature and process of teacher education will have to be worked out differently. Existing teacher education programme is divided into different academic papers and sections. Usually the academic papers are principles of education and educational psychology etc. While teaching these courses, the Teacher-Educators emphasize information aspect only (having no relevance to class room teaching or school problems). The student teachers are never taught "how to use the information for solving problems related to school education in general and teaching in particular."

Keeping in view the limitations of discipline oriented approach the Teacher-Educators should visualize problems oriented approach. Comprehensive list of various problems faced by various functionaries be developed through field based working. The role of Teacher-Educators today is to mend the existing system with vision to help teacher education grow as a professional course and produce quality teachers for school.

Teacher-Educators: Manager Leaders

As a result of the debate and discussion starting from the grass root level to the climax level, in 2005, the NCERT developed a National Curriculum Framework (NCF), with advocacy for a shift in the instructional designs from teacher-centeredness to learner-centeredness. This has been further supported by advancing a plea for invoking a construction approach to learning in which learner has been visualized as a pro-active explorer of newer frontiers of knowledge, information and skills. The role envisaged for the learner is that of a seeker of knowledge rather than the recipient as is traditionally insisted upon in our educational contexts. In order to realize this end, as also hinted in the NCF (2005), search for a new leadership style for teacher educators is urgently called for.

The vision of a teacher-educator has to be essentially that of a guide and facilitator by playing both manager and leader roles. There are certain basic theories and models advocated in respect of effective managerial and leadership roles that have been considered in the content of teacher education especially for secondary school level.

Leadership and Managerial role defined: Bennis (1989) observed, "To survive in the 21st century we are going to need new generation of leaders – leaders, not managers. The distinction is an important one. Leaders conquer the context – the volatile, turbulent, ambiguous surrounding that sometimes seen to conspire against us and will surely suffocate us if we let them – while managers surrender to it." Characteristics of Leaders against Managers: Important characteristics of leader as against managers may be indicated in terms of several important parameters. A leader innovates and develops whereas a manager administers and maintains; a leader inspires, trusts and has a long-range perspective, while a manager relies on control and has a short range view; a leader asks what and why, whereas a manager asks how and when. The leader challenges that status quo has an eye on the horizon while the manager accepts the status quo and has an eye on the bottom line.

The twin Role of Teacher-educator as a Leader and Manager: A teacher-educator while envisioning the twin role of leader and manager has to assimilate attitudes and values and accept the leadership issues by addressing the day-to-day problems and challenges as well as futuristic approach to the issues confronting him.

In this broad framework, a teacher-educator has to equip himself with the abilities and motivational skills to deal both with the present and the future. As a manager, he has to learn to address the issues which are directly concerned with the conditions of teaching and learning while as a leader, he has to develop capabilities for inspiring his team to seek newer horizons in respect of the knowledge which is fast emerging in the content of rapidly advancing technological and communication network. Since leadership is concerned basically with ability to make an impact on other, the teacher-educator has to acquire, assimilate and internalize such powers by pursuing the educational goals most vigorously. In performing managerial role, he has to acquire the competencies and skills which enable him to empower his student teachers to be able to face the challenges in the most competent manner possible. For

Teacher-Educators to be able to perform an effective leadership role, it will be imperative under the path-goal theory to develop their knowledge level, enhance their experience in addressing difficult and challenging situations and acquiring an internal locus of control.

New Role of Teacher and Teacher-Educators

The International Society for Technology Education has re-released its educational technology standards for teachers. These standards include 21st century skills. Some of these skills are:

- Finding and managing resources.
- Publishing on the web.
- Connecting with colleagues, students, parents and local and global communities.

Teachers must be proficient in these skills in order to model good practices for their students and help students include these skills for learning. Activities may be organized which will allow collaborative work for Teacher-Educators with full knowledge on using and integrating ICT in the educational process.

Professional Competency of Teacher-Educators

Professional competency focuses on the professional role of the Teacher-Educators as it relates to instructional planning, instructional delivery and instructional evaluation (Miller and Miller, 1998). Teacher-Educators must be able to demonstrate not only general and specific knowledge and skills of their technical specialty; they must also demonstrate ability to translate the knowledge and skills into pedagogy. Teacher-Educators must demonstrate competency in:

- ***Communication***: An ability to interact, which is able to transmit his/her thoughts to other person.
- ***Analysis***: An ability to be a clear thinker, who can fuse experience, reason and training into considered judgment.
- ***Problem Solving***: An ability to find solutions of a problem through critical analysis.
- ***Values within Decision-Making***: An ability to reflect and to habitually seek to understand the moral dimensions of decisions and to accept responsibility for the consequences of actions.
- ***Social Interaction***: An understanding of how to get things done in committees, task forces, team prosiest and other group efforts.
- ***Global Perspectives***: An ability to articulate, inter connections between and among diverse opinions, ideas and beliefs about global issues.

- ***Effective citizenship***: An ability to make informed choice and develop strategy for collaborative involvement in community issues.
- ***Aesthetic Responsiveness***: an ability to make informed responses to artistic work, which are grounded in knowledge of the theoretical historical and cultural content.

Continuous Professional Development of Teachers and Teacher Educators

The teacher education programme seeks to provide conceptual framework through the following specific outcomes:

- ***Subject Matter***: Teacher-Educators will demonstrate a thorough knowledge of their subject matter.
- ***Pedagogy***: Teacher-Educators will demonstrate level of instructional skill and learner characteristics, sufficient to systematically design and deliver instructions.
- ***Assessment***: Teacher-Educators will design, implement, analyse and interpret the students' assessment.
- ***Technology***: Teacher-Educators will demonstrate the ability to use appropriate instructional technology for information management, communication and instructions.
- ***Professional***: Teacher-educators will demonstrate the professional dispositions and knowledge of school operations necessary to be successful in classroom.

It may be concluded by the golden saying that a poor teacher 'tells', an average teacher 'explains', a good teacher demonstrates and a great teacher 'inspires'.

REFERENCES

Goswami, Sarita. (2009). An appraisal of norms and standards of NCTE regarding teacher education based on attitude of teacher educators. In *Journal of Teacher Education and Research*, Vol. 4, No. 2, Dec. 2009.

Ministry of Human Resource Development (1986). Government of India, New Delhi – May 1986 National Policy on Education 1986,

Ministry of Human Resource Development (1992). National Policy on Education, 1986 (Revised), New Delhi: Government of India

Ministry of Human Resource Development (1992). Programme of Action, New Delhi: Government of India, Department of Education.

National Council for Teacher Education, (1998). *Competency based and Commitment Oriented Teacher Education for Quality School Education*. New Delhi: NCTE.

National Council for Teacher Education. (1998). *Curriculum Framework for Quality Teacher Education*, New Delhi: NCTE

National Council for Teacher Education. (1998). Policy Perspectives in Teacher Education, *Critique and Documentation: Recommendations of various commissions and committees on teacher education (1998)*. NCTE Document 98/23, New Delhi: NCTE.

National Council of Educational Research and Training (2005). *National Curriculum Framework 2005*, New Delhi: NCERT.

National Council for Teacher Education. (2009). National Curriculum Framework for Teacher Education (Draft for Discussion) New Delhi, NCTE, from http://www.teindia.nic.in/Files/national curriculu-for-teacher-education -2009.pdf

Richard, P. Tisher and Mariv F. Wideen. (1990). Research in Teacher Education, *International Perspectives*, The Falmer Press, Taylor &Francis Inc., 1990, Frost Road, Suite 101, Bristol, P.A. 19007 (USA)

20
Secondary Teacher-Training Curriculum and its Transaction

Vimal Kishor

Curriculum is the very heart of educational process. Other aspects of education exist so that there may be an effective curriculum. Curriculum is generally defined as the educational experiences that children have in school. This is a broad definition and includes far more than mere outline of facts, skills, attitudes or ideals, though these are important, too. The personalities of the teacher, the principal and the janitor, must be included. In fact, the whole community — and beyond that the total culture — affect the children in school and, to the extent what they do, are a part of the curriculum. The curriculum, in specific, is a medium that translates socio-educational philosophies into teaching procedures and teaching outcomes. In other words, curriculum is an attempt to communicate the essential principles and features of an educational proposal in such a form that it is open to critical scrutiny and capable of effective translation into practice.

In this competitive world, students need to become more professional to meet the needs of globalization. The society is expecting quality education so that youngsters achieve top placements nationally/internationally. It is the teachers who are called as the nation builders. It is in the school where the teachers modify/develop the students' mental set-up and prepare them for the forthcoming competitions. These teachers who prepare the future themselves are prepared by a professional course called B.Ed. The B.Ed. Programme is now offered in majority of the universities. The over-all objective of teacher education is to equip the prospective teacher with necessary skills, knowledge and technique/strategies for the education of the child (or to assist the child in his learning).

Major Objectives of Bachelor of Education Programme

The main objectives of the undergraduate level programme in Education at present as given in the syllabus of the various universities are as follows:

- To develop an awareness of the role of teacher in realizing the objectives of school education;

- To develop competence to teach at least two school subjects on the basis of the accepted principles of learning and teaching;
- To develop skills for continuously evaluating pupil growth;
- To develop understanding, interest, attitudes and skills which would enable him to foster all-round growth and development of the pupils under his care;
- To develop competence to act not only as a leader of the children but also as a guide of the community and as a liaison between school and the community;
- Making student teachers understand not only the subject but also the unity of knowledge among different subjects;
- Developing among student teachers an integrated and holistic approach in the teaching of social sciences and technology;
- Developing among student teachers the competencies in the use of locally available educational resources;
- Empowering student teachers to know how learners construct knowledge and to facilitate the process;
- Developing among student teachers the skills of communication and language proficiency;
- Helping student teachers to acquire repertoire of strategies, competencies and skills for transaction and evaluation;
- Appreciating the impact of various changes taking place in the society i.e. Liberalization, Privatization and Globalization (LPG), etc. on different aspects of life and their imperatives;
- Enabling student teachers to promote self-learning/mutual learning in and outside the classroom in order to eventually become independent learners;
- Inculcating among student teachers social, cultural, aesthetic, moral and spiritual values and scientific approach and the skill of integrating and transacting these;
- Making student teachers appreciate India's unity in diversity;
- Enabling student teachers to integrate values in all subjects/activities;
- Developing among student teachers awareness and sensitivity towards environment concern and promoting skills for meeting environmental challenges;
- Enabling student teachers to develop competencies for an error free, responsive and transparent evaluation.

Researchers' Views Regarding B. Ed. Curriculum

The teacher-training programme is conceived as the crucial one for creating a large number of teachers imbibed with requisite professional skills and competencies. The present day society needs teachers who can really face the multifarious challenges of the teaching-learning process and can infuse higher morale as well as spirit of inquiry among the learners. In view of this the B.Ed. curriculum need to be properly designed and implemented so as to enable the teachers to perform their duties and responsibilities with competence.

The researchers have, in general, pointed out certain drawbacks in the existing Secondary Teacher Education Programme being run in India as well as abroad. These include the following:

- There was great diversity regarding aims, titles, combinations, content classification, practical work, etc. in the foundational courses prescribed for B.Ed. Degree.
- The comprehensive B.Ed. curriculum was not effectively implemented due to time-shortage, semester-system and internal-assessment, etc.
- There was no significant difference between the classroom performance of trained and untrained teachers irrespective of the subject taught.
- The curricula of Secondary Teacher Education lack uniformity and clear-cut definition. B.Ed. syllabus was found to be inadequate since it was more theoretical in nature.
- There was an obvious disconnect in the programme between the theoretical components and the realities of the classroom.
- The main purpose of teacher-education programme is to develop values skills, professional attitude and personality as an individual, which is not possible within a short duration of one year or effective eight to nine months.

On the basis of their studies and personal professional experience, different researchers and authors have forwarded certain constructive suggestions for the improvement of Secondary Education Teacher Education Programme that include the following:

- The duration of the Secondary Teacher Education Programme should be two academic sessions.
- The aspects of Secondary Teacher Education Programme (STEP) should be: (a) educational theory, (b) practice teaching, (c) community work, (d) work experience, (e) sessionlal work, and (f) co-curricular activities.
- The theory load should be cut down and the ratio of the theory and practice teaching should be 50:50.
- It is practice teaching or practical skill in teaching which was found to be more helpful than the rest of the teacher education programme in developing abilities, especially skills.

- It will be important in this era of intense focus on single measures of teacher education outcomes to press for the use of multiple measures that allow a comprehensive view of what candidates learn and what a programme contributes to their performance.
- Teacher training programme can have lasting impact only if parallel and simultaneous inputs are provided to related sub-systems like provision of infrastructural facilities, curriculum reform, efficient systematic management, use of communication technology and due recognition of teacher's status.
- The curriculum for teacher-education should be developed with co-ordinated effort of all the three agencies NCTE, UGC and NCERT by involving field level agencies and institutions.
- A clear-cut plan with detailed activities is needed for monitoring and evaluation of the programme.

Transaction of B.Ed. Curriculum

The simple construction of curriculum is not enough unless there are clear specifications for its mode of application i.e., transaction in the real classroom situations. Generally, the curriculum prepared for any level of education is implemented by means of following some specific methods as well as techniques. Any suggested curriculum may reflect the intensions of its framers but, is the quality of its transaction which determines the extent to which curricular objectives are realized, and this will largely depend on the sincerity and motivation of the persons responsible for transaction and on the appropriateness of the methodologies used by them. Modes of curricular transaction pertain to the channels adopted for providing learning experiences to trainees. These act as the real 'links' between the expectations placed on a teacher education programme on the one hand, and on the other, the process of enabling teacher trainees to absorb the essentials and actualize these expectations. To put it differently, the modes of transaction represent an operationalization of the various components of teacher education programmes. The mode of training to be adopted for any educational programme has to be determined on the basis of certain criteria. These include: the purpose or goals of programme, the characteristics of the clientele, the nature of the substance to be transacted, the nature of learning activities to be provided, the infrastructural arrangements available and the organizational inputs required. At a deeper level, selection of training modes involves other factors concerning individuals, the community, administrative initiative, professional compulsions, market forces etc. The process of curriculum transaction also brings into focus the role of hidden curriculum which is as important as the manifest curriculum so far as achievement of curricular objectives is concerned. This would mean carrying out those educational activities in teacher education institutions which would develop in student teachers a comprehensive view of the educational experiences. The NCFSE-2000 has made specific recommendations for the transaction of curriculum and evaluation of outcomes at school stage which have considerable implications for teacher education. The major focus has been on understanding 'child as the constructor of knowledge', harnessing potential of information and communication technologies for improvement of learning of children, besides emphasis on mastery of the required content and skills, commensurate with the development of children.

The mode selected has to act as a channel to cater to all these. This is what makes it a crucial act. In teacher education, transactional modes have essentially been of two categories, viz., the face-to- face mode and the distance mode. The face-to-face mode refers to instructional interactions in which learners and the teacher transact a curriculum in a face-to-face situation. This mode includes inputs like seminars, discussions, lectures, demonstrations and any activity involving direct interaction between the learners and the teacher. The distance mode, as the term indicates, pertains to all kinds of interactions between the teacher and learners in which they are not in direct contact with one another and require a third channel or medium for contact. These include the print, audio, video, or any other mode. The face-to-face mode is the oldest and most widely accepted mode. Obviously, at a time when electronic media were not available and even the print medium was unknown, the most easily accessible channel for transmission of knowledge and for communication was face-to-face interaction with the teacher. With printing and the public the school system, text books became available and assumed significance. Over the years, the print medium has provided support to oral communication with the teacher as the main focus in schools. Correspondence education acquired significance as an alternative to 'teacher talk' in India, with increased availability of printing facilities.

Surprisingly, ever since the inception of teacher education programmes in India, more particularly in the post-independence period, dissatisfaction with the ineffectiveness of the 'conventional face-to-face mode' has often been expressed. Irrespective of which institution they came from, all school teachers, with the possible exception of a handful, agree with the 'logic' of the B.Ed Programme but not its effectiveness. After becoming 'regular' teachers, they need not follow the method they have learnt during their training. Further, entrant teachers undergoing the course and teacher educators know the non-receptivity of school teachers to accommodating the 'practice teaching' component in their schools. The secondary teacher education programmes represented by B.Ed. courses are mainly intended for 'preparing' entrants for the teaching profession, with substance of the course constructed on the premise that the prospective teacher needs to be initiated to concepts and understanding so far unknown to him/her and to the requisite skills and technology. In order to enable an entrant teacher to absorb these, a logically arranged theoretical understanding and opportunity to practice what is learnt are provided. Extending this logic would mean that any field experience would by itself enable the entrant to perceive the field differently. Personal experience would provide, no doubt, some understanding of the concepts and factors involved. If this is accepted, the 'substance' of B.ED. may have to be constructed differently.

With regard to the status and role of teacher in community, Secondary Education Commission (1952) headed by Dr. A. Lakshmanswami Mudaliar, Vice-Chancellor, Madras University, noted:

In the preceding chapters of our Report we have referred to the various steps to be taken to improve the quality and standards of Secondary education and to make it a worthy medium for the balanced development of the students' personality. We are, however, convinced that the most important factor in the contemplated educational reconstruction is the teacher — his personal qualities, his educational qualifications, his professional training and the place that he occupies in the school as well as in the community. The reputation of a school and its influence on the life of the community invariably depend on the kind of teachers working in it. Priority of consideration must, therefore, be given to the various problems connected with the improvement of their status.

Report of the Education Commission (1964-66, 124) headed by Dr. D.S. Kothari describes the role and importance of Teacher in the following words:

> A sound programme of professional education of teachers is essential for the qualitative improvement of education. Investment in teacher education can yield very rich dividends because the financial resources required are small when measured against the resulting improvements in the education of millions. In the absence of other influences, a teacher tries to teach in the way in which he himself was taught by his favourite teachers and thus tends to perpetuate the traditional methods of teaching. In a situation like the present when new and dynamic methods of instruction are needed, such an attitude becomes an obstacle to progress. It can be modified only by effective professional education which will initiate the teachers to needed revolution in teaching and lay the foundations for their future professional growth. First-rate teacher-training institution can thus play a crucial role in the development of education.

The National Policy on Education, 1986 in this context stated that:

> The status of the teacher reflects the socio-cultural ethos of a society; it is said that no people can rise above the level of its teachers. The Government and the community should endeavour to create conditions, which will help motivate and inspire teachers on constructive

> and creative lines. Teachers should have the freedom to innovate, to devise appropriate methods of communication and activities relevant to the needs and capabilities of and the concerns of the community.

Position Paper on National Curriculum Framework, 2005 visualizes Teacher Education as:

Teacher education has to become more sensitive to the emerging demands from the school system. For this it has to prepare teachers for a dual role of:

- encouraging, supportive and humane facilitator in teaching-learning situations who enables learners (students) to discover their talents, to realize their physical and intellectual potentialities to the fullest, to develop character and desirable social and human values to function as responsible citizens; and,
- an active member of the group of persons who make conscious effort to contribute towards the process of renewal of school curriculum to maintain its relevance to the changing societal needs and personal needs of learners, keeping in view the experience gained in the past and the concerns and imperatives that have emerged in the light of changing national development goals and educational priorities.

Position Paper on National Curriculum Framework, 2005 further elaborates the role of Teacher in the context of above expectations:

> These expectations suggest that teacher operates in a larger context, and its dynamics as well as concerns impinge upon her functioning. That is to say, teacher has to be responsive and sensitive to the social context of education, the various disparities in background of learners as well as in the macro national and global contexts, national concerns for achieving the goals of equity, parity, and social justice as also excellence. To be able to realize such expectations, Teacher Education has to comprise such features as would enable each of its learners, i.e., student teachers, to:
>
> - care for children/learners and who love to be with them;
> - understand children within social, cultural and political contexts;
> - view learning as a search for meaning out of personal experience;
> - understand the way learning occurs, possible ways of creating conducive conditions for learning, differences among students in respect of the kind, pace and styles of learning;
> - view knowledge generation as a continuously evolving process of reflective learning;
> - necessarily view knowledge as an external reality embedded in textbooks but as constructed in the shared context of teaching learning and personal experiences;

- be sensitive to the social, professional and administrative contexts in which they have to operate;
- be receptive and constantly learning; own responsibility towards society and work to build a better world;
- develop appropriate competencies to be able to not only seek the above understandings in actual situations, but also be able to create them;
- have a sound knowledge-base and basic proficiency in language,
- identify their own personal expectations, perceptions of self, capacities and inclinations;
- consciously attempt to formulate one's own professional orientation this will determine his role as a teacher in situation specific context.

In this context, the teacher-training programme is conceived as the crucial one for creating large number of teachers imbibed with requisite professional skills and competencies. The present day society needs teachers who can really face the multifarious challenges of the teaching-learning process and can infuse higher morale as well as spirit of inquiry among the learners. In view of this the B.Ed. curriculum need be properly designed and implemented which can enable the teachers to perform their duties and responsibilities with competence.

Very often it is seen that B.Ed. curriculum happens to be more theoretical and less practical. Such a state of B.Ed. Curriculum leaves the teachers nowhere making them crippled in the classroom situation. Therefore, as per the recommendation of National Curriculum Framework, 2005 a linkage need be established between theory and practice. Further, it also gives stress upon linking classroom knowledge to situations outside the classroom as well as discouraging the method of rote learning. In view of such changing needs and demands in philosophy of teaching-learning process, there is an urgent need to study the utilitarian aspect of the B.Ed. Curriculum as viewed by the teachers concerned.

Conclusion

The observations of the above mentioned reports indicate the necessity of having quality teachers at every stage of our educational system. However, good teachers can be produced only when we have good and effective teacher-education programmes supported by well-balanced teacher-education curriculum. It is presumed that the teacher-education curriculum must develop among student teachers a thorough understanding of physiological and psychological development as well as sociological background of learners to identify children having special needs and providing appropriate measures for their education.

But the matter of concern is that to what extent the teacher-education curriculum has the potential to meet the requirements of the teacher-trainees on one hand and to what extent the teacher trainees are really capable of implementing the taught concepts in the real classroom teaching-learning process on the other hand. It may be pointed out here that no programme can be given the credit of being successful if it does not have any utilitarian value. As such, the teacher education curriculum is expected to be appreciated by the teachers as relevant if it has the potential to solve the teaching-learning related problems of the teachers. As teacher-education programme is considered as the key programme for the human resource development of the country, evaluative research need be conducted regarding the relevance of this curriculum. However, it should not be based on the type and amount of curriculum but on the basis of how far it is useful to teachers in their day-today classroom activities. As such, the B.ED. curriculum need be relevant one with regards to the real classroom teaching practice and should also be appreciated by the teachers as the utilitarian one.

REFERENCES

Ackerman, Elaive (2004). Effective teacher preparation programmes from the perspective of first year teachers. Gonzaga University, pp. 315. *Dissertation Abstracts International*, Vol. 66, No. 3, September, 2005, p. 960-A.

Anderson, Vernon E. (1956). *Principles and Procedure of Curriculum Improvement.* New York: The Ronald Press Company, pp. 7-11.

Behri, Alka (1998). Analysing Teacher Education Curriculum in the Context of Requisite abilities for Effective Teaching. *Indian Educational Review,* Vol. 33, No. 1, New Delhi: NCERT, January 1998, pp. 93-104.

Bhatia, Ranjana (1987). Evaluation of New B. Ed. Curriculum in the colleges of Education Affiliated to the University of Bombay. Ph. D. Edu., Bom. U. *Fourth Survey of Research in Education (1983-88),* Ed., M.B. Buch (1991). New Delhi: National Council for Educational Research and Training, Sri Aurobindo Marg, Volume II, p. 923.

Chandra, Soti Shivendra, Beri, Anoop and Beri, Nimisha (2008). Re-equipping Teacher Education. *University News: A Weekly Journal of Higher Education*, Vol. 46, No. 16, April 21-27, 2008.

Gupta, M. Sen (2007). Teacher Training—Any Impact? *University News: A Weekly Journal of Higher Education,* Vol. 45, No. 10, March 05-11, 2007.

Hammond, Linda Darling (2006). Assessing Teacher Education—The Usefulness of Multiple Measures for Assessing programme Outcomes. *Journal of Teacher Education,* Vol. 57, No. 2, March/April 2006, pp. 120-138.

Hemambujam, K. (1983). A Critical Study of Teacher Education at the Secondary Level in Tamil Nadu. Ph. D. Edu., Kar. U. *Fourth Survey of Research in Education (1983-88),* Ed., M.B. Buch (1991). New Delhi: National Council for Educational Research and Training, Sri Aurobindo Marg, Volume II, p. 943.

Jones, Mildred Albertha (1991). An evaluation of classroom performance and pedagogical knowledge of trained and untrained teachers in Barbadian secondary schools.

University of South Florida, pp. 130. *Dissertation Abstracts International*, Vol. 53, No. 2, August, 1992, p. 390-A.

Kakkad, G.M. (1983). Secondary Teacher-Education Curriculla- An Analytical study and Developing Teacher-Education Programme. Ph. D. Edu., Nag. U. *Fourth Survey of Research in Education (1983-88),* Ed., M.B. Buch (1991). New Delhi: National Council for Educational Research and Training, Sri Aurobindo Marg, Volume II, p. 947.

Maheshwari, Amrita (2008). Crucial Issues and Emerging Concerns in Teacher Education. *University News: A Weekly Journal of Higher Education,* Vol. 46, No. 12, March24-30, 2008.

National Focus Group on Teacher Education for Curriculum Renewal (2005). *National Curriculum Framework: Position Paper.* New Delhi: National Council of Educational Research and Training, 2006

National Policy on Education (1986). *Government of India, Ministry of Human Resource Development, Department of Education.* New Delhi-110001, Part IX, pp. 31-32.

Report of the Education Commission (1964-66). *Education and Development. National Council of Educational Research and Training,* Sri Aurobindo Marg, New Delhi-110016. Chapter IV, Teacher Education, p. 124.

Secondary Education Commission (1952). *Government of India, Ministry of Human Resource Development, Department of Education,* New Delhi-110001, Chapter XII (Improvement of the Teaching Personnel), p. 151.

Sharma, G.P. (1982). A Study of the Foundational Course Prescribed for B.Ed. Degree of Indian Universities. Ph. D. Edu., Agra. U. *Third Survey of Research in Education (1978-83),* Ed., M.B. Buch (1986). New Delhi: National Council for Educational Research and Training, Sri Aurobindo Marg, p. 838.

University Grants Commission (1990). *Reports of Curriculum Development Centre in Education,* Vol. II (B. Ed.) Course, New Delhi: UGC, pp. 6-15.

Verma, Mahesh (2006). *Teacher Education.* New Delhi: Murari Lal and Sons, pp. 65-72.

Walia, K. (1992). Secondary Teachers Education Programme in Northern India: An Evaluative Study. *Fifth Survey of Educational Research*, Vol. I, New Delhi: National Council for Educational Research and Training, p. 454.

21

Preparing Future Teachers: Transacting the Curriculum for Teacher Education

Ritu Bakshi

Why India is still a developing country and what is stopping it from being a developed country? Most probably, the answer is education system that is not able to achieve its target of inculcating appropriate skills in the people. India is going to experience a paradox of nearly 90 million people joining the workforce but most of them lack requisite skills and the mindset for productive employment according to a report. India has about 550 million people under the age of 25 years out of which only 11 per cent are enrolled in tertiary institutions as compared to the world average of 23 per cent. Today, in India, it is difficult to decide how the agenda for teacher education and its reform can be taken forward. The Right to Education will succeed only if teachers are able to work to ensure that all children do become educated by attending school; effectively, this means that the Centre has placed the onerous responsibility of ensuring the realization of the right on teachers.

Existing pre-service teacher education programmes for future teachers are ill-equipped to achieve this, even in places where they are conducted sincerely. Dominant Bachelor of Education (B.Ed) formats are oriented to teaching 'textbooks', they lack grounding in contemporary understanding of childhood, child development and learning theory. So a reformed and robust programme of teacher education has a bearing on realising the right to education is obvious.

Teachers as Assets

Teachers are the greatest assets of any education system. They are accepted as the backbone of education system. Teacher quality is therefore crucial and has been globally accepted to be significantly associated with the quality of education in general and students' learning outcomes in particular. The Education Commission (1964-66) of India accepted this influence of teachers in powerful words, "No system can rise above the status of its teacher..." Research shows that teacher quality is significantly and positively correlated with pupil attainment and it is the most important within school aspect explaining students' performance. Teachers help in shaping and reshaping the society and determine the quality of life in the community and the nation. Each society, therefore, makes some provision for pre-service education and continuous professional development of teachers in order to help them contribute in the growth of society.

If we analyse teacher education systems in different countries from this perspective we will find majority of teacher education reform efforts centered on reforming the knowledge base of teachers, and similarities can be observed in teacher education curriculum across various societies.

Teacher Education Curriculum Reforms and Policy initiatives

The pre-service teacher preparation programmes remain the important determinant of how teachers learn and succeed in the dynamic circumstances of real classroom and school. India has made concentrated efforts to modify and modernize teacher education curricula to suit the requirements of contemporary educational needs of the society and instill greater professionalism and commitment in practicing teachers through pre-service and continuous in-service teacher education programmes. The National Policy of Education (NPE, 1986) reflects this commitment by considering pre-service and in-service teacher education as a continuous process and two ends of a continuum. A number of educational committees, commissions, professionals who have been advocating for achieving or enhancing quality in education, will have to acknowledge the importance of the role of teacher in bringing about the expected change. More than thirteen decades have passed since the Hunter Commission (First Indian Education Commission) has made its recommendation for having trained teachers followed by a variety of recommendations by various committees. We have also not stopped at recommendations but have made certain major leaps in our endeavor of bringing about quality in teacher education. The NPE, 86 has provided the greatest momentum in bringing about revolution in teacher education. It has resulted in the establishment of the NCTE. Teacher Education is also included under the Centrally Sponsored Schemes. These stressed on the need for flexibility, and local specificity; and strongly felt, that the whole teacher education programme needs to be remodelled to strike more balance between the theory and practice, and assessment of students' performance. All the commissions, committees, and study groups expressed concern over the irrelevance of teacher education programme. However, in reality, even after approximately five decade of the observation made by the Education Commission (1964-66) in this context that "Vitality and realism are lacking in the curriculum and programme of work which continue to be largely traditional with disregard for the present day need and objectives" (Para.4 02; p. 68) remains relevant, though, a number of policy initiatives have been taken by the government, from time to time, to modernize and bring qualitative improvement in teacher education curriculum of the country.

So we still find that somewhere the gap is still continuing, reflecting on the present system of education. Who can offer an explanation to this? The answer lies in the observations of the University Education Commission that 'Teaching' in this country is not recognized as a profession and that of the Kothari Commission that teacher training is conducted in 'isolation'.

National Curriculum Frameworks for Teacher Education: A Move Towards Teacher Preparation

Teacher development is considered as the continuous process of developing and maintaining professional competence in teachers through pre-service, induction training, in-service training and on-going professional development programmes. Pre-service is the first step in the ladder of developing professionalism in teachers that, in turn, is dependent on the professional preparation of teachers through well designed teacher education courses suited to the needs of contemporary educational system. Teacher education has a symbiotic relationship with the school education.

Developments and changes in both the sectors mutually reinforce the concerns necessary for the quality improvement of entire system of education. Therefore, any reform in educational system should ideally be accompanied by reforms in teacher preparation courses also. India has tried to put this theoretical ideology into practice. Consequently, with change in the curriculum framework for school education we find subsequent efforts to adjust the teacher preparation curricula accordingly. Four such major attempts have been made by the policy planners of the country so far to provide conceptual directions in uniformity and quality of teacher education curriculum according to the socio-culture, and socio-economic ethos of the country. The first comprehensive attempt was made in 1978 with the publication "Teacher Education Curriculum: A Framework" by the National Council for Teacher education (NCTE), and recommendations of this Framework included:

- Relevance of the Curriculum to the personal and social needs of children and schools; as well as aspirations of people and ideology of nation.
- Task-oriented teacher education. Teacher education must be treated as an "exercise of training a teacher for handling a variety of tasks inside and outside the classroom."
- Reform in practice teaching. The framework suggested that student teachers should be put through a series of simulating, microteaching situations before being pushed into actual classrooms.

- Semester system was suggested to replace the year wise course.
- Evaluation system to be made more reliable and valid.
- Promotion of research and experimentation in teacher education institutions.

Another significant attempt to bring qualitative improvement in teacher education curricula was made in 1988. This framework consolidated developments that had taken place in preceding years, and emphasized the need to accommodate the developments taken place in knowledge and technology in the teacher education curricula. The changing role of teacher had been strongly emphasized in this framework as "The Future teacher will be a competent professional and a skilled teacher as always has been expected, but this will now mean that he will also need to be an effective communicator, a designer and user of learning resources, a learning facilitator, and active participant in community life"

Dialectic Approach: Theory and Practicum

The need for having a balance between theory and practice was manifested in the Framework as "The curriculum should emphasize integration of theoretical understanding with their practical application without overdoing one over the other". Central place to practicum or field work with appropriate weightage was also suggested by this Framework. The course content therefore included: Foundation Courses, emphasizing mainly the philosophical and social perspectives, and psychological bases of education at the stage concerned; Stage- relevant specializations, emphasizing understanding of the professional functions of the teacher in a general way relevant to the stage and competencies and skills of teaching relevant school subjects. Field Work or Practicum, emphasizing application of theory in classroom teaching and in the practical activities involving students, parents and the community.

However, in spite of three curriculum frameworks, and recommendations of National Policy on Education (NPE, 1986) for complete overhauling of teacher education programmes (Para 9.4; p. 44) the teacher education system of the country is often criticised for its quality. Though there have been widespread efforts to modify teacher education curriculum of the country over the years, only cosmetic changes have been made in reality, and majority of teacher education programmes remained satisfied with providing a 'chefs salad' of information about various concepts to perspective teachers, including concepts like human rights education, education for sustainable development, peace education, and culture specific pedagogy etc. Way back in 1985 an important document 'The Challenges of Education,' which preceded the NPE (1986) made statement: "We are on the threshold of development of new technologies likely to revolutionize teaching in classroom. But unfortunately, the process of updating the curricula of teacher education has been very slow. Much of the teacher education is irrelevant even to contemporary requirements, leave alone those of the future. We, therefore, face a paradox of having better books, and research but progressively more indifferent teachers". (p. 54) The situation has not changed much even today. The changes suggested by these curriculum frameworks have not been fully implemented at the ground level.

Teacher education curriculum is expected to develop dispositions among teachers to discharge their duties effectively. As in any other professional education programmes, the teacher education curriculum has to have a knowledge base which is sensitive to the needs of field applications and comprise meaningful, conceptual blending of the theoretical understanding available in different cognate disciplines. The existing curriculum, however fails miserably to bring to the surface this applied aspect of various philosophical, sociological and psychological ideas, and hence the whole teacher education programme remains theoretical and divorced from the grass root realities of classrooms. It fails to develop an understanding among the students about Education as independent discipline in itself and it's inter-linkages with various cognate disciplines.

Un-relatedness of the Theoretical Course in Real Classroom Practices: A Major Issue

A major problem facing teacher education programme in India is the un-relatedness of the theoretical discourses at the training college and classroom realities of schools. This divorce between the classroom realities a teacher has to face and the teacher education programmes he/she receives also finds an expression in the World Bank.

The orientation provided in teacher education institutions through foundation courses is often too theoretical and provides only unrelated and fragmented knowledge to teachers. It fails to develop a deeper understanding in student teachers about the learners, their socio-cultural environment, their developmental stages, physical and psychological changes they are undergoing, and influence of these factors on their learning styles. Therefore considerable diversity is needed in content and pedagogy to develop reflectivity in teachers. Teachers in the existing socio-cultural context of the country need to be logical and reflective because of increasing racial, ethical, and cultural and linguistic diversities in the schools and in society which demands broad minded citizens and also because a number of empirical evidence suggests that teacher's own beliefs play a major role in how they respond to the diversity in their classroom situations. Teacher education curriculum, therefore need to be planned and organized to develop the spirit of inquiry, initiative, scientific temper, conceptual clarity and linguistic skills through rigorous practice teaching and/or internship which has so far remained a neglected area of teacher preparation.

Pedagogical Reform of Teacher Education: The National Curriculum Framework for Teacher Education, 2009

A major effort to reform school education as well as teacher education towards modernization, contextualization and professionalization has been made in 2005 and 2009 through the National Curriculum Framework for School Education (2005), and National Curriculum Framework for Teacher Education (2009) respectively. During recent years the epistemology of learning has undergone a major change; i.e., learning does not involve discovering the reality, but constructing the reality. Knowledge and cognitions are to be constructed and effects are to be felt. Learning is no more a passive absorption of knowledge and ideas, but the construction of ideas developed on one's personal experiences. Emphasis has, now, shifted towards constructivist approach of learning. Learning is also perceived as an integral part of learner's physical, social, and cultural contexts. This concept has come to be known as situated cognition and is the guiding principle of the National curriculum Framework for School Education (2005) developed by NCERT. The NCF 2005 expects a teacher to be the facilitator of students' learning in a manner that helps them to construct knowledge and meaning utilising their individual experiences. The whole pedagogical approach of teacher education programme, therefore, needs to be reoriented from traditional behaviourist to constructivist discourses. The National Curriculum Framework for Teacher Education (2009) developed by NCTE tries to ensure that teacher education courses are reoriented to align with the epistemological shift envisaged in the NCF 2005 and develop teachers as facilitators of learning. It includes the contexts, concerns and visions of teacher education which calls for preparing teachers for learning society, empowering teachers in learning to learn, and making teacher education liberal, humanistic and responsive to the to the demands of inclusive education. It has tried to incorporate the changing school contexts and demands in the light of recently implemented Right to Education Act (RTE 2009), issue of academic burden of students, and universalisation of secondary education that have implication for teacher education. The major concerns addressed by this framework include inclusive education, ensuring equitable and sustainable development, utilising community knowledge in education, and integration of ICT and e-learning in the curriculum of teacher education which is in tune with the thrust of NCF 2005 and the needs of contemporary Indian society. Therefore, the traditional approach to teacher reparation based on philosophical, sociological and psychological orientation of courses has given way to 'carefully crafted curriculum design that draws upon theoretical and empirical knowledge as well as student teachers' 'experiential knowledge' (NCFTE 2009, p. 24). Three broad curricular areas identified by this Framework are:

- Foundations of Education which includes courses under three rubrics, namely, Learner Studies, Contemporary Studies and Educational Studies;
- Curriculum and Pedagogy including Curriculum Studies and Pedagogic Studies; and
- School Internship, leading to the development of a broad repertoire of perspective, professional capacities, teacher sensibilities and skills (NCFTE 2009, p. 24). An attempt has been made through this Curriculum Framework to not only address the issues, concerns and pedagogical shifts visualised by NCF 2005, but also organize the entire teacher education curriculum as an organic and integrated whole. It also tries to address the criticism regarding the unrelatedness of theoretical discourses of teacher education institutions to the classroom realities by incorporating the socio-cultural contexts of education, giving more weightage to the field experience of student teachers in all courses through practicum, visits to innovative centres of pedagogy and learning, classroom based research.

Conclusion

How to effectively prepare future teachers for educating a diverse student population in today's global society is a critical issue facing teacher educators. On investigation of teacher preparation programmes across the nation, and the resulting teacher retention rate, it appears evident that teacher preparation programmes in schools of education must prepare pre-service teachers for the "real" classroom—one that is diverse in many ways—ethnically, culturally, socio economically, as well as other forms of diversity. This raises concerns about who will teach our children and how will the quality of education they would receive.

Teachers in the 21st Century must be prepared for the classroom in ways beyond what is presented in textbooks. In an ever-increasing diverse society, the acquisition of content knowledge and limited field experience by pre service teachers fall short of preparing them for teacher effectiveness in the diverse classroom. They must be equipped with knowledge and skills that are not articulated in textbooks. Teaching and learning strategies, classroom management skills, and diversity sensitivity ought to be integral parts of any and all pre service teacher training programs. An early, substantial, and varied field experience, then, is a critical component of any teacher preparation programme to ensure successful transitioning from pre service teacher to teacher practitioner.

The curriculum for teacher candidates must include courses related to diversity to help these teacher candidates recognize and work against situations that perpetuate inequality. These courses need to be relevant to the world the teacher candidates will face. Hence any effective teacher education curriculum calls for systematic task analysis of teachers at various levels and inclusion of relevant contents, which alone can infuse confidence among the prospective teachers to negotiate the school curriculum in classroom. The present teacher education programme is inadequate to meet the challenges of diverse Indian socio-cultural contexts and the paradigm shift envisaged in the NCF 2005. The pedagogic reform from this perspective need to invest on building on teachers capacity to act as autonomous reflective groups of professionals who are sensitive to their social mandate and to the professional ethics and to the needs of heterogeneous groups of learners. The National Curriculum Framework for Teacher Education (2009) promises to translate the vision into reality and prepare humanistic and reflective teachers that have the potential to develop more professional teachers and improve the quality of education.

- There should be equal emphasis on all the components of training—theory, practice and application (internship).
- Along with the theory and practical work related to each theory paper, the students may be required to do case studies, a project or action research.
- The existing B.Ed course may be made a 2 year modular programme—a combination of Foundation and Skill Training Programme:
  - First year for foundation courses
  - Second year for Skill training and Action Research

Hence, investment in reviewing and reforming pre-service teacher education may give desired results and be helpful in proper implementation of CCE and RTE. So it's a wake-up call now for immediate reforms in teacher education with systematic investment and follow up, since as all is not well with present education system. We as educators have to safeguard it from being hijacked by shortsighted alternatives.

REFERENCES

Ferguson, R.F. (1991a): Paying for public education: New evidence on how and why money matters. *Harvard Journal of Legislation*, 28(1), pp. 1-35.

Ministry of Human Resource Development (MHRD): *Learning Without Burden* (Yashpal Committee Report). New Delhi, India.

National Commission on Teachers-1 (1983-85): *Teacher and society*. Delhi, Government of India Press.

National Council for Teacher Education (1998): *Curriculum Framework for Quality Teacher Education*, New Delhi, NCTE.

NCERT (1978): *Teacher Education Curriculum: A Framework*. New Delhi, NCERT.

NCTE (1988): *National Curriculum Framework for Teacher Education*, New Delhi, NCERT.

22
Total Quality Management and its Commitment in Teacher Education: An Issue of Concern

Puja Gupta

Quality is regarded as a prime requisite to develop human skill in the "knowledge era". It is becoming an essential aspect, and in coming years, it would be an essential requirement for the survival of the organization. It needs to be nurtured through positive attitude and quality culture in an organization. Lifelong learning is a process that can be done in almost every aspect of life. Institution is a place to learn continuously. At work, we learn how to accomplish certain tasks, how to decisions, how to treat other people within the organization and how to cope with the everlasting changes. 'Gurukula system' of education was probably the best example of quality management in education. This quality in education was lost during the medieval and the modern colonial period. The students want institutions to equip them to deal with a very uncertain future. Employers require greater learning skills, teamwork and self motivation based on a good grasp of basics. Government is under intense pressure to reduce public spending. In these circumstances, quality is the answer, not the problem. It is the only way to increase outputs and reduce costs. Once an institution adopts a Total Quality Programme for itself and its learners, the quality problem might disappear and unexpected disturbance and failure in managing the classes become rare occurrences. Total Quality Management is one of the many things that people learn at work place.

Concept of Quality

It is difficult to give a comprehensive definition of quality. However the quest for quality has been the major concern of the entire human civilization. Quality is not an act; it is a habit. It generally signifies the degrees of excellence. It is the totality of features and characteristics of process that bear on its ability to satisfy stated needs.

Total Quality Management: Concept

Total Quality Management (TQM) was developed by an American, Edwards Deming, to improve the quality of production and services. TQM is a management approach of an organization based on quality and the participation of all its members, aiming at long term success. It is a way of thinking about goals, organization processes and people to ensure that the right things are done right the first time. This thought could change attitudes, behaviour and results for the betterment. It is not a system, a tool or even a process. All these are employed to achieve Total Quality Management.

Total quality management (TQM) is a recent concept popular among the management circles. Its application to education is well articulated by NAAC in its Total Quality Management for Tertiary Education (2003). Total Quality Management considers quality primarily as that perceived by the customers of service or product. In education it means meeting of changing demands of students, employers, knowledge producers and society. Total Quality Management is therefore, "a people driven process. It involves change in people's attitude primarily. In addition, it deals with process orientation and continuous improvement of the process. It strives for empowerment and autonomy of the people involved in using processes of production. It asks people to continuously look for new ways to adopt to the changing environment. It is a continuous improvement plan with an effort to bring out the best for the organization" (NAAC, 2003).

Total Quality Management is based on the assumption that quality cannot be inspected into a product rather it must be built into it. It is a fundamental shift, the systematic analysis and blue printing of operation; process of habitual improvement where control is embedded within and is driven by the culture of the organization. Managing quality is the job of each and every member of an organization.

Total Quality Management in Teacher Education

Teacher devotes his entire life to learning and is a living embodiment of lifelong learning. The quality of teacher education determines the quality of teachers. The number of teachers produced at different levels is increasing to meet the demands of education. In this enormous expansion of the teacher education system in the country, quality was not the major concern. Teacher education institutes should be properly equipped and staffed so that they have necessary orientation and commitment for preparing teachers for various levels of school education. Teacher education is an important element influencing the quality of education imparted to students at all levels. Teacher education is a complex professional task. Its major components include pre-service education and in-service education of teachers; it also includes induction programme and staff development programmes.

Quality of human resources and man power is largely dependent on the unfolding of human personality and increased opportunities for transmission of their interests, attitudes and values. This task is best performed by a sound system of education, as it is only education which can unlock all doors for progress. Teachers don't enter the classroom as finished products. Most of teachers who remain in the profession grow over time and become better. Good teachers produce good students. A teacher's most important task is contributing to and enhancing the learning and achievement of his/her students. Teacher education is the heartland of any education system. The future world lies in the hands of the teachers. Teacher education is involved in the process of preparing teachers and support them throughout their careers.

Teacher education system in India has long been considered weak among higher education degree programmes: one that lacks high standards and strong contacts with the field. Unlike the professional education course for doctors, engineers etc, the professional education course for teachers is often found to be not only short in duration, but also very limited in exposing the teacher trainees to the practical realities of classroom teaching in varied school contexts. In this regard, critics point out that teacher education courses lack both academic rigor and professionalism that is often seen in other professions such as medical, legal etc. It is said that the best gift a teacher can give his students is making education effective and thereby promoting learning. This can be possible if existing practices are reworked from time to time in the light of new developments and changing requirements.

Total Quality Management in Teacher Education refers to the enforcement process of an administrative approach in which each human resource involved in the process of education participates actively in the process of decision making.

Total Quality Management in Educational Institutions: Why?

The concept of Total Quality Management is applicable to academics. Many educators believe that it provides guiding principles for needed educational reform. The need for adoption of Total Quality Management can be explained in following points:

- *(i)* ***Value Erosion***: The value erosion among students is a matter of concern today. There is increased deterioration of respect for teachers in the society. The teachers themselves are responsible for the situation. Misuse of the position and corruption that is rampant in other areas of society is reflected in the field of education also.
- *(ii)* ***Lack of Sense of Accountability***: Teacher educators are running away from their responsibilities and are just working to earn their livelihood which in turn degrades the quality of education.
- *(iii)* ***Management Interference***: Another important reason which arises the need for TQM is management interference now and then which prohibits the teacher educators to give their best.

(iv) ***Attitude of Teacher Educators and Prospective teachers***: Both the teacher educator and prospective teachers are going towards pessimism day by day due to various reasons such as government legislations, explanation in terms of economy etc.

Total Quality Management in Teacher Education: How?

Adopt New Philosophy

Demands and opportunities for teachers are constantly changing. The existing model of teacher education has the following feature:

Trainees after admission are told of various theories related to teaching and learning. Then to have practice for the development of various skills, they go for teaching practice under the supervision of their teachers. The practice is under controlled conditions, as they have to take two classes per day. But after the training when they get employed and go to the field (Schools) for teaching they face the real situation and problems and being unable to tackle these problems they fail in their real professional work.

To cope with this problem, the concept of 'Wholistic Teacher Education' model as proposed by A.K. Paliwal and B.K. Passi can be followed:

Problem-Practice-Theory

In this proposed model, firstly the trainees are sent to the field to face the actual problems. This will enrich them in experience and they will have a glimpse of the real world of teaching. Then they start practicing teaching, go to class and try to use their experiences gained while facing actual situation, and finally they are motivated to construct their own theory of teaching learning based on their observations.

Constancy of Purpose

The purpose of life is improvement. So we must "Commit to CAN-Constant and Never ending improvement" (Anthony Robbins). In TQM organization, teams and individuals are constantly working for improvement. The concept of services being "good enough" is now outdated. To achieve the aim of "the best" we have to club talent and experience. For this, personal interaction between teachers and students should be positive and teachers should try to foster teacher-student and student-student relationships as no man is an island in himself or herself. So teamwork collaboration will help in achieving our purpose. This means a teacher imparts, instructs, and raises awareness of something, but also has to be a jack-of-all-trades.

Cease Dependence on Mass Inspection and Numerical Standards

If we want to achieve optimum quality in teacher education, we have to abolish the harmful effects of rating people. We have mainly to focus on learning and enrichment of experience and not on rating. It will encourage creativity and experiments. As there are various defects in our examination system, they are doomed due to subjectivity of the examiners. This causes adverse effects on teaching methods, results in moral degradation and has bad effect on health. These mass inspections fail to test the real knowledge. We must have in our mind the concept of individual differences while rating the students.

Drive out Fear

If teachers and trainees do not have burden of rating and grading then they will put great inputs, speak freely and can take risks. This can make their work a pleasure. This will inculcate confidence and they can have stamina to meet the obstacles and overcome them.

Quality of Incoming Material

The success of an institution depends upon the incoming material. Here, in the scenario of education our incoming materials are students. These is a famous saying, "Planting of good seeds got good plants." This means that the students chosen for teacher training courses must have teaching aptitude and they must have patience to learn. As Tagore remarked "*A lamp can never light another lamp unless it continues to burn its own flame.*"

Become Competitive

William Arthur Ward said: "*The mediocre teacher tells, The good teacher explains, The superior teacher demonstrates, The great teacher inspires.*"

A teacher has to inspire his/her students for healthy competition so that the students have all-round development of their personality. A teacher has to create competitive atmosphere and assign right duties to the students without any bias and subjectivity. Competition is a great force behind the success in life and as the saying goes *"Good timber does not grow with ease. The stronger the wind stronger the trees."*

Eliminate Boundaries in an Organization

If we have to make a place in this world then we have to abolish the hierarchy so that each and every individual feels belongingness to the institution. For this, all the members must be given equal opportunities to hone their skills so that they can keep abreast of times and educate their learners in a better way. As it is said, "As are the gods so are the worshippers." And with we-feeling we can step towards path of success.

Change in Attitude

Unless and until the attitudes are changed in utilizing TQM in classroom instruction we can't imagine of quality. Attitudes such as open mindedness, will to learn something new, will to evaluate teaching learning progress, will to learn about new instructional devices etc.

Provision of Resource Book

There is a need for a resource book for teacher educator that spells out different methods, which need to be followed to improve training programmes quantitatively as well as qualitatively.

Reformation of Curriculum

The curriculum for teacher education must be reformed and reconstructed. Practical work must be emphasized in spite of loading the minds with the theoretical knowledge.

More Emphasis on Practice Teaching

The practice teaching period must be increased. It must be conducted in three phases i.e. for three months. In April the students teach for one month under the supervision of teacher educator followed by another two months of internship in July and August during which the prospective teacher is supervised by school authorities.

Teachers Performance Evaluation

Periodic appraisal of teachers is very necessary. It can be based on peer evaluation, student evaluation, and principal's evaluation and if it is conducted objectively might help the teacher to improve professionally. Once the quality is assured by an organization a total commitment for its sustenance is very essential. Quality commitment can usually be regarded as an ongoing programme which is basic to Total Quality Management. Sound human relations both within the organization and the society is a must.

Basis of Total Commitment to Quality

Total commitment to quality is based upon three basic aspect:

1. Sound Quality Policy
2. Careful Quality Planning
3. Enlightened Quality Management

1. ***Sound Quality Policy***: The first and foremost aspect of total commitment to quality by an organization is to form a sound quality policy. Various aspects related to quality must be focused. Policies must not only be theoretical in these existences but must be practical enough to ensure its usage.

2. ***Careful Quality Planning***: Education planners must have strong determination and deep insight regarding the planning. Each and every aspect related to teacher education must be taken into consideration and then proper planning must be ensured.

3. ***Enlightened Quality Management***: Policies and planning remains in vain unless and until the management has the positive attitude towards the adoptance of the Quality Programmes. Commitment towards the quality can only be ensured it the managers are enlightened enough regarding the assurance of quality.

Activities for Achieving Total Commitment to Quality

- ***Quality Education and Training***: The development of personnel in all functions and at all levels can be ensured by quality education and training. Both are based on various principles such as quality problem centered, focus on the needs of the teacher education, up gradation of human resources etc.
- ***Development of Quality mindedness in human resources***: Human satisfaction is the main tool which provides quality mindedness. Human climate must be provided which indirectly motivates the individual. Both transparency within the working culture and clear communication are the pre-requisites for quality mindedness.
- ***Participative Approaches***: An idea of commitment to the quality can flourish only if there exist the feeling of team building and be-longingness. Its an universal fact that group action is effective. The gap between the employer and employee must be bridged in order to develop the feeling of belongingness. Various important decisions must be taken as a joint venture and not by the management itself.
- ***Appreciation and Encouragement***: Demoralization is one of the important constraint in the commitment to quality. In order to ensure the commitment of human resources towards quality, the only step is appreciation and encouragement. Appreciate the work done by the educators and motivate them by rewarding their dedication either in tangible or non tangible forms.
- ***Provide Stress free Working Culture*:** Stress is the biggest obstacle in the commitment to quality. When stressful atmosphere exist in the working environment then whatever the input be the output is always low. So management must see that the organizational stressors are reduced to the minimum extent.
- ***Accountability of All:*** Commitment to the quality can be ensured if all the human resources are held equally accountable in each and every decision of an organization.
- ***Managing Change*:** Change can be defined as an alteration in the existing field of forces. The change if not properly organized can affect the quality aspect of an organization. An optimistic approach towards change is necessary among the human resources. This is only possible if an organization has internal flexibility and creativity.

- ***Planning to Achieve Objectives***: Teacher-Educators with specialization in education or excellent teacher-educators of different teacher education institutions should be taken for policy implementation. A high level council comprising representatives of state, apex bodies, experts, teacher associations, representatives of teacher-educators, and universities may be constituted. Unnecessary expenditure in the name of false programmes for eradication illiteracy etc. should be stopped. Commercialization and privatization of teacher education should be stopped to ensure quality improvement and proper man-power planning.
- ***Change in Culture***: Commitment to Total Quality Management requires a change in culture. This is notoriously difficult to bring about and takes time to implement. It requires a change of attitudes and working methods. The staff in institutions needs to understand and live the message if Total Quality Management is to make an impact. The latter is characterized by an understanding that people produce quality. Two things are required for the staff to produce quality. First, the staff needs a suitable environment in which to work; then they need the tools of the trade and they need to work with systems and procedures, which are simple.

Benefits of Implementing and Being Committed towards Total Quality Management

- Total Quality Management enhances the morale of teacher educator and other employees working in the teacher-training institute.
- There will be a change in values and attitudes of the institution as the people lower down are also involved in the decision-making process.
- It encourages effective participation of the employees as it stresses on teamwork.
- It helps to provide better use of resources since the process is studied and reviewed periodically.
- It increases the employees' awareness of the institution's mission and their part in accomplishing it.
- It increases efficiency and effectiveness which ultimately saves time and money.

In a nutshell, the need of today is teachers who can ensure quality education with professional perfection; this can be attained through an application of total quality management and its commitment forever. For this we have to improve teacher education with the application of total quality management by redefining the roles, create staff developments, involve all, eradicate mass inspection, remain open for the adoption of new philosophies and create conducive environment and work culture based on trust and shared decision making. This will help us achieve our goal of being the best in all spheres of education.

REFERENCES

Abrham, J. (2006). *Quality of Teacher Education. Programs: Some Suggestions*, New Delhi: Edutracks.

Kothari Education Commission. (1966). *Government of India Document*, New Delhi: Ministry of Education.

Mangal, S.K. (2008). "Educating the Teacher Educators", *Edutracks*, 1(5) 6-12.

Mukhopadhyay, Maramar, (2009). *Total Quality Management in Education*, New Delhi.

Narang, S.K. (2006). *The Bright and Their Education*, New Delhi: Prime Publishers.

Reddy, G.S. (2009). "Barak Obama on Education", *Edutracks*, Jan. 2009 Vol. 8, No. 5.

Saxena, N.R. and Mishra, B.K. (2009). *Teacher Education*, Meerut: R. Lal Book Depot.

Websites Accessed

www.naac-india.com
www.ncte-in.org
http://www.msn.com
http://www.ed.psu.edu/
www.ugc.ac.in/orgn/staffcollege.html
www.totalqualitymanagement.wikepedia.com
www.teachersmagazine.org.

23
Teacher Education in India: Evolutionary Five Year Plans for Development

Suruchi Soni

After independence, a new era ushered in as a sequel to the efforts of various important commissions and committees appointed by the Central and State Governments. In 1948, just after independence, the Ministry of Education, Government of India appointed University Education Commission under the chairmanship of Dr. S. Radhakrishnan. The Commission, as per Notification, was expected to make recommendations on aims of university education, university teaching staff, courses of study, standard of teaching, post-graduate training and research and other aspects of university education. The Commission was of the view that in order to improve their qualitative ethos, we should not only set forth a higher standard in high school and intermediate examinations bur also raise the level of teaching also. It rightly suggested that we cannot raise examination standards unless we improve the quality of teaching. Secondary education can be improved only if a large number of good qualities of teachers are available. University standards can be improved by improving the quality of teaching in schools and intermediate colleges. For this universities should provide continuous supply of highly trained and efficient teachers for these institutions. The Commission also recommended refresher courses for high school and intermediate college teachers as a measure of reform.

The Committee on Higher Education for Rural Areas: Rural Institutions (1954) under the chairmanship of Shri K.L. Shrimali; the National Committee on Women's Education (1958) under the chairmanship of Smt. Durga Bai Deshmukh; the Review Committee on Education (1960) set up by the UGC under the chairmanship of Prof. N.K. Sidhanta and later Prof. K.G. Saiyidain: the Committee on Emotional Integration (1961) under the chairmanship of Dr. Sampurnanand; the Study Team for Selected Educational Schemes (1961) appointed by the Planning Commission under the chairmanship of Shri B.N. Jha; the Study Group on Training of Elementary Teachers in India (1961) under the chairmanship of Shri Raja Roy Singh; the Committee on Education as an Elective subject at the Undergraduate Stage (1963) appointed by the UGC under the chairmanship of Prof. A.R. Wadia; and the Study Group on the Study of

English in India (1964) under the chairmanship of Prof. VK Gokak. All these committees gave recommendations and suggestions for teacher education as well as research in education.

Then the National Commission on Teachers I (1983) was set up under the chairmanship of Prof. D.P. Chattopadhyaya for the teachers of school stage. This Commission indicated that the

- training of teachers demands urgent attention;
- every training programme should enable a trainee to acquire basic skills and competencies of a good teacher;
- the minimum length of training for a secondary teacher should be five years, following the completion of class XII. Such an integrated programme, spread over five years, will give the much needed time and experience to produce the kind of new teacher the country needs;
- Each state may introduce an Education Department in their existing colleges alongwith their other programmes, allowing for a section of their students to opt for teacher education.

A document entitled 'Challenge of Education: A Policy Perspective' (1985) was brought out for reviewing and reshaping education system to enable it to meet the challenges of the future and also improve its efficiency and quality. Teacher, teacher training and teacher education related to different aspects and challenges were also discussed in this document. The views expressed and suggestions made were carefully studied and the National Policy on Education (1986) was adopted by the Parliament. This Policy consists of XII parts covering different aspects of education. Keeping in view the requirements of the 21st century, the National Policy on Education (1986) was drafted with a very broad outlook. Along with other issues of concern, consolidation and restructuring of teacher education was strongly emphasized for an overall quality control in the education sector.

After that in 1990, a Committee was set up under the chairmanship of Acharya Rama Murti to review the National Policy on Education and to make recommendations for its modifications. The Committee submitted its report in December 1990. Certain modifications were made in the year 1992. The content and process of teacher education in accordance with this review stood conceptualized as follows:

- Teacher Education is a continuous process, and its pre-service and in-service components are inseparable.
- The new programmes of teacher education will emphasise on continuing education and the need for teachers to meet the thrusts envisaged in this policy.

- District Institutes of Education and Training (DIETs) will be established with the capability to organize pre-service and in-service courses for elementary school teachers and for the personnel working in non-formal and adult education.
- Selected Secondary Teacher Training Colleges will be upgraded to complement the work.

In accordance with the National Policy on Education and Programme of Action, 1986, a centrally sponsored scheme of Restructuring and Reorganization of Teacher Education was taken up in 1987 to create a strong institutional infrastructure and academic and technical resource base for orientation, training and continuous upgradation of knowledge, competence and pedagogical skills of elementary school teachers in the country. The scheme envisaged setting up of District Institutes for Education and Training (DIETs), one in each district, to provide academic and resource support to elementary education teachers and the instructors in non-formal and adult education. It also envisaged upgradation of Secondary Teacher Education Institutions into Colleges of Teacher Education (CTEs) and Institutes of Advanced Study in Education (IASEs) for organizing pre-service and in-service training for secondary teachers and providing extension and resource support to secondary schools. The Central Government provided financial assistance to the States and UTs for setting up DIETs/CTEs/IASEs and strengthening of SCERTs. DIETs were established either by upgrading existing Elementary Teacher Education Institutions (ETEIs) or by setting up new ones in districts which had no existing institution. Land for the purpose was to be provided by state governments free of cost. IASEs and CTEs were set up by upgrading existing Secondary Teacher Education Institutions (including University Departments of Education). In the backdrop of the above recommendation and a steady urge for quality education, as highlighted in the International Conference on Secondary Education in Delhi (1993) and on Higher Education at Paris (1998), the NCTE published a Curriculum Framework for Quality Teacher Education in 1998.

After achieving independence, India adopted the planning process for its economic and social development through Five Year Plans. The First Five Year Plan was formulated and its implementation was started during the financial year 1951-52. Education was included as one of the human social development components right from the First Plan. Teacher education covering training of elementary and secondary level school teachers has been assigned due importance in the planning process of school education. Outlays were earmarked for teacher education related programmes over the different Five Year and Annual Plan periods.

First Five Year Plan—Expansion of Training Facilities for Teachers

It was observed that a very large percentage of teachers were untrained. In 1949-50, the percentage of untrained teachers was 41.4 in primary schools and 46.4 in secondary schools. For the purpose of educational reorganization, most of the trained teachers also required considerable retraining. Expansion of training facilities, therefore, deserved very high priority. There was also dearth of women teachers who were especially suited for balwadis (including pre-schools and day nurseries) and primary schools. The scales of pay and conditions of service of teachers were generally very unsatisfactory to constitute a major cause of the low standards of teaching.

It may be observed that teachers' training facilities expanded differently at different levels. While the number of trained teachers during the year increased only by 15 per cent in the case of primary teachers, it increased by 54 per cent in the case of secondary schools and 62 per cent in the case of basic teachers. The low percentage increase in the case of primary teachers was explained by the fact that with the policy of ultimately converting all primary schools into basic schools, most of the States were taking steps to convert their primary teachers' training colleges into basic training colleges. The percentage of untrained teachers in 1950-51 was 37 in the case of primary schools, 45 in the case of junior basic schools and 44 in the case of secondary schools. As a result of expansion of training facilities during the Plan period, the percentage of trained teachers rose by 3 per cent in the case of primary teachers; 15 per cent in case of junior basic teachers and 6 per cent in case of secondary teachers respectively.

Second Five Year Plan—Intensification of Expansion of Training Facilities

Teacher is viewed as the pivot in the system of education. This was specially the case during the period of basic change and reorientation. Improvement in the conditions of teachers was, therefore, considered to be an important issue for progress in education. Measures which were necessary, whether by way of better training or better salaries and conditions of service, were held back because of the large number of teachers involved. Thus, the number of teachers had risen from 7.3 lakhs before the first plan to 10.24 lakhs in 1955-56 and was expected to further increase to 13.56 lakhs in 1960-61. In the Second Plan, Rs. 17 crores were provided for increasing training facilities for teachers and, besides expanding existing institutions, it was proposed to establish 231 training schools and 30 training colleges. At the end of the Second Plan, it was expected that the proportion of trained teachers would increase to 79 and 68 per cent in primary and secondary schools respectively. The number of basic training colleges was to be increased from 33 to 71 and of basic training schools from 449 to 729.

Third Five Year Plan—Teacher Training for Basic Education

The most important measure for the expansion of basic education was the provision of larger facilities for the training of teachers for basic schools and the reorganization of existing training centres. At the end of the second plan, elementary school teachers were being trained in 1307 institutions, of which about 70 per cent were already organized on the basic pattern. It was supposed that by the end of the Third Plan, the number of training institutions would increase to 1424 and all of them would impart training on basic lines, the number of pupil teachers on roll being about 200,000 as compared to 135,000 in 1960-61. For teachers, who had not been trained in basic education, short-term courses of training in the simpler aspects of basic education were to be provided.

Fourth Five Year Plan—Correspondence Courses for Untrained Teachers and Enrichment of In-service Programmes

At the elementary stage, the number of teachers was estimated to have increased from about 1.09 million in 1960-61 to about 1.60 million in 1968-69. There had been a steady expansion of teacher training facilities so that the number of elementary trained teachers during the period increased from about 0.71 million to about 1.24 million, raising the percentage of trained teachers from 65 to 77. Further, during the period 1966-69, owing to financial stringency, some of the States were unable to employ all the teachers who had passed out of the training institutions. This had led to considerable unemployment among trained teachers in some States. During this plan period, correspondence courses for untrained teachers working in schools were in focus and the State Institutes of Education cooperated in respect of implementation of these programmes.

At the secondary stage, the number of teachers in 1968-69 was estimated at 0.525 million, of whom 0.381 million or 73 per cent were trained. The training facilities available at this stage were considered adequate and could be easily expanded according to the perceived need. The correspondence courses organized by the Central Institute of Education, Delhi and the four Regional Colleges of Education facilitated the process of speeding up the training of untrained teachers. Funds were placed at the disposal of the University Grants Commission to improve physical facilities of the departments of education in universities and secondary training colleges and to upgrade the professional competence of the teacher educators working in them. These programmes were coordinated with those of the National Council of Educational Research and Training, State Institutes of Education and State Institutes of Science Education.

Fifth Five Year Plan—Curricular Re-orientation

It may be noted that the plan outlays for education during the first three years of the plan had been somewhat modest because of the economic constraints but the growth in the total governmental expenditure on education, both plan and non-plan, must be considered substantial. In addition to the expansion of educational facilities, provision could also be made for curricular re-orientation, work experience and strengthening of educational institutions for teachers.

Under the 20-Point Socio-Economic Programmes, three components namely—provision of books and stationery to students at cheaper rates, supply of essential commodities to hostel students at subsidized prices and expansion of apprenticeship training programmes—were undertaken. The capacity of the textbook printing presses was enhanced, book banks continued to be established in educational institutions and the coverage of apprenticeship scheme was expanded.

Sixth Five Year Plan—Enhancing Holding Power of Schools

It was realized that the elementary school teachers have to play a vital role and their services should be utilized not only for teaching the children who come to school but also to bring non-attending children to school and to see that they do not drop out. It was rightly suggested that programmes of qualitative improvement in elementary education help the programmes of expansion by enhancing and attracting the holding power of schools. It was emphasized to allocate adequate funds for several programmes of qualitative improvement such as introduction of socially useful productive work, curricular reform so as to link education to the environment and to make it relevant and interesting to children, relating school vacations to climate and agricultural conditions, provision of equipment and provision of cheap but effectively useful buildings constructed, as far as possible, out of local materials by local communities, improvement in the quality of school books, adoption of dynamic methods of teaching and evaluation, emphasis on better teaching of the basic subjects of language, arithmetic and science, creation of scientific awareness and inculcating scientific attitude, better pre-service and in-service education of teachers and improvement of supervision.

Seventh Five Year Plan—ICT Input for In-service Training of Teachers

The major concern during the period was that the training of teachers should comprise, apart from pedagogy, the use of mass media, science and technology, planning and curriculum design for local environment-based courses, mobilization and use of community resources and other relevant subjects. A special emphasis was required to be laid on teaching methods and other measures particularly needed for first generation learners and for reducing the number of drop-outs. Teacher training institutions were to be developed and strengthened accordingly. Considering the number involved (over 2.5 million teachers), institutionalized in-service education of teachers was difficult to manage not only due to the huge costs involved but also due to lack of facilities for training.

It was, therefore, necessary to think of a variety of training arrangements. Among others, these included, in-service education by utilizing the mass media; adoption of schools of lower levels of education by institutions of higher levels for upgrading of teacher competencies; dispatch of teacher guidance notes by training schools; publication of bulletins informing teachers of new developments; and use of correspondence course materials supported by occasional contact.

Eighth Five Year Plan—Establishment of NCTE as a Statutory Body to Augment Standards of Teacher Education

During this period, an important development took place. It was articulated that statutory status be accorded to the National Council for Teacher Education (NCTE) to lay down and maintain standards in institutions and courses of teacher education; the schemes of DIETs, STEIs and IASEs be continued and their coverage expanded with a view to strengthening institutional infrastructure and programmes of teacher education; and the scheme for strengthening of SCERTs be implemented and suitable measures for selection and professional development of staff in SCERTs, DIETs and IASEs be undertaken. It was projected that a large number of teachers were to be covered through in-service programmes—both institutional and distance education—and reputed professional organizations were to be encouraged to conduct in-service anti refresher courses for teachers. Open universities at the national and state level were to be encouraged to introduce induction teacher training courses to supplement efforts of the existing training institutions. The bulk of seats in teachers' training colleges were to be reserved for rural women.

Ninth Five Year Plan—Upgrading Infrastructure and Curricula

It was observed that the number of teachers working in elementary and secondary schools recorded a six-fold increase from 7.5 lakhs in 1951 to 45.28 lakhs in 1996, with female teachers constituting 34.3 per cent of the total number in 1996. The budgeted expenditure on education had recorded an increase from Rs. 644.6 crores in 1951-52 to Rs. 36,529.29 crores in 1996-97. It was proposed that the North-Eastern States, which have a larger percentage of untrained teachers in elementary schools, would initiate programmes to cover this gap by adopting the following measures:

- A Diploma Programme for Primary Education developed by Indira Gandhi National Open University (IGNOU) to be launched in collaboration with the State Governments;
- NCTE to establish a Regional Committee for North-Eastern States to provide the necessary fillip to the teacher training institutions;
- Induction programmes of 4 to 6 weeks duration by DIETs to enrich the capabilities of freshly appointed teachers.

The process of strengthening Teacher Education Programmes is given further impetus by upgrading the physical and academic infrastructures of:

- National Council for Teacher Education (NCTE);
- Departments of Education in Universities;
- State Councils of Educational Research and Training (SCERTs);
- Colleges of Teacher Education (CTEs);

- Institutes of Advanced Study in Education (IASEs);
- District Institutes of Education and Training (DIETs); and
- Block Resource Centres/Cluster Resource Centres.

Tenth Five Year Plan—Strengthening Professional Development of Teachers

The Tenth Five Year Plan (2002-07), placed an exclusive emphasis on teacher education. For professional development of teachers, the focus given has been on:

- Ensuring pre-service training to all elementary school teachers so that all untrained teachers can be trained within a period of three years, including the distance learning mode;
- Enhancing pre-service training facilities in selected districts where the present capacity is not adequate;
- Improving the quality of pre-service elementary teacher education;
- Extending the provision of pre-primary teacher training by strengthening existing institutions that provide, or are willing to provide, pre-service education for the pre-primary stage;
- Developing two-months to one-year duration specialized correspondence courses, for elementary teachers in collaboration with open universities, higher education institutions.
- Development of courses for in-service education of teachers that may carry credits and linking these to promotions and benefits.
- In January 2004 the revised Teacher Education Scheme for the Tenth Plan period has been circulated to states and Union Territories having the following objectives:
    - Speedy completion of DIET/CTE/IASE/SCERT projects sanctioned but not completed up to the end of the IX Plan period;
    - Making DIETs, CTEs, IASEs sanctioned (and SCERTs strengthened) upto the Ninth Plan period optimally functional and operational;
    - Sanction and implementation of fresh DIET/CTE/IASE/SCERT projects to the extent necessary;
    - Improvement in the quality of programmes being undertaken by DIETs etc., especially those of pre-service and in-service training so as to enable them to effectively perform their nodal role of improving the quality of elementary and secondary education in their respective jurisdiction, as measured in terms of the levels of learner achievement.

National Council for Teacher Education

In 1973, the Government of India constituted a non-statutory National Council for Teacher Education, with secretarial support provided in the Department of Teacher Education of the National Council of Educational Research and Training. The National Council for Teacher Education was to:

- advise the Government of India on all matters concerning Teacher Education, including pre-service and in-service training, and periodical review of progress in revising curricula;
- advise State Governments on any matter referred to the Council by them;
- review the progress of plan schemes, both Central and States, concerning teacher education;
- advise the government on ensuring adequate standards in teacher education;
- any other matter entrusted to the Council by the Government of India.

The Programme of Action 1992 indicated that the National Council for Teacher Education be accorded a statutory status. Accordingly, a Bill was drafted for this purpose and was introduced in the Parliament. The Bill envisaged a Council, an Executive Committee and Regional Committees. The objectives envisaged were to:

- create mechanism for determination and maintenance of standards of teacher education;
- regulate institutions of teacher education with a view to phasing out sub-standard and malpractising institutions:
- lay emphasis on continuing education of teachers;
- reduce the gap between supply and demand of trained personnel.

After due deliberations, the Parliament passed the National Council for Teacher Education Bill and the National Council for Teacher Education Act (No. 73), 1993 came into being. The Act provided the establishment of National Council for Teacher Education to:

- Achieve planned and coordinated development of teacher education system throughout the country;
- Regulate and maintain norms and standards in the teacher education system;

The NCTE commenced its statutory functioning with effect from 17th August 1995. This was a historic landmark in the development of teacher education in the country. The NCTE was assigned the functions stated below:

- undertake surveys and studies relating to various aspects of teacher education and publish the results;

- make recommendations to the Central and State Governments, Universities, University Grants Commission and recognized institutions in the matter of preparation of suitable plans and programmes in the field of teacher education;
- co-ordinate and monitor teacher education and its development in the country;
- lay down guidelines in respect of minimum qualifications for a person to be employed as a teacher in schools or in recognized institutions;
- lay down norms for any specified category of courses or training in teacher education, including the minimum eligibility criteria for admission thereof, and the method of selection of candidates, duration of the course, course contents and mode of curriculum;
- lay down guidelines for compliance by recognized institutions, for starting new courses or training, and for providing physical and instructional facilities, staffing pattern and staff qualifications;
- lay down standards in respect of examinations leading to teacher education qualifications, criteria for admission to such examinations and schemes of courses or training;
- lay down guidelines regarding tuition fees and other fees chargeable by recognized institutions;
- promote and conduct innovations and research in various areas of teacher education and disseminate the results;
- examine and review periodically the implementation of the norms, guidelines and standards laid down by the Council, and suitably advise the recognized institutions;
- evolve suitable performance appraisal systems, norms and mechanisms for enforcing accountability on recognized institutions;
- formulate schemes for various levels of teacher education and identify recognized institutions and set up new institutions for teacher development programmes;
- take all necessary steps to prevent commercialization of teacher education; and
- Perform such other functions as may be entrusted to it by the Central Government.

Every institution offering or intending to offer a course or training in teacher education has to seek permission under this Act. The Act has given power and authority to the Regional Committees, which at· present are four, namely—Eastern, Western, Northern and Southern—to grant recognition or to refuse permission for running a teacher training programme.

In order to promote quality concerns, NCTE has developed norms and standards for 12 teacher education programmes, namely:

1. Pre-School Teacher Education
2. Nursery Teacher Education
3. Elementary Teacher Education
4. Bachelor of Elementary Education
5. Secondary Teacher Education
6. Master of Education Programme
7. Certificate in Physical Education
8. Bachelor of Physical Education
9. Master of Physical Education
10. B.Ed. (Open and Distance Education Learning System)
11. M.Ed. (Open and Distance Education Learning System)
12. M.Ed. (Part-Time)

Sarva Shiksha Abhiyan has been launched by the Government of India to attain universalization of primary education by 2007 and universalization of elementary education by 2010. Needless to stress that to attain this objective requires a huge number of additional teachers at the elementary level during the Tenth Five Year Plan. In order to facilitate establishment of adequate number of teacher training institutions at these levels, the National Council for Teacher Education decided in January 2004 to dispense with the requirement of No Objection Certificate (NOC) from State/UT Government, for a period of three years for those institutions already running B.Ed. programmes recognized by the NCTE and to such other institutions keen to start a course or training in pre-school nursery teacher education.

National and International Collaboration

Few MoUs have been entered into action initiated for promoting and sustaining this drive at the institutional level.

NCTE-IGNOU MoU

National Council for Teacher Education (NCTE) and Distance Education Council (DEC), an authority of Indira Gandhi National Open University (IGNOU), signed a Memorandum of Understanding (MoU) on 2nd May, 2001 and renewed the same on 30th April, 2004. The second MoU focuses on ensuring cost-effectiveness while maintaining quality and, for this purpose, NCTE and DEC jointly endeavour to design and develop self-instructional materials and also aim at faster development of quality of teacher education in distance mode in the country at all levels.

NCTE-NAAC MoU

In order to evolve suitable performance appraisal systems, norms and mechanisms for enforcing accountability on recognized institutions for quality assurance of Teacher Education, NCTE entered into a Memorandum of Understanding with National Assessment and Accreditation Council (NAAC) w.e.f.

16th August 2002 for executing in right earnest the process of assessment and accreditation of Teacher Education Institutions recognized by NCTE. NCTE and NAAC jointly developed a manual for accreditation of teacher training institutes offering pre-service courses in the field of teacher education.

NCTE-RCI MoU

NCTE has also initiated collaboration with Rehabilitation Council of India (RCI) for educational interventions in training of teachers who teach children with special needs, besides sensitizing all the teachers in service. A Memorandum of Understanding in this regard was signed between NCTE and RCI on 19th January 2005 to develop an action plan and to take up further course of action for education of children with special needs, focusing on minimum standards, course curriculum and research studies for the promotion of inclusive education with disability-specific specialization and other related matters.

NCTE-SACTED Collaboration

Another initiative which is directly addressed to promoting international collaboration pertains to the venture to boost regional cooperation and launch joint activities in teacher education. The South Asian Consortium for Teacher Education and Development (SACTED) consisting of Bangladesh, Maldives, India, Pakistan and Sri Lanka, set up in November 2004, has explicit objectives of developing capabilities of teacher education system so that it can provide quality inputs to schools and teacher education.

Finally, the role and concerns of the NCTE have increased in recent years, the broad mandate given to the NCTE is to achieve planned and co-ordinated development of teacher education system in the country and regulating and maintaining norms and standards, since teacher education system has already witnessed mushrooming of a large number of institutions. Improving the quality of the graduates of teacher training institutions prior to the NCTE's existence, who are already in the system, is also a major challenge. The NCTE has been playing a catalytic role in developing resource material in print and electronic forms and distributing them to teacher training institutions. This is extremely important because we owe it to the nation to provide a qualified, competent and a caring teacher to every classroom.

In the 21st century, teachers are to play a catalyst role in the altered frame of reference, with an emphasis on the basic function of teachers in shaping tomorrow's world. Delors (1996) commended the concept of learning throughout life as one of the keys to the 21st century teaching-learning continuum, as the world is increasingly coming into the classroom and correspondingly, the classroom too must increasingly go out into the world. Education, to be relevant and effective, must move into the community to help education change the world into a knowledge society.

Last, but not the least, we should develop in them an ever-growing thirst for knowledge. Every teacher or person involved in this profession must be fully equipped to seize learning opportunities throughout life, by developing one's own approach and a set of the best suitable skills to act as a specialist in gathering knowledge, retaining, disseminating and transmitting it. This may be developed through active participation in orientation courses, seminars, workshops, conferences treated as essential to maintain one's professional acumen.

REFERENCES

Acts, Rules and Regulations (Compiled and updated upto 30th April, 2005), National Council for Teacher Education.

Delors, J. (1996), *Learning the Treasure Within*—Report of the International Commission on Education. UNESCO, Paris.

Envisioning Teacher Education. In the 10th Plan and Beyond (2003), National Council for Teacher Education, New Delhi.

Five year plans, Government of India, Planning Commission, New Delhi.

Kothari, D.S. (1966), *Report of Education Commission* (1964-66). Government of India, New Delhi.

MHRD (1986), *National Policy on Education* 1986. Government of India.

Mudaliar, A.L. (1953), *Report of Secondary Education Commission* (1952-53). Government of India, New Delhi.

Mukerjee, S.N. (1968), *Education of Teachers in India.* S. Chand & Company, New Delhi.

National Policy on Education 1986 (As modified in 1992), Government of India, Department of Education, Ministry of Human Resource Development, New Delhi.

NCTE (1998) Curriculum Framework for Quality Teacher Education, National Council for Teacher Education, New Delhi.

Policy Perspectives in Teacher Education—Critique and Documentation (1998), National Council for Teacher Education, New Delhi.

Report of the Education Commission (1964-66), Education and National Development, Ministry of Education, Government of India, New Delhi.

The Teacher and Society, Report of the National Commission on Teachers-I (1983-85), Ministry of Education, Government of India, New Delhi.

Contributors

Ajay Kumar Attri (Dr.), Assistant Professor (Education), ICDEOL, Himachal Pradesh University, Summer Hill, Shimla, Himachal Pradesh. Email: ajayattri76@gmail.com

Bimal Charan Swain (Dr.), Senior Lecturer in Education, Radhanath Institute of Advanced Studies in Education, Cuttack (Odisha).
Email: bimalswain@yahoo.com

Chetna Bajwa (Ms.), Assistant Professor, Aravali College of Advanced Studies in Education, Faridabad. Email: sonal.chabra77@gmail.com

Dillip Kumar Khuntia, Assistant Professor in Education, BM College of Education, Sonepat, Haryana.

Gyanendra Kumar Rout (Dr.), Assistant Professor in Education, Govt. Degree College, Rikhnikhal, Pauri Garhwal, Uttarakhand. Email: gkr75@yahoo.co.in

J.D. Singh (Dr.), Asst. Professor, GV (PG) College of Education (CTE), Sangaria, Rajasthan. Email:drjdsingh@gmail.com

Kuldeep Singh Katoch (Dr.), Assistant Professor, Department of Education, ICDEOL, Himachal Pradesh University, Shimla, Himachal Pradesh.
Email: kuldeepkatoch@gmail.com

Laxmidhar Behera (Dr.), Assistant Professor in Education, RIE (NCERT), Bhubaneswar, Odisha. Email: behera17@yahoo.co.in

Mayadhar Sahu, Assistant Professor in Education, Ravenshaw University, Cuttack, Odisha. Email: mayadharsahu104@gmail.com

Nityananda Pradhan (Dr.), Head, Department of Education, Ravenshaw University, Cuttack, Odisha. Email: npradhan17@rediffmail.com

Peeyush Kumar Garg (Dr.), M.M. College of Education, M.M. University, Mullana, Haryana. Email: peeyushkumar.garg@gmail.com

Puja Gupta, Lecturer in Education, Krishma P.G. College of Education, Nerchowk, Mandi, H.P. Email: gupta.puja16oct@gmail.com

Rajalakshmi Das (Dr.), Senior Lecturer in Education, Radhanath Institute of Advanced Studies in Education, Cuttack (Odisha). Email: bimalswain@yahoo.com

Ramakanta Mohalik (Dr.), Assistant Professor, Department of Education, Regional Institute of Education, Bhubaneswar. Email: ramakantamohalik@ rediffmail.com

Ranjan Kumar Rout, Lecturer in Education, Ravenshaw University Cuttack. Odisha. Email- rout.ranjan@yahoo.co.in

Ritu Bakshi, Sharan College of Education for Women, Gurkari, Kangra, HP.

Sabita Mishra Dr. (Mrs.), Lecturer in Education, Ravenshaw Junior College, Cuttack, Odisha. Email: sabita.mishra9@gmail.com

Sangeeta Barwal (Dr.), Assistant Professor, Krishma P.G. College of Education, Nerchowk, Mandi, H.P., Email: drsangeeta92@gmail.com

Sangeeta Solanki (Dr.), Lecturer, Mangalmay Institute of Management & Technology, Greater Noida. Email: shree280@gmail.com

Sankar Prasad Mohanty, Lecturer & Research Scholar, Department of Education, Ravenshaw University, Cuttack, Odisha. Email: spmcuttack@gmail.com

Sesadeba Pany (Dr.), Principal, Krishma P.G. College of Education, Dadour, Dist-Mandi, Himachal Pradesh. Email: drpany_s@yahoo.com

Shri Kant Dwivedi (Dr.), Lecturer, Mangalmay Institute of Management & Technology, Greater Noida. Email: shree280@gmail.com

Sonal Chabra (Ms.), Research Scholar, Guru Gobind Singh Indraprastha University, Delhi.

Suruchi Soni, Lecturer in Education, Krishma P.G.College of Education, Nerchowk, Mandi, H.P. Email: suruchi_emailid@yahoo.co.in

Taruna Malhotra (Dr.), Assistant Professor, Vaish College of Education, Rohtak, Haryana. Email: drtaruna.malhotra@gmail.com

Vimal Kishor, Lecturer in Education, Jupiter College of Education, Mairi, Una, Himachal Pradesh. Email: vimalkishor88@yahoo.com